Introduction to PostgreSQL for the Data Professional

First Edition

By Ryan Booz & Grant Fritchey

Published by Red Gate Books 2024

Title: Introduction to PostgreSQL for the data professional.

Authors: Grant Fritchey and Ryan Booz

Technical Reviewer: Robert Treat

Copy Editor: Louis Davidson

Edition: Preview Edition

Publication Year: 2024

Publisher: Red Gate Books
Cavendish House, Cambridge Business Park
Cambridge, CB4 0XB
United Kingdom

ISBN: 978-1-3999-9678-5

Library of Congress Cataloging-in-Publication Data

Introduction to PostgreSQL for the data professional. / Grant Fritchey and Ryan Booz.
Includes bibliographical references and index.
ISBN 978-1-3999-9678-5

1. PostgreSQL 2. Database Management 3. SQL

Printed in United States of America

Table of Contents

About the Authors.. x

About the Tech Editor.. xi

Forward xii

Preface xiv

Chapter 1: An Introduction to PostgreSQL... 1

What's in a Name 2

How It All Began 3

    Going Open-Source 4

    PostgreSQL Governance 5

Commitfest 7

Why PostgreSQL and Why Now 10

Conclusion 11

Chapter 2: PostgreSQL Basics and Differences.................................13

Feature Comparison...13

    Extensibility...14

    Built-in Job Scheduler 15

    Query Hints...16

    Query Plan Cache..16

    Execution Plan Viewer 17

Terminology Differences..18

    Cluster vs. Instance..18

    Role vs User 18

    Tuple vs. Row 19

    Literal Object Qualifiers..19

    COPY vs. BULK INSERT 20

    TOAST...20

SQL Differences 20

Data Types 21

Conclusion 30

Chapter 3: Installing PostgreSQL...31

Minimum Hardware 31

Where To Get the Bits 32

Linux Install 34

Windows Install 36

Containers 43

Conclusion 44

Chapter 4: PostgreSQL Tools...45

psql 45

Installing psql 46

Connecting to PostgreSQL from psql..48

Using psql 48

pgAdmin 51

Installing pgAdmin 52

Using pgAdmin 54

DBeaver 59

Installing DBeaver 59

Using DBeaver 60

Azure Data Studio 65

Installing Azure Data Studio 66

Working With Azure Data Studio 68

Conclusion 72

Chapter 5: Sever Configuration...73

Memory Settings 73

Modify Configuration Settings in PostgreSQL 75

Caching Data Pages..75

Query Memory..76

Number of Connections 78

Ongoing Maintenance and Backup/Restores 78

Query Plan Settings...80

    Random Page Cost...80

    Effective Cache Size 81

    Just-In-Time Compilation...82

Conclusion 82

Chapter 6: Roles and Privileges **83**

Host-based Authentication..83

Cluster, Databases, and Roles 86

    Roles 87

    Users and Groups..87

    Role Attributes 88

    The Superuser Role 90

Role Privileges 91

    GRANT and REVOKE...93

    The PUBLIC Role..97

    Object Ownership..98

    Conclusion 105

Chapter 7: Creating Databases **107**

What Is a Database 107

Creating a Database..109

Modifying a Database 113

Removing a Database 116

Database Templates...117

Tablespace..120

Conclusion 122

Chapter 8: Extensions **123**

The History of Extensions 123

What Are Extensions? 124

Available Extensions...126

    Installing Extensions 128

    Updating an Extension 129

    Dropping an Extension 130

Making Extensions Available for Use 130

    Extension Registries 131

    Pre-made Docker Containers 132

    Linux Package Managers 133

    Cloud-Hosted Databases 134

Two Words of Caution 134

    Extensions Across Environments..135

    Extension Backup and Restore 135

Extensions to Try...136

    pg_stat_statements..136

    postgis 137

    pg_hint_plan 137

    pg_cron..138

    postgres_fdw 139

    pg_partman..140

    pg_trgm 141

    hypopg...142

Vector and AI Extensions...142

    pgvector...143

    pgai..143

    azure_ai...144

Conclusion 144

Chapter 9: Core Object Types in PostgreSQL **145**

SQL Examples 145

Object Ownership 146

Core Object Types...146

    Databases...146

    Schema 147

    Tables..147

    Sequences..152

    Indexes 153

    Functions 158

    Procedures 159

    View...160

    Materialized View 161

    Foreign Table..161

    Trigger 162

    Types...162

    Domains 163

Conclusion 163

Chapter 10: Introducing PL/pgSQL **165**

Purpose of a Procedural Language...166

Basic PL/pgSQL Syntax 166

    Blocks..167

    Variables..168

    Error Handling...169

Procedural Language 171

    IF/THEN...172

    CASE...173

    Loops...174

Creating Procedural Objects..179

    Functions 179

    Procedures 183

Cursors 186

Conclusion 189

Chapter 11: Query Tuning and Indexes **191**

EXPLAIN..191

Estimated Query Plans...192

EXPLAIN Options...193

Adding run-time statistics 193

BUFFERS...195

Query Cost and Actual Time..198

Primary Node Types...199

Scan Nodes 199

Join Nodes...200

Other Nodes 201

Additional Areas to Troubleshoot 201

First things first – work_mem..202

External Sort Disk 202

Indexes 205

B-Tree Deduplication...206

Functional Indexes 208

Partial Indexes 209

Composite Indexes 210

Covering Indexes 213

Logging Query Plans 214

Auto Explain..214

Reading Execution Plans from the Log 217

More Resources 217

Chapter 12: Backup and Restore **219**

Restore Strategy 220

Database Backups 221

SQL Dump..222

File System Backup 225

Base Backups...225

Comparing Backup Mechanisms 227

Restoring a Database 228

Restoring to a Point in Time...231

WAL Archiving 232

Recovery To a Point In Time 233

Conclusion 235

Chapter 13: MVCC, VACUUM, and ANALYZE **237**

MVCC in PostgreSQL..238

Row Versions 239

Row Versions in Practice...240

Row Visibility...241

Transaction ID Space..242

The Vacuum Process 243

VACUUM and autovacuum 243

Dead Tuples and Table Bloat 245

Freezing Live Tuples 247

ANALYZE and autoanalyze 247

Configuration and Maintenance Tasks 249

maintenance_work_mem 249

Reindexing...250

Fill Factor...251

Heap-Only Tuples 252

Conclusion 254

Chapter 14: Replication and HA **255**

Cloud Hosted Databases 255

Replication 256

Physical Replication 256

Logical Replication 258

Replication Slots 258

Setting Up Streaming Replication 260

Setting Up Logical Replication 267

Conclusion 275

Chapter 15: Monitoring PostgreSQL **277**

Knowledge Drives Decisions..278

Collecting Server Information..279

Error Logs...279

Cumulative Statistics System 283

Query Performance Metrics 290

Query Metrics at Execution 290

Monitoring Query Metrics 292

Conclusion 295

Chapter 16: PostgreSQL on the Cloud...**297**

Why the Cloud?..298

Why Platform as a Service (PaaS)?...299

PaaS Services..300

AWS 300

Azure Database for PostgreSQL 303

Google Cloud Platform 305

Conclusion 308

Chapter 17: Where To Go For More Learning **309**

PostgreSQL Documentation 310

Books on PostgreSQL 313

The Art of PostgreSQL..313

Database Administration: The Complete Guide to DBA Practices and Procedures.............313

PostgreSQL Query Optimization: The Ultimate Guide to Building Efficient Queries 314

PostgreSQL Events 314

    User Groups and Meetups 315

    Local Events 316

    International Events 317

Online Resources 319

    Aggregations 319

    Podcasts 320

    Blogs 321

    Webinars 321

Conclusion 322

Index 323

About the Authors

Ryan Booz

Ryan is an Advocate at Redgate focusing on PostgreSQL. Ryan has been working as a PostgreSQL advocate, developer, DBA and product manager for more than 22 years, primarily working with time-series data on PostgreSQL and the Microsoft Data Platform. Ryan is a long-time DBA, starting with MySQL and Postgres in the late 90s. He spent more than 15 years working with SQL Server before returning to PostgreSQL full-time in 2018. He's at the top of his game when he's learning something new about the data platform or teaching others about the technology he loves.

Grant Fritchey

Grant Fritchey is a Data Platform MVP and AWS Community Builder with over 30 years' experience in IT, including time spent in support and development. Grant works with multiple data platforms including PostgreSQL and SQL Server, as well as multiple cloud platforms. He has also developed in Python, C#, and Java. Grant writes books for Apress and Redgate. Grant presents at conferences and user groups, large and small, all over the world. He joined Redgate Software as a product advocate in January 2011.

About the Tech Editor

Robert Treat

Robert Treat is a seasoned database professional with nearly three decades of experience working on mission critical, data intensive systems. A passionate open-source advocate and contributor, he is probably best known for his work with Postgres, where he has been recognized as a Major Contributor. His career has traversed a diverse set of organizations including DoorDash, Etsy, Amazon, National Geographic, and WebMD, where he has worked in both leadership and practitioner roles, honing his expertise in databases management and operations. As an independent community advocate, he dedicates his time to fostering open-source initiatives, speaking on a wide variety of topics including open source, devops, and scalable web operations, with a goal of empowering others and driving innovation and operability within the field.

Foreword

It is with great pleasure that I introduce this comprehensive guide to PostgreSQL, authored by two very respected figures in the database community, Grant Fritchey and Ryan Booz. Together, they have produced many blog posts and books about databases for years and years. As you read this book, this is very evident, making it a valuable resource. I have read this book as closely as I have any other book because I served as the copy editor for most of the book.

I have known one of the authors for over 15 years, and the other for 2 now, but I have learned so much about PostgreSQL (and SQL Server and other topics) from them both over these years.

Grant Fritchey, known for his extensive work with SQL Server, has over the past few years, added PostgreSQL to his skill set and brings a wealth of knowledge and practical insights about both to this topic. His experience is not just theoretical; it is grounded in real-world applications and challenges, making his contributions both relevant and actionable. Grant has been a part of the database community for many years now and has always been a wonderful teacher and all-around nice person to deal with.

I met Ryan Booz through working with him at Redgate and he has taught me a lot about how PostgreSQL works (and as a SQL Server expert myself, there are some very interesting differences that aren't always as obvious as you might expect, which is a part of why this book was written!) Everything I have said about how great it is to work with Grant goes exactly the same for Ryan.

Ryan has been instrumental in educating the community through his regular online seminar series, "PostgreSQL 101," and his numerous articles on Simple-Talk.com. His passion for PostgreSQL and his ability to break down complex concepts into understandable terms have made him a trusted voice in the community.

This book is a testament to their hard work and dedication. It provides a very nice introduction to PostgreSQL and includes hints throughout on how it is similar and different from other RDBMS, covering everything from installation and configuration to advanced performance tuning and optimization. Whether you are new to PostgreSQL or looking to deepen your understanding, this book offers valuable insights and practical advice that will help you succeed.

I will go so far as to say that this book was one of the easiest I have ever had the pleasure to edit, and that includes all my own books as well. I am confident that readers will find this book to be an essential addition to their technical library and am proud to admit that here in this foreword.

Louis Davidson (Simple Talk Editor)

Preface

There is no denying that PostgreSQL is growing in popularity. You can look at the history of its growth on the DB-Engines Ranking web site if there's any doubt. As more and more organizations begin to manage some, or all, of their data in PostgreSQL, a growing number of people are going to have to know how PostgreSQL works. We're writing this book for you. Whether you're a Database Administrator (DBA) who has to learn how to maintain a whole new data platform, a developer looking for new and better ways to manage information persistence, or even someone fresh in the IT field looking to expand your skill set, this book is for you. However, that said, we do assume a certain amount of knowledge of databases in general. We have comparisons to other data platforms, frequently Microsoft SQL Server, but others as well, to help establish context. So, this book is more a "beginners in PostgreSQL" rather than a "beginners in databases" in general style book.

Your authors have a very large amount of accumulated knowledge of databases, database management, and database development. We tried to add as much of that into the book as we can. There's guidance for best use of PostgreSQL in a lot of the chapters, not simply descriptions of how things work. We know, based on our own blunders and learning curve, that why you're doing something matters as much as how. So, we put that into the book as well.

Since this is very much an introductory book for PostgreSQL, the best way to get the maximum value from the book is to follow the flow of the book. This is especially true because we use code and structures introduced in earlier chapters, later in the book, so skipping around could cause confusion. However, most chapters stand on their own, for the most part. While it is certainly possible to skip around, you may hit snags when you run the sample code. Speaking of sample code, you'll generally see it looking like this:

Listing X-1. This is sample code

```
SELECT cola FROM sometable;
```

The code will be introduced in some manner, you'll see it in a different format, and you'll see the Listing caption with a chapter and the number of the listing within the chapter. This makes it possible to refer back to code within a chapter. You will also see code that's shown in-line with the text, just like `sometable` here. You'll note that this has a different font, to help set it apart from the rest of the text. Speaking of Notes, and Warnings, you'll see this throughout the book:

NOTE/WARNING/CAUTION: These are points that we don't want to get lost in the text because they're important. This way, you can spot them easily.

We broke the chapters down into sections that will have headings to let you know what they're about. Hopefully this helps navigation as you read the book.

We are both excited to share this book with you. There are several reasons for this. While writing a book is somewhat difficult, and very time consuming, when you're done, there's a real sense of accomplishment. Also, both of us have run into issues while learning PostgreSQL and thought to ourselves, if only someone had pointed this out for me. Well, we've tried to do that throughout the book in order to help you on your journey. Finally, and most important, we both really enjoy being able to help others. We enjoy it even more when it's helping others get going on the PostgreSQL data platform, because we've had a lot of fun exploring this space. Our goal is to help you on that journey too. Thanks for reading.

1
An Introduction to PostgreSQL

PostgreSQL is unique among other popular databases both in its foundations and in the way that it is developed and maintained. For users primarily experienced with commercial relational databases, this can sometimes be a point of intrigue… and confusion.

PostgreSQL was, has been, and will continue to be a true open-source database run by the community. This means that no one person, group of people, or organization owns PostgreSQL. Anybody can use it without paying a license, and anybody can derive new work and other databases with the code as they see fit. (Spoiler alert: hundreds of companies and organizations have created database variants using the PostgreSQL source code over the years.)

If you are new to PostgreSQL and are planning to use it for upcoming projects, it's useful that you understand some of the background that makes PostgreSQL what it is today. This history gives you background on how the project works, how the community has evolved, and what you can expect for support and feature updates in the future. Plus, it's just an interesting project that many of us have come to rely on and it's fascinating to understand the differences from what you know today with whatever RDBMS you're using.

What's in a Name

Let's get one thing out of the way. How in the world do you pronounce PostgreSQL and what alternative names are "accepted" by the community and contributors. Since the project became open source in 1996 and the name was changed slightly, there has been much debate over this topic. However, unlike the most ubiquitous answer in most technology fields, the name and pronunciation of the project, "it depends" isn't the correct answer.

The project can officially be referenced by two names:

- PostgreSQL, pronounced *Post-gres-Q-L*

- Postgres, pronounced *Post-gres*

Contrary to popular belief, the following common variations are *not* officially acceptable names or pronunciation of the project:

- Postgre SQL, pronounced *Post-grey-SQL*

- Postgre, pronounced *Post-grey*

- Postgres SQL, pronounced *Post-gres-SQL* (two "s")

Does any of this really matter? Not for any technical reason, no. Nobody will be harmed if you use the wrong name, and your database instance won't lose any data.

The reason to consider this is simply because of the community and contributors, many of which have spent thousands of hours (in some cases) developing and supporting PostgreSQL, care about the name of the project they have invested in. When you ask for help or offer assistance to others, using the correct spelling and pronunciation of the name shows that you care enough about the project to call it by its official name. At least, that's our take.

Throughout this book we will mostly use the longer form, PostgreSQL, although don't be surprised if there are references to Postgres, either.

How It All Began

PostgreSQL has existed in its current form since 1996. But that's not where PostgreSQL began.

In the early 1970s, researchers at UC Berkley received funding to develop a geographical database for the university's economics group [1] called Ingres, the **In**teractive **G**raphics **R**etrieval **S**ystem. However, Michael Stonebreaker, the lead researcher, used the funding to develop a larger-scale project focused on a new relational database model like IBM's System R. They kept the name and started development.

Ingres was actively developed until 1985 and was kind of open source, unofficially. As the project developed, anyone (mostly other universities) could get a copy of the code on tape for a nominal fee. Ahead of its time even back then.

The other differentiating feature was that Ingres didn't support SQL which was growing in popularity among some other database projects, most notably Oracle. Instead, Stonebreaker believed that a language based on relational mathematics was better suited for complex querying which they called QUEL. In many ways QUEL did have advantages over SQL, particularly in its powerful aggregate capabilities. It also introduced the original COPY command, still found in PostgreSQL today.

As the Ingres project ended, Stonebreaker returned to Berkley and started a new project to improve upon flaws he saw in the contemporary database systems of the day, primarily dealing with the ability to define new data types, something databases at the time didn't support.

Because this project came after Ingres and built on some of the same foundations, they called the new project POSTGRES, literally meaning *after Ingres*. Clever, eh?

POSTGRES didn't use any of the Ingres code but did incorporate many of the original features and concepts. At the same time, POSTGRES added support for datatypes and a method for user-defined relationships to make the system better at finding related data, especially with the POSTQUEL language modeled after QUEL.

During the late 80s and early 90s, Oracle became the dominant database in the commercial space, while POSTGRES was becoming more popular in academics and research. Over time, many of the original POSTGRES developers in academia moved on to other projects, particularly many went to work on a commercial fork known as Illustra. Eventually the POSTGRES project became too popular for the remaining academics, with increased requests for support and new features, and so the project ended in 1994 with one final release, version 4.2. The code was made available under an MIT style license, which opened it up for anyone to use and modify.

Going Open-Source

The release of the code under the MIT-style license allowed two of the graduate students that had already been working on the POSTRES project to complete their work to replace POSTQUEL with SQL. It was finally released in September of 1995 under the new name Postgres95. Aside from SQL, the final major change in this new release was the change to the *Postgres license* shown below, a simpler, more liberal license that permitted the software to be freely modifiable. At the time, this type of license was generally unheard of. It has remained unchanged since 1996.

```
PostgreSQL is released under the PostgreSQL License, a liberal Open Source
license, similar to the BSD or MIT licenses.

PostgreSQL Database Management System
(formerly known as Postgres, then as Postgres95)

Portions Copyright © 1996-2024, The PostgreSQL Global Development Group
Portions Copyright © 1994, The Regents of the University of California

Permission to use, copy, modify, and distribute this software and its
documentation for any purpose, without fee, and without a written agreement is
hereby granted, provided that the above copyright notice and this paragraph and
the following two paragraphs appear in all copies.

IN NO EVENT SHALL THE UNIVERSITY OF CALIFORNIA BE LIABLE TO ANY PARTY FOR DIRECT,
INDIRECT, SPECIAL, INCIDENTAL, OR CONSEQUENTIAL DAMAGES, INCLUDING LOST PROFITS,
ARISING OUT OF THE USE OF THIS SOFTWARE AND ITS DOCUMENTATION, EVEN IF THE
UNIVERSITY OF CALIFORNIA HAS BEEN ADVISED OF THE POSSIBILITY OF SUCH DAMAGE.

THE UNIVERSITY OF CALIFORNIA SPECIFICALLY DISCLAIMS ANY WARRANTIES, INCLUDING,
BUT NOT LIMITED TO, THE IMPLIED WARRANTIES OF MERCHANTABILITY AND FITNESS FOR A
PARTICULAR PURPOSE. THE SOFTWARE PROVIDED HEREUNDER IS ON AN "AS IS" BASIS, AND
THE UNIVERSITY OF CALIFORNIA HAS NO OBLIGATIONS TO PROVIDE MAINTENANCE, SUPPORT,
UPDATES, ENHANCEMENTS, OR MODIFICATIONS.
```

It doesn't get any simpler than that.

The final change in the organization and development of Postgre95 came in 1996 when the project was renamed to PostgreSQL and The PostgreSQL Global Development Group (PGDG) was formed to maintain and guide the development of PostgreSQL into the future. For 28 years (at the time of this writing), the PGDG has consistently worked with developers across the globe to add new features, make enhancements, fix bugs, and support the project, consistently releasing a new major version nearly every year since 1997.

PostgreSQL Governance

PostgreSQL is a global project, hence the PostgreSQL Global Development Group. Coordinating developers, patches, ideas, releases, support, bug fixes, and more with distributed team is never easy, even in our remote-first modern times. For the first 10+ years of the PostgreSQL project, it was a major undertaking. In many cases, developers might not meet for years, or only at a yearly hackathon.

Therefore, the PGDG decided to divide responsibilities and management of the project among a few key groups.

The Core Team

The Core Team is an appointed board of key contributors and supporters throughout the years. Since its inception, the positions have been filled through appointments by the core team itself. There is no specified number of members, however, historically there have been seven members as it currently stands today.

The team is not responsible for setting a roadmap of features. That is accomplished through the mailing lists and based on what features contributors are interested in working on.

Instead, the core team is primarily responsible for:

- Setting release dates
- Dealing with confidential project matters
- Acting as spokespeople for the project
- Arbitrating any unresolved community decisions.
  (a great example of this arbitration from the 2007 mailing list archives, specifically dealing

with what to call the project, leading to the two options discussed earlier. -
https://www.postgresql.org/message-id/473D7617.6070900@postgresql.org)

While there is a lot of important and necessary work that the core team does, just remember that they are not project managers in the typical sense. As code contributors they may work on a specific feature of interest to them, but they do not directly decide what the features of PostgreSQL will be. That is left to the community through proposals and discussions.

Code Contributors

Code contributors are any community member that submit patches for consideration and feedback. This is a long list of people spanning almost three decades, which is an impressive feat for any project.

It's worth noting, however, that code contributors don't have direct access to the source repository. As for 2024, all PostgreSQL patches must first be submitted through the `pgsql-hackers` mailing list for consideration. (We'll talk more about the mailing lists in a bit.) If the patch garners enough interest and support, it is added to the next *Commitfest* so that all future work and feedback can be tracked through the email list thread specific to this patch.

There are hundreds (thousands?) of patches that have been started over the years and not included. Sometimes the patches were proof-of-concept patches to start a discussion, sometimes they just went without any feedback, and other times the original author lost interest, and the patch never made further progress. Although there's nothing stopping another contributor from picking up that patch later (even years later!) and having another go.

In total, PostgreSQL wouldn't be the database system it is today without the hundreds and hundreds of code contributors that have dedicated time and effort to the project creating patches and reviewing or testing others. While some of the processes may seem outdated by modern standards ("why can't we just do a pull request on GitHub?"), there are valid reasons and, in some ways, those reasons have kept the project stable for nearly 30 years.

Code Committers

This group is a much smaller list of individuals throughout the world. They have been identified and recognized by their peers as someone that can be trusted with commit access to the repository, and they're often charged with working on patches in a specific area(s) of the code base.

All the people on this list are active developers, while being charged with more responsibility. As patches are submitted through the mailing list and added to a Commitfest. Contributors need to get the support of a committer to shepherd their patch through the review, modification, and eventual commit process. If no committer will take charge of the patch, it's unlikely to be added to an upcoming PostgreSQL release.

When a patch is finally added to the main PostgreSQL code repository, it will be the name of the committer, not the contributor, that is shown in the commit log. The commit comments will list the original contributor along with any significant reviewers and contributors, but the name associated with the commit will be the person that has access to modify the repository.

Without these dedicated volunteers, all the amazing features that others contribute would never make it into the codebase and releases would take significantly longer and contain fewer features.

Commitfest

We've talked about the core team, worldwide code contributors, and the select group of committers that all work together to help PostgreSQL keep innovating and fixing bugs. But how do they actually coordinate and accomplish this work multiple times each year? Commitfests.

Many years ago, the core team decided to aim for yearly major releases and multiple times throughout the year to release minor updates. To manage the plethora of patches being submitted, reviewed, and committed, the concept of an organized Commitfest was implemented. As the name implies, these are focused times when those that can commit patches to the source code work with contributors to commit the patches that are deemed complete and ready to ship.

As you might expect with an open-source project, Commitfests are transparent and open to the world so that anyone can see exactly what's happening with each patch and proposal. At any point in time, you can view the status of ongoing work at commitfest.postgresql.org, shown in Figure 1-1.

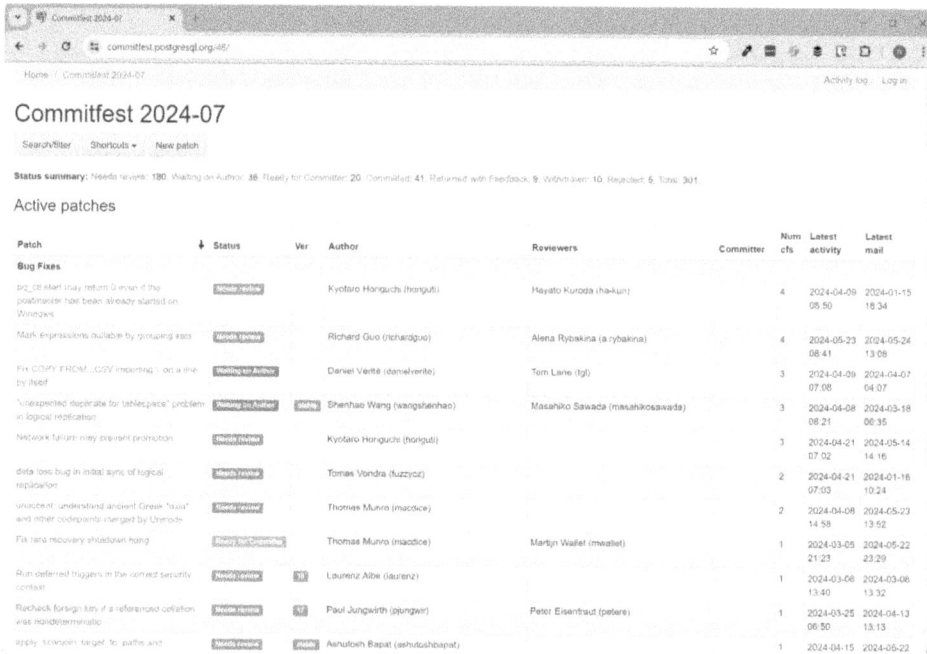

Figure 1-1. PostgreSQL Commitfest web application for tracking ongoing work on current and future releases.

Every patch has a clickable link which will display details about the history of work completed and its status throughout various Commitfests, shown in Figure 1-2. Any email threads from the `pgsql-hackers` mailing list are also attached as a link to the conversation. This allows you to read about the origin of the patch, all discussion, and any final resolutions. It can be very fascinating to look at old email threads for major features or long-awaited improvements, gaining a better understanding for how they were implemented and what choices had to be made along the way.

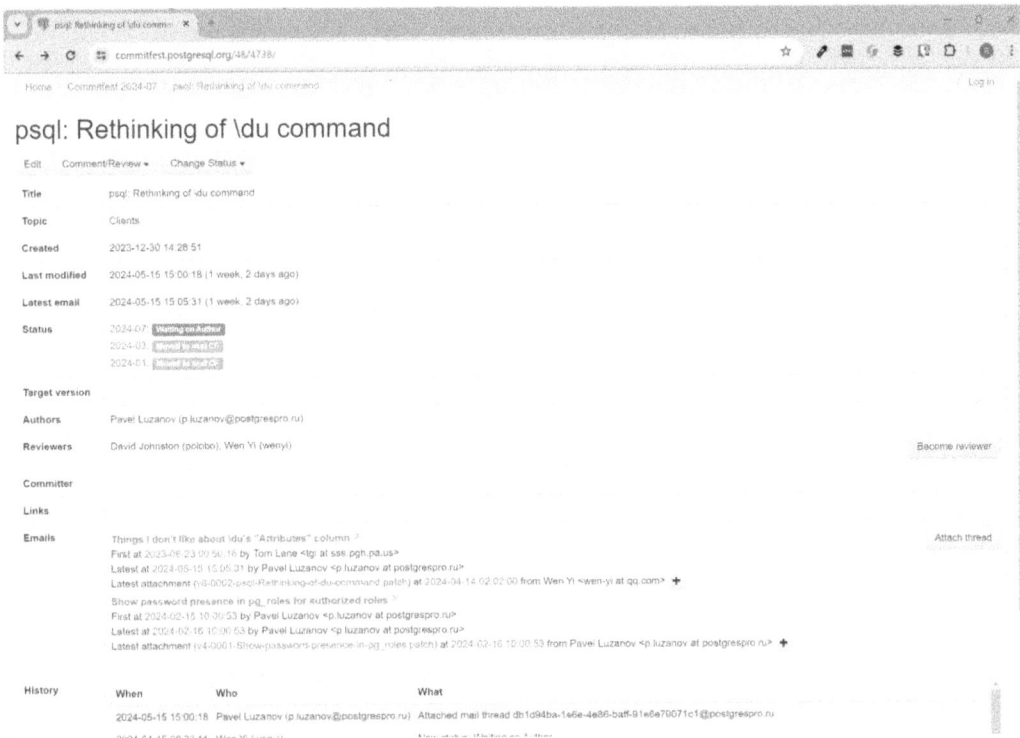

Figure 1-2. Detailed information for an individual patch within the commitfest.

Commitfest Cadence and Manager

The final thing to understand about PostgreSQL Commitfests is that they happen at a regular, consistent cadence. There are five events each year, generally two months apart. During each Commitfest, work is completed on bug fixes, minor version enhancements, and upcoming features for the next release. Any patch that would result in a breaking change to a current version of PostgreSQL is only included in the next major release.

The Commitfest that starts in March, however, typically runs for an extra month, although that's not officially mandated. Having this additional time allows the contributors to focus primarily on the major features that are likely to be included in the upcoming major release. Generally, starting in late May, beta versions of the next major release start to become available for testing by anyone.

By the end of the July Commitfest, major features are nearly solidified for the next version, and incomplete patches are moved to the next Commitfest which begins the yearly cycle all over again.

Coordinating work during a Commitfest doesn't happen automatically. Each Commitfest is led by a Commitfest manager (or managers). As part of the global community of contributors, this is a volunteer assignment that happens at least five times a year, for many years running! This is not a paid position and technically anyone can volunteer (although there's an expectation that they have likely contributed to the source in the past).

Their job is to verify the patches that are currently assigned, help coordinate reviewers, and generally just keep things moving along. It's essential work that most people in the world that use PostgreSQL will never know about. But now *you* do!

Why PostgreSQL and Why Now

Great. So now you know a lot more than you did a few minutes ago about how PostgreSQL started, is developed, about the community surrounding it, and how the very permissive license has fueled its growth and popularity. But it has essentially been around in its current form for nearly 30 years. Why does it seem to have reached the tipping point? Why, particularly if you've been a relational database/SQL developer or administrator for most of your career using a different platform, are you reading this book now?

While there are many reasons ("it depends" after all), in our opinion, the prevailing factors are twofold.

First and foremost, licensing. PostgreSQL has the most permissive licenses of almost any open-source project. Regardless of where you host a PostgreSQL database, on-prem or in the cloud, features are not tied to a license. It doesn't matter how many processors or cores you have, if you do concurrent index builds (i.e. online index builds), or if you want to use five different extensions, there is no license conversation to have. Yes, you still need to pay for servers, processor time, storage, and more, but there's no license component.

Second is extensibility. PostgreSQL is the only database among all the major relational databases to support extensions. In this chapter we discussed how the core database engine is developed and made available to the world. But many years ago, knowing that there would never be enough time or developers to see every feature request come to fruition, they created the ability for other developers to add capabilities without modifying the core code by adding small programs called extensions to their PostgreSQL installation.

Extensions allow PostgreSQL to be used in many ways, customized to the use case and needs. Extensions can create new index types, add powerful geospatial data capabilities, become a relational vector database for LLM, and even create distributed database architectures.

The extension ecosystem is growing very quickly, and the future is bright for what PostgreSQL will be capable of next.

Conclusion

The history, community, and dedication around PostgreSQL can be confusing to new users, and awe-inspiring the more that you understand the project. The database that millions of people know and love today, is built on the backs of an army of dedicated volunteers improving the database one patch at a time.

If you are able to attend a PostgreSQL-focused event sometime, you're almost guaranteed to meet some of these people. Thank them for their work, ask why they got involved, and encourage them to keep going.

2
PostgreSQL Basics and Differences

Now that you have an overview of how PostgreSQL began and the unique process for developing and maintaining features, it's time to start making a few comparisons between the knowledge you already have, and how it translates to PostgreSQL.

Fortunately, moving from one relational database system to another already puts you at an advantage because you know a dialect of SQL, understand the basics of schema design, and principles like backups and high availability. However, without a little help upfront, it can be challenging to figure out what the differences are which may unexpectedly trip you up as you begin your journey to learn PostgreSQL. This chapter aims to help uncover, at a high level, some of the major features and syntax differences to give you a head start.

Feature Comparison

Trying to highlight all the differences between relational databases could easily fill an entire book. Because we both come from SQL Server backgrounds, we'll be specifically comparing features in SQL Server to narrow the focus. We want to highlight features you may currently be using that work differently (or don't exist at all), and some features that PostgreSQL brings to the table that a database platform like SQL Server doesn't have.

Extensibility

While we'd prefer to start this chapter talking about features in SQL Server and their counterparts (or not) in PostgreSQL, talking about the extension capabilities in PostgreSQL are essential for some of the comparisons that follow.

At the end of Chapter 1 we briefly discussed two of the reasons why PostgreSQL has enjoyed so much popularity and fervor over the last decade. Aside from licensing, the ability to use extensions to add functionality or modify how a process within Postgres behaves has proven to be extraordinarily powerful for a wide array of use cases.

To a user of SQL Server, this kind of flexibility is unheard of. As a licensed product from Microsoft, users are dependent on their timeline and feature goals. If adding new AI features will be helpful and potentially profitable, it's likely that the next release will have a significant amount of effort dedicated to making AI accessible within the database. However, if it was important to you that SQL Server supported more native datatypes for geospatial data, including special indexes that make searching and correlating that data easier, you may be out of luck. That's not a specific critique of SQL Server or the development team (you're doing great!). It's often just an economic decision.

With PostgreSQL, however, that geospatial workload is easily employed by installing the PostGIS extension. This extension creates new datatypes and bindings to special indexes that work better with geospatial data. It also creates dozens of functions that are unique to geospatial data and allow a myriad of features to find the distance between two points, convert geospatial datatypes, do nearest neighbor search of points, and more.

The same goes with features like indexes. PostgreSQL has a set of hooks that any extension developer could take advantage of to create new index types. Other extensions might create a listener so that when a query plan is being created, the extension has an opportunity to modify something about the plan because of the kind of data the query is accessing.

Extensions can be created in any supported language on the server (including SQL) and can be used for special or mundane tasks. Many PostgreSQL administrators create extensions that simply install a known set of administrative functions that their teams use across the estate. Because extensions are versioned, it's an easy and safe way to determine if a particular database has the latest version of maintenance functions specific to that company or team.

The growing extension landscape within the PostgreSQL community is a powerful way to add functionality that wouldn't otherwise be possible, all without waiting on the (often) multi-year cycle for adding new, major features to the core PostgreSQL engine. While that may sound scary, the most popular extensions have been very well vetted for functionality, stability, and security best practices.

Talking more deeply about extensions, how to install them, manage them, and use them effectively could easily take a few dozen pages of a book all by itself. However, all major cloud providers support the most popular extensions and provide excellent documentation to help get you started. As of this writing, there are over 1,000 known extensions in the wild, but only about 50-75 that are heavily used to help solve common problems.

There are multiple places to find extensions, however, as of 2024, there is still no one central place to find, download, and install all of them. A few places to start include:

- PGXN, the Postgres Extension Network (pgxn.org)

- Postgres Trunk (pgt.dev)

- Postgres Extension Repos List (https://github.com/joelonsql/postgresql-extension-repos)

- Linux package managers (rpms, Debian, homebrew, etc.)

The main takeaway is that PostgreSQL supports extensions which can provide new functionality or enhance existing features of PostgreSQL. No other relational database supports this kind of feature and is a primary, distinguishing factor of PostgreSQL. You'll hear about a few extensions in the next few sections.

Built-in Job Scheduler

SQL Agent jobs are a mainstay of how so much background work is accomplished in the management of SQL Server and tasks that keep your data workflows in good working order. Whether you run Ola Hallegren's maintenance scripts or schedule some type of

ETL jobs, having a built-in scheduler as part of the server is convenient and often essential. With SQL Agent jobs you also benefit from features like notifications or server email integration. In our experience, agent jobs are used on nearly every production SQL Server.

PostgreSQL doesn't have an internal, out of the box, job scheduling mechanism. Instead, this functionality can be provided by numerous extensions.

The most popular, and supported by all major cloud providers, is pg_cron. There is no graphical interface for setting up the scheduled jobs, and that currently holds true for any of the popular extensions that provide this functionality. But, with minimal effort, the extension can be installed and jobs created with very specific cron-like scheduling parameters.

Query Hints

Love them or hate them, query hints are a necessity for many of the things we do in SQL Server. Whether MAXDOP, OPTIMIZE FOR, RECOMPILE, or NOLOCK (sorry, we had to do it), there are good and valid reasons for many of the hints when used appropriately.

PostgreSQL does not come with native support for query hints. You cannot force a specific join type, degree of parallelism, or point to a specific index when writing PostgreSQL queries. Unless, of course, you install the pg_hint_plan extension, also available on most major cloud providers.

With pg_hint_plan installed in the database you can add Oracle-style query hints to your queries. Hints are added to the SQL query as comments with specific commands that can direct the planner to join tables in specific ways, use an index, modify row estimates for a relation, and more.

Query Plan Cache

In SQL Server, the query plan cache is an essential feature that helps reduce compilation overhead for queries. Rather than compiling a plan on every execution, the query planner can pull a matching query plan out of the cache in some circumstances and get on with execution. There are pitfalls with the query plan cache that still exist today like parameter sniffing of stored procedures, but any time work can be reduced on the query planning and execution process is a win.

PostgreSQL does not have a query plan cache. Every execution of a query produces a new plan, unless you specifically prepare a query statement and reuse that plan for future queries. Admittedly, however, how and why you would use prepared statements is a slightly complex topic and one you should study before implementing in specific workloads you might have.

The idea that every query requires compilation is a foreign concept to SQL Server developers and DBAs. We're taught over and over that the plan cache is essential to reduce overhead for the server to reduce every possible CPU cycle of work. Interestingly, query planning is rarely the issue that slows down a query or overloads the server in PostgreSQL.

We don't currently know of any plans to support a query cache in PostgreSQL core, nor any popular extensions that do. However, some cloud vendors have implemented their own features that do something similar (i.e. AWS Aurora PostgreSQL query plan management), and there are a few publicly available extensions that attempt to implement similar functionality, although none of them are regularly discussed or unavailable in hosted environments.

Execution Plan Viewer

This falls more under tooling than a deficiency in viewing query plans, but having graphical viewers that provide various metric breakdowns is a staple for SQL Server developers. The ease of opening any plan in a detailed viewer is front and center in SQL Server Managements Studios (SSMS) and even Azure Data Studio. Because these tools are included as part of the products supported and maintained by the team developing SQL Server, it's an integrated experience that we often take for granted.

Depending on the IDE that you use with PostgreSQL, a graphical query plan viewer may be available. PGAdmin has included one for many years, and there are multiple online tools that will turn the text-based plans into a visual plan, but it's just not as seamless as what you know in SSMS or the handful of other go-to tools.

Regardless of the tool or method you might use to produce a visual plan, you'll still be better served in the long run to become familiar with text based EXPLAIN plans. It's not as scary as it sounds once you know a few basics. We'll explore some of the basic concepts and a few online tools to help parse query plans in Chapter 11: Indexes and Query Tuning.

Terminology Differences

Although PostgreSQL and SQL Server are both relational databases that support many features of the ANSI SQL standard, knowing the correct terminology for similar concepts is essential, particularly as you search documentation or ask for help from the community. In the next section, we'll look specifically at differences in SQL concepts.

Cluster vs. Instance

Like the choice to rename the project to PostgreSQL, forever confusing users about how to pronounce it, the term used to identify the running PostgreSQL process is slightly confusing, too.

Technically, as referenced in the official documentation, the running process is called a *cluster*, not *instance*. You can have multiple running clusters on a host, each listening to a different port, and configured differently. Obviously, this can cause some confusion when all distributed database systems are a cluster of, well, clusters. We hear more people call an individual PostgreSQL process an instance as time goes by, but it's worth noting that when you typically see the word "cluster" in reference to a PostgreSQL server, that's just a single running process unlikely to be connected to other instances.

Role vs User

In PostgreSQL, all principles that can connect to a database are called *roles*. There is no technical difference between a role that functions as a user, and a role that functions as a group. By convention, all user roles are allowed to login, while group roles are not. However, there's nothing that enforces that in PostgreSQL. Depending on how a role is configured, it may be able to grant membership to other roles, so even if the role can login (i.e. a "user" role), it might still offer membership to a group of other roles.

One other thing of note is that although roles are created at the cluster level, a user role can only establish a connection to a database. Even if you supply the correct credentials, if the role doesn't have at least one database that it has the privilege to connect to, they will not be able to establish a connection.

Chapter 6 is dedicated to roles and security.

Tuple vs. Row

In SQL Server, a row, is a row, is a row… for the most part. In PostgreSQL, however, you'll often hear the word *tuple* to describe the individual rows of data returned from a table. They essentially mean the same thing, but there's a (historically) academic reason why the word tuple is still used.

A tuple refers to the schema (column types, widths, order, etc.) of a row. Rows are instances of tuples. But using the word tuple means that you're not talking about just an abstract set of data being returned. It must match and adhere to the constraints of the schema of the table, which is the definition of a tuple.

It's a very minor difference, and honestly doesn't matter in the grand scheme of things, but you'll hear the word tuple a lot, so it's worth understanding that it's just a row, which is a representation of the schema from the table.

Literal Object Qualifiers

The ANSI SQL standard says that double quotes should be used to qualify objects (generally), but especially when objects don't adhere to the naming rules, like adding spaces in an object name. Unfortunately, not all databases adhere to this standard and choose other qualifying characters.

By default, SQL Server uses square brackets to qualify names (left) and PostgreSQL uses double quotes (right).

```
[Table One] vs. "Table One"
```

This is especially noteworthy when migrating to PostgreSQL with lots of legacy SQL that uses a different qualifier.

COPY vs. BULK INSERT

Loading lots of data from external sources is necessary for almost every database project in modern applications. Dating back to the original, open-source research project that is the foundation for PostgreSQL, there has been a special SQL command called COPY that only PostgreSQL supports.

COPY is generally supported by any database which is derived from PostgreSQL and is the preferred method for inserting lots of data quickly. The binary COPY protocol is also supported by most modern language SDKs to assist with the speedy loading of data.

TOAST

The term TOAST stands for "The Oversized Attribute Storage Technique". (Clever, eh?)

TOASTing data is essentially off row storage for data that cannot fit into a single 8Kb page. Any variable length data type can be toasted, which writes the data to other pages on disk and then creates a pointer in place of the data within the row. Any time a query requests that specific data, it is accessed outside of the row, materialized, and returned.

TOASTed data is automatically compressed, with recent versions of PostgreSQL supporting user-selectable compression algorithms if they are made available during the compilation of the PostgreSQL kernel.

While that doesn't sound like anything fancy (all database servers need a way to store large data outside of a data page), the unique feature in PostgreSQL is that there are access methods which extensions can hook into when data is toasted. With this hook, extensions like TimescaleDB can implement a proprietary data compression feature which stores data off in an aggregated form which can help time-series type workloads.

Just don't get out the butter and jam when someone using PostgreSQL starts talking about TOAST.

SQL Differences

Finally, we want to spend just a few pages discussing some of the first SQL differences that are likely to trip you up if you're coming from SQL Server.

Data Types

PostgreSQL has many built-in data types and more can be added through extensions or through direct SQL statements. New index types can also be created to assist the query planner in retrieving data more efficiently. However, the standard set has a few surprises that we wanted to highlight.

TEXT

PostgreSQL does support the CHAR/VARCHAR datatypes, but over the years there has been a lot of testing and discussion around the need for anything other than TEXT. As counter intuitive as it may sound, there's almost never a reason to use a character datatype instead of TEXT. It's UTF-8 by default, automatically takes care of any toasting and off-row compression, and it simplifies schema development.

One of the main reasons SQL Server developers have been told time and again *not* to use VARCHAR(MAX), which would essentially be equivalent of using TEXT, is because the query planner can do unexpected things with memory grants if all text fields are set as "big" fields.

PostgreSQL doesn't deal with query memory in the same way, so this isn't a concern. Also, disk storage and data retrieval are not negatively impacted when using text fields. If you require a specific maximum width for a text column, add the appropriate constraint to prevent wider data from being saved to the text field. Using a constraint also has the added benefit of being able to widen or remove the constraint at any time without having to modify the datatype and potentially cause a table re-write.

TIMESTAMP (WITH TIME ZONE)

TIMESTAMP (`timestamp`) or TIMESTAMP WITH TIME ZONE (`timestamptz`) are generally equivalent to the DATETIME/DATETIMEOFFSET datatypes in SQL Server. Like SQL Server, time zone aware datatypes will store the data in UTC.

The output of a TIMESTAMP WITH TIME ZONE will be converted to the time zone set within the session. Depending on the tool/IDE you use to query `timestamptz` data, your time zone may be read from your computer locale or from a configurable setting.

Using `psql`, the queries in Listing 2-1, 2-2, and 2-3, demonstrate how the time zone of the session modifies the output of a query.

Listing 2-1: *Show the current time zone of the session*

```
SHOW timezone;

TimeZone|
--------+
Etc/UTC |
```

Listing 2-2: *Timestamp with time zone value stored as UTC*

```
SELECT last_update FROM bluebox.customer
ORDER BY customer_id LIMIT 1;

last_update                |
---------------------------+
2023-10-13 20:41:34.320464+00|
```

Listing 2-3: *psql displays output of the timestamptz column at session time zone*

```
SET TIME ZONE 'EST';

SELECT last_update FROM bluebox.customer
ORDER BY customer_id LIMIT 1;

last_update                |
---------------------------+
2023-10-13 15:41:34.320464-05|
```

The problem with the time zone used for the output is that different tools handle it different ways. For example, we often use DBeaver to execute queries in PostgreSQL. Unfortunately, it sets the time zone at startup based on the locale of your computer. Attempting to set the time zone of the session as shown above does not affect the output formatting without additional configuration. Therefore, someone else running the same query in a different time zone will get a different output with a different offset value. The timestamp value itself has not changed; it just looks different since each user will "see" the data in their locally specified time zone.

If you need to guarantee that the output is formatted using a specific time zone offset, then you must cast the value within the query. The SELECT statement in Listing 2-4 will produce the same timestamp value and offset for anyone that runs it, regardless of their session time zone.

Listing 2-4: *Cast a timestamptz to a specific time zone*

```
SELECT last_update AT TIME ZONE 'EST' FROM bluebox.customer
ORDER BY customer_id LIMIT 1;

last_update                |
---------------------------+
2023-10-13 15:41:34.320464 |
```

Storing and querying dates and timestamps can be complicated at times. However, for consistency and ease, using TIMESTAMP WITH TIME ZONE (`timestamptz`) to store timestamp values is the most reliable. It's flexible and will always output the appropriate value given a specific time zone.

ARRAY

One of the most controversial datatypes, specifically from users coming to PostgreSQL from a different database, is the array datatype. Any datatype in PostgreSQL can be represented in array form as a column type. It certainly takes some getting used to, and it's not a datatype to be used without purpose, but it can be powerful when used correctly.

Arrays should (generally) never be used as a replacement for a linking table, but when a list of items can be associated with an object, this has a few advantages.

First, arrays are type aware. Rather than using a text field to store a comma-separated list of values that might store text, integers, floating points, timestamps, and more, arrays know the type and will error if a user tries to insert integers into a text field.

Arrays can also be indexed in a way that goes beyond a comma-separated text field and there are specific built-in functions to query and manipulate arrays. Also, as helpful as array types can be when used correctly to store data in a table column, it's often a game changer to be able to use array datatypes in pl/pgsql (analogous to TSQL for SQL Server) for development.

Case Rules

PostgreSQL uses case sensitive collations which means that all object names are case sensitive. However, PostgreSQL automatically transforms all object names to lowercase unless they are qualified with double quotes. If you don't know about this ahead of time, especially coming from SQL Server, a lot of queries will start to fail in unexpected ways.

For instance, let's say that you create a table using the code in Listing 2-5.

Listing 2-5. Creating a table object without qualifying the name

```
CREATE TABLE CamelCase (c1 text);
```

Because the table name is not qualified with double quotes, any of the select statements in Listing 2-6 will return data because the name is stored in lowercase, and all object references in these queries transform the table name to lowercase.

Listing 2-6. Unqualified object names will query as lower case

```
SELECT * FROM CamelCase;
SELECT * FROM camelcase;
SELECT * FROM CAMELCase;
SELECT * FROM CaMeLcAsE;
```

However, the SELECT statement in Listing 2-7 will fail because the qualified table name instructs PostgreSQL to find that exact table, with the exact name and case.

Listing 2-7. The qualified object name doesn't exist because it was created unqualified

```
SELECT * FROM "CamelCase";

ERROR:  relation "CamelCase" does not exist
LINE 1: select * from "CamelCase";
```

This is especially troublesome when two different developers execute SQL to generate tables but one qualifies the name and the other doesn't. Listing 2-8 shows how two different tables will be created with no errors.

Listing 2-8. Mixing qualified and unqualified object names

```
-- This results in a table with the matching case
CREATE TABLE "CamelCase" (c1 text);

-- This results in a table with the object name of "camelcase"
CREATE TABLE CamelCase (c1 text);
```

Instead of using camelCase for object names, the majority of PostgreSQL functions and schemas utilize lower snake case to name objects, using underscores between words rather than uppercase letters. This means that the preferred method of creating the example table above would be to use the naming shown in Listing 2-9.

Listing 2-9. Most PostgreSQL developers prefer snake case object names

```
CREATE TABLE camel_case (c1 text);
```

Between object name qualifiers and the automatic transformation to lowercase, we've seen many queries rewritten from TSQL that produce errors simply because of this principle.

Don't use camel case in PostgreSQL. You will have to qualify the name on creation of the object and every query that ever references that table, column, function, and more.

LIMIT vs. TOP

To select a limited number of rows in a query, SQL Server users instinctively use type `SELECT TOP(10) FROM…` and it's a hard habit to break. Instead, PostgreSQL uses the more standard LIMIT keyword to limit the number of rows returned from a query. Listing 2-10 and 2-11 demonstrate how to select 10 rows of data from the rental table from each database.

Listing 2-10. Retrieve 10 rows from the rental table in SQL Server

```
SELECT TOP(10) * FROM [Bluebox].[Rental] ORDER BY RentalID;
```

Listing 2-11. Retrieve 10 rows from the rental table in PostgreSQL

```
SELECT * FROM bluebox.rental ORDER BY rental_id LIMIT 10;
```

DATE_PART vs DAY/MONTH/YEAR

Like the TOP function in SQL Server, we're guessing that most of you have some muscle memory around how you get the parts of a date out of a timestamp-like value. The sensible functions DAY(), MONTH(), and YEAR() are clear and commonplace in everyday TSQL. PostgreSQL on the other hand uses the date_part() function to return various parts of a timestamp or date value. (SQL Server has a datepart() function as well).

Slightly more cumbersome at first glance, but this function also accommodates a few dozen parameter values to extract every part of the source value: day, month, year, century, doy, epoch, and others that allow you to get just the data you need.

For example, a query that counts the number of DVD rentals per year is shown in Listing 2-12 for SQL Server and Listing 2-13 for PostgreSQL.

Listing 2-12. Extracting the year from a timestamp in SQL Server

```
SELECT COUNT(*), YEAR(RentalStart) RentalYear
FROM BlueBox.Rental
GROUP BY RentalYear
ORDER BY YEAR(RentalStart) DESC;
```

Listing 2-13. Extracting the year from a timestamp in PostgreSQL

```
SELECT COUNT(*), DATE_PART('year',rental_start) rental_year
FROM bluebox.rental
GROUP BY rental_year
ORDER BY rental_year DESC;
```

Note that in PostgreSQL, you can use the function alias in both the GROUP BY and ORDER BY clauses. In SQL Server, aliases are only allowed in the ORDER BY clause.

INTERVAL vs DATEADD

PostgreSQL has an INTERVAL datatype which represents an interval of time. And although there are functions like `date_add()` and `date_subtract()`, PostgreSQL Date/Time values support direct math using an INTERVAL.

To query for the last week of data from the rental table using dynamic date math, Listings 2-14 and 2-15 show how this can be accomplished in SQL Server and PostgreSQL.

Listing 2-14. Dynamic date math in SQL Server using DATEADD

```
SELECT COUNT(*), YEAR(RentalStart)
FROM BlueBox.Rental
WHERE RentalStart > DATEADD(MONTH,-1,SYSDATETIME())
GROUP BY YEAR(RentalStart)
```

Listing 2-15. Dynamic date math in PostgreSQL using the INTERVAL type

```
SELECT COUNT(*), DATE_PART('year',rental_start) rental_year
FROM bluebox.rental
WHERE rental_start > NOW() - INTERVAL '1 month'
GROUP BY rental_year;
```

LATERAL vs APPLY

As you grow in skill developing against SQL Server, eventually you learn about the APPLY operator in TSQL joins. It's an effective (and often efficient) way to iterate over each row in an outer query against a secondary query that references data from the outer row. If you ever want the most recent value for each item in a query, APPLY is usually the easiest way to do that, no extra function required.

PostgreSQL subscribes to the ANSI SQL standard approach to this called a LATERAL query. While there are a few minor differences in how LATERAL queries can be written and used, the overall concept is the same.

Listing 2-16 and 2-17 show an example query to retrieve the customer ID from each store with the most recent rental for SQL Server and PostgreSQL respectively.

Listing 2-16. SQL Server In-line code

```
SELECT StoreID, CustomerID, RentalStart
FROM BlueBox.Store s1
CROSS APPLY (
  SELECT TOP(1) CustomerID, RentalStart
  FROM  BlueBox.Rental
  WHERE StoreID = s1.StoreID
  ORDER BY RentalStart DESC
) r1;
```

Listing 2-17. SQL Server In-line code

```
SELECT store_id, customer_id, rental_start
FROM bluebox.store s1
INNER JOIN LATERAL (
  SELECT customer_id, lower(rental_period) AS rental_start
  FROM bluebox.rental
  WHERE store_id = s1.store_id
  ORDER BY rental_start DESC
  LIMIT 1
) r1 ON true;
```

Anonymous Code Blocks

Last but not least, we need to talk about writing ad hoc, inline code with variables, functions, loops, and more. SQL Server developers and DBAs are used to doing this everywhere. Whether in SSMS or a TSQL script that will be run as part of a deployment, we create code blocks liberally, because it's just so useful to efficiently doing complex work.

The challenge is that this kind of procedural programming within a SQL script is not supported by the ANSI SQL standard. Any time you write scripts using variables and more for SQL Server, they are being executed by the TSQL engine which understands that some of the code is treated differently to provide added value. This works because SQL Server defaults to executing SQL files with the TSQL engine unless indicated otherwise. We just never have to think about it.

PostgreSQL treats SQL as the declarative language that it is, without inherent ability to execute procedural code. Instead, PostgreSQL expects most procedural code to be written in a function which declares the procedural language to use. Using variables and other procedural code directly in the script simply won't work.

However, you can declare what's known as an anonymous code block (sometimes called "DO" blocks) directly in your SQL script to accomplish some of the same functionality. This is meant for one-off situations and imposes some annoying limitations, like not allowing the block to return a set of data.

As a very simple example, Listing 2-18 and 2-19 demonstrates how to declare a variable, select a value into it, and then print the results.

Listing 2-18. SQL Server In-line code

```
DECLARE @LimitedDescription AS NVARCHAR(50);
SELECT @LimitedDescription = LEFT(Overview,50)
  FROM BlueBox.Film
  WHERE FilmID = 100;

PRINT @LimitedDescription;
```

Listing 2-19. PostgreSQL Anonymous Code Block

```
DO $$
   DECLARE limited_description TEXT;
BEGIN
  SELECT LEFT(overview, 50) FROM bluebox.film
  WHERE film_id = 100
  INTO limited_description;

  RAISE NOTICE '%', limited_description;
END;
$$
```

Certainly not as straightforward as you might be used to, and as we said, there are other limitations that will probably encourage you to just write a function. But when you need to do some ad hoc data processing that doesn't require the return of a dataset, anonymous code blocks are very helpful.

Conclusion

In this chapter we tried to highlight some of the main differences between PostgreSQL and SQL Server. As we mentioned at the beginning of the chapter, your current skills writing SQL and using a relational database give you nearly all the tools you need to effectively use PostgreSQL. Often just knowing what to call something can make all the difference when you are starting out or need to ask for help.

There are plenty of other things that differ between the two database platforms, but we wanted to keep this chapter focused and give you some new tools to start exploring with.

3
Installing PostgreSQL

PostgreSQL can run on almost any operating system and almost any set of hardware. The complete list of supported platforms is available in the PostgreSQL documentation (http://tinyurl.com/pgintrobook). For this book, we're going to concentrate on three different ways to get PostgreSQL up and running on your own hardware:

- Installing to Linux

- Installing to Windows

- Using containers

There are a number of additional operating systems that can be used, which may come with changes to the methodology for installing PostgreSQL. However, most people fall into one of these three categories. We'll be using PostgreSQL version 16 throughout the book. Some examples might not run on earlier versions.

One more possible mechanism for getting started with PostgreSQL is to host your cluster on one of the cloud platforms. We'll address using the cloud in Chapter 16.

While PostgreSQL can run almost anywhere, there are a few minimum hardware requirements that we should address up-front.

Minimum Hardware

As was already stated, PostgreSQL can run on just about anything from an Edge unit like a Raspberry Pi up to the very largest servers. However, as with any software, there are a few minimum requirements that you must meet in order for PostgreSQL to work. PostgreSQL doesn't have a published minimum set of requirements. However, there are suggestions for minimums in various locations online. Here, we'll outline a few.

For the CPU, the minimum recommended processor speed is 1 GHz, but obviously, slower speeds will only result in slower processing. Here are the architectures currently supported: the x86 family of chips, ARM and SPARC, PowerPC, S/390, MIPS, RISC-V, and PA-RISC.

The minimum amount of memory is quite a bit more ambiguous. The general suggestion for minimal performance is at least 2GB of ram. Just as with the minimum processor speed, this amount of memory will result in quite poor performance for most use cases. More memory is better.

The amount of storage you have directly impacts the amount of data you can keep. However, the minimum amount of space you need to get PostgreSQL off the ground is 50KB. That doesn't include data storage, and this will be a very truncated installation of PostgreSQL, but it will function.

Clearly, an average laptop can readily run PostgreSQL, so for learning, training, and testing purposes, just about anything you have available should work well enough.

Where To Get the Bits

As we explained in Chapter 1, the PostgreSQL community is organized in a manner that is different from most commercial database systems you may be familiar with. Those differences extend to distribution of the core code itself. The community found at postgresql.org and the "hackers" group that actively works on the core codebase on the PostgreSQL mailing lists, primarily focuses on distributing just the core code itself, making it available from the PostgreSQL source repository.

However, most people make use of one of the many different packaging systems, binary distributions, or other alternative methods of acquiring PostgreSQL. You should know that these packages are also made by independent groups of volunteers, or in some cases, companies, that coordinate with the greater PostgreSQL community. These groups packaging PostgreSQL have a significant level of independence and control over how the software is ultimately installed on your systems. While this can lead to surprising differences in how PostgreSQL operates across those different systems, the theory behind this process is that individual packaging teams know what makes the most sense for their needs, and the PostgreSQL developers don't have the time or resources to police this across every platform they support.

You can go and download the code directly and compile it yourself. It's available from https://git.postgresql.org. However, as this is an introductory book, we're not going to make you compile the code to get started. Instead, we'll use the installation packages found here: https://www.postgresql.org/download/. You'll want to select the appropriate operating system as shown in Figure 3-1:

Figure 3-1. Operating systems installation packages on postgresql.org

Depending on the operating system, you'll get a second set of menus. For example, if we pick Linux, I'll then be asked to pick which flavor of Linux I'm interested in as you see in Figure 3-2:

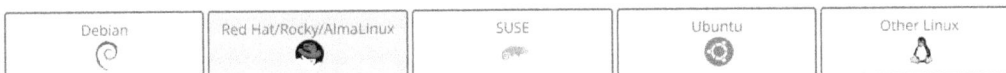

Figure 3-2. Selecting the appropriate distribution of Linux

Then again, depending on the OS, you'll be taken to the various versions of PostgreSQL available to that OS as well as instructions in how to get the appropriate installation packages. For example, selecting Windows takes us to a download link, as well as documentation for which versions of PostgreSQL run on which versions of Windows. If we pick Ubuntu, the instructions are on how to use the Apt repository to get a different version of PostgreSQL. Generally speaking, PostgreSQL is available within many Linux flavors using the distributions native packaging system. However, it may not always be the version you want, so you'll have to go through an install before you can get PostgreSQL up and running.

Linux Install

Every variation of Linux is a little bit different. Because of this, there's not a single path through the process of getting PostgreSQL installed on Linux. We're going to document how to install using Ubuntu and Debian because they're two of the more popular distributions on desktops.

The process is straight forward. We're going to pull down the correct PostgreSQL install using the installation and maintenance program built into Ubuntu, APT:

Listing 3-1. *Install PostgreSQL from Linux packages*

```
sudo apt install -y postgresql
```

That will install and/or update PostgreSQL on Ubuntu and Debian. Next, to ensure we're connected to the PostgreSQL APT repository, we'll run one more command, added by the PostgreSQL install:

Listing 3-2.

```
sudo /usr/share/postgresql-common/pgdg/apt.postgresql.org.sh
```

This way, you can use APT to get PostgreSQL updates and extensions from the repository maintained by the Global Development Group.

To check the status of PostgreSQL, to see if it is it running, we'll run another command using the system control tool:

Listing 3-3

```
sudo systemctl status postgresql
```

In our system, we see that the service is loaded, but that it is not running, so we'll start it up using the same system control tool:

Listing 3-4

```
sudo systemctl start postgresql
```

With that, PostgreSQL is installed, up and running on our Linux machine. However, we won't be able to connect to it locally without first adding a client, so we'll also run this:

Listing 3-5

```
Sudo apt install postgresql-client
```

We'll talk more about tools in Chapter 4, but to finish getting PostgreSQL configured, we need to create a user and a database for them to connect to. In this, we're not using the 'postgres' user because that's a good security practice. We'll talk more about security in Chapter 6.

Listing 3-6

```
sudo -u postgres createuser -s $USER
createdb mydb
psql -d mydb
```

The first command creates a user based on my login on the Ubuntu system. You can obviously pick another user for that. We then created a database. With the database created, we connected to it using the client we installed above, psql. You should see something like Figure 3-3:

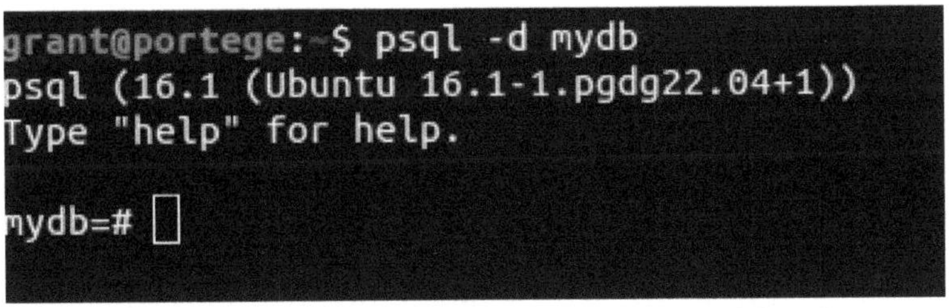

Figure 3-3. Successfully connected to our PostgreSQL cluster

The tool psql will allow me to run a query as follows:

Listing 3-7.

```
SELECT * FROM pg_catalog.pg_tables;
```

Typing this into psql, be sure you have the terminator, the semi-colon, and then hit enter. You should see results similar to Figure 3-4:

schemaname	tablename	tableowner	tablespace	hasindexes	hasrules	hastriggers	rowsecurity
pg_catalog	pg_statistic	postgres		t	f	f	f
pg_catalog	pg_type	postgres		t	f	f	f
pg_catalog	pg_foreign_table	postgres		t	f	f	f
pg_catalog	pg_authid	postgres	pg_global	t	f	f	f
pg_catalog	pg_statistic_ext_data	postgres		t	f	f	f
pg_catalog	pg_user_mapping	postgres		t	f	f	f
pg_catalog	pg_subscription	postgres	pg_global	t	f	f	f
pg_catalog	pg_attribute	postgres		t	f	f	f
pg_catalog	pg_proc	postgres		t	f	f	f
pg_catalog	pg_class	postgres		t	f	f	f
pg_catalog	pg_attrdef	postgres		t	f	f	f
pg_catalog	pg_constraint	postgres		t	f	f	f
pg_catalog	pg_inherits	postgres		t	f	f	f
pg_catalog	pg_index	postgres		t	f	f	f
pg_catalog	pg_operator	postgres		t	f	f	f
pg_catalog	pg_opfamily	postgres		t	f	f	f
pg_catalog	pg_opclass	postgres		t	f	f	f
pg_catalog	pg_am	postgres		t	f	f	f
pg_catalog	pg_amop	postgres		t	f	f	f
pg_catalog	pg_amproc	postgres		t	f	f	f
pg_catalog	pg_language	postgres		t	f	f	f
pg_catalog	pg_largeobject_metadata	postgres		t	f	f	f
pg_catalog	pg_aggregate	postgres		t	f	f	f
pg_catalog	pg_statistic_ext	postgres		t	f	f	f
pg_catalog	pg_rewrite	postgres		t	f	f	f
pg_catalog	pg_trigger	postgres		t	f	f	f
pg_catalog	pg_event_trigger	postgres		t	f	f	f
pg_catalog	pg_description	postgres		t	f	f	f
pg_catalog	pg_cast	postgres		t	f	f	f
pg_catalog	pg_enum	postgres		t	f	f	f
pg_catalog	pg_namespace	postgres		t	f	f	f
pg_catalog	pg_conversion	postgres		t	f	f	f
pg_catalog	pg_depend	postgres		t	f	f	f
pg_catalog	pg_database	postgres	pg_global	t	f	f	f
pg_catalog	pg_db_role_setting	postgres	pg_global	t	f	f	f
pg_catalog	pg_tablespace	postgres	pg_global	t	f	f	f

Figure 3-4. Results from pg_catalog.pg_tables

And that's all there is to it when it comes to a Linux install of PostgreSQL.

Windows Install

To get started with a Windows install, you first have to download the proper executable for the version of PostgreSQL you intend to install, and the chip set you're going to install it on. The download page is located here: http://tinyurl.com/3u9z9ky3 (this takes you directly to the same page you can get to from postgresql.org when choosing Windows, hosted by EDB). Double clicking on the executable opens the install wizard.

During installation, you'll have to pick what parts of PostgreSQL you wish to install. For your average server, you may only install PostgreSQL itself. Some may want to choose to install the command line utilities as well. For a development machine, it's probably a good idea to go ahead and install all of the tools including pgAdmin and Stack Builder. For the purposes of the book, the Server (obviously) and command line tools are all you need, however, the choice is yours. Our selections when installing can be seen in Figure 3-5:

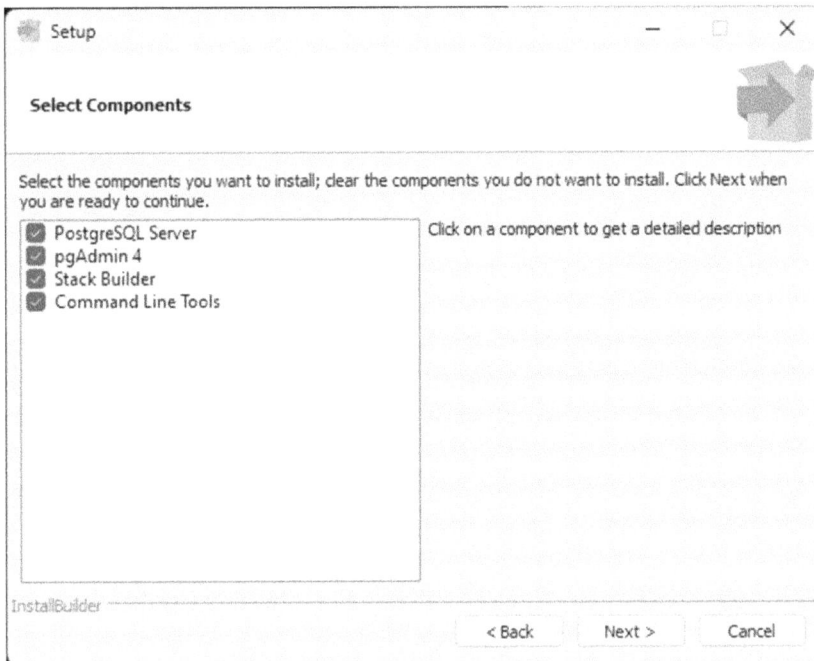

Figure 3-5. Selecting which components to install

We chose these tools so that we can show a variety of tools throughout the book, not just the more limited set. Lots of people are much more comfortable using a graphical user interface for example, so we included pgAdmin.

The next screen lets you decide where to store your actual databases that you define and manage within PostgreSQL. We'll cover some of these types of choices in more detail in Chapter 7. It's fairly common to separate the location of database files from the location of your PostgreSQL code. For demo purposes we are simply accepting the defaults as shown in Figure 3-6:

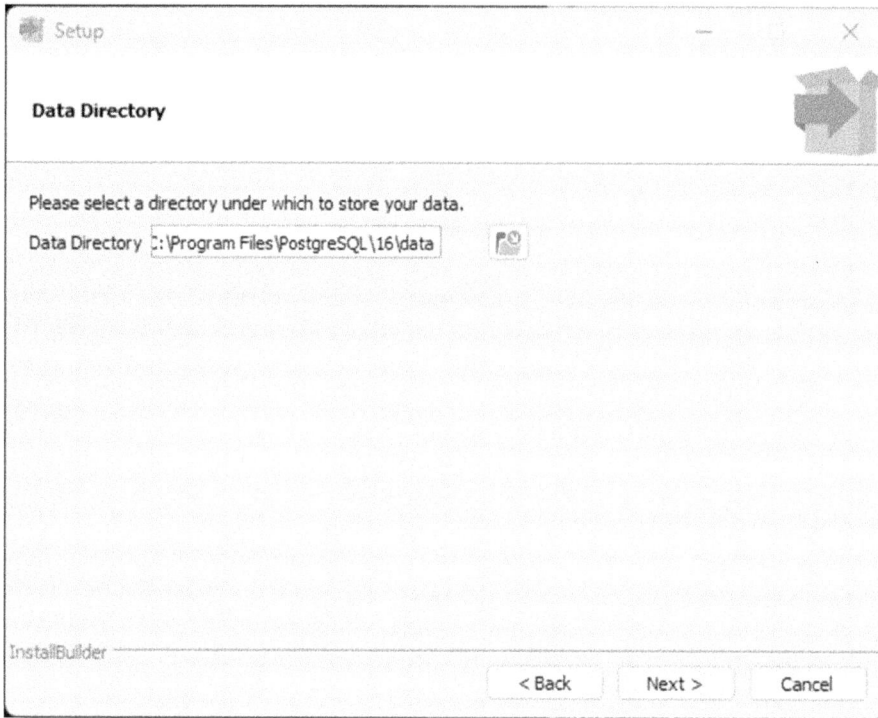

Figure 3-6. Selecting the location of PostgreSQL databases

Unlike with the Linux install, for Windows we do need to define the password for the 'postgres' default user. While we're going to address security in more detail in Chapter 6, we'll just note here that it is a good practice to disable the postgres login, or, at the very least, don't use it regularly to manage your clusters. Regardless, be sure you retain this password in some fashion for the short term while finishing the install and your setup of PostgreSQL:

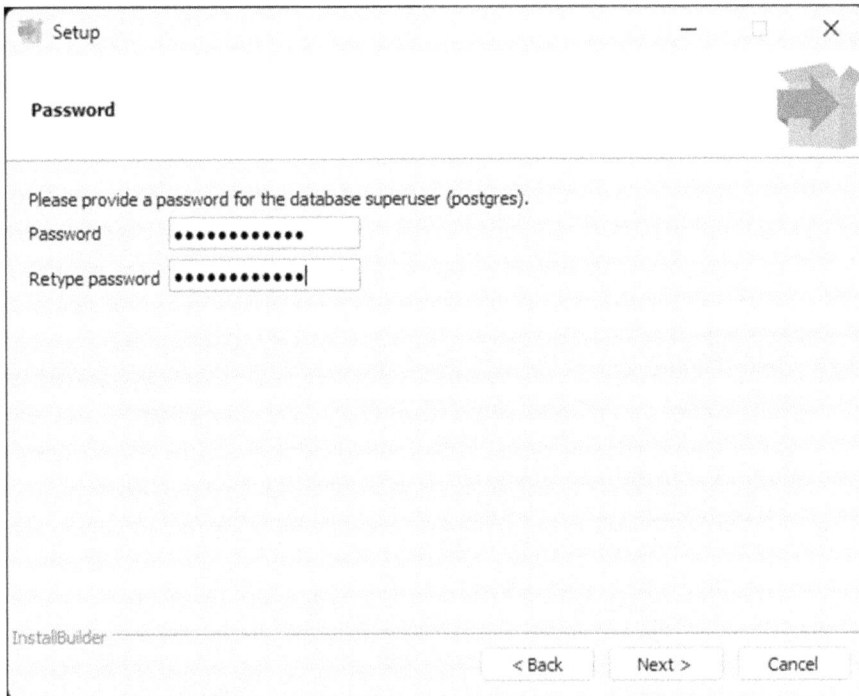

Figure 3-7. Setting the postgres password

Next, you'll be picking the port. The default port is 5432. If you need to run more than one cluster of PostgreSQL on a server, you'll need to define more than one port. Figure 3-8 shows that we're letting the default stand for this install:

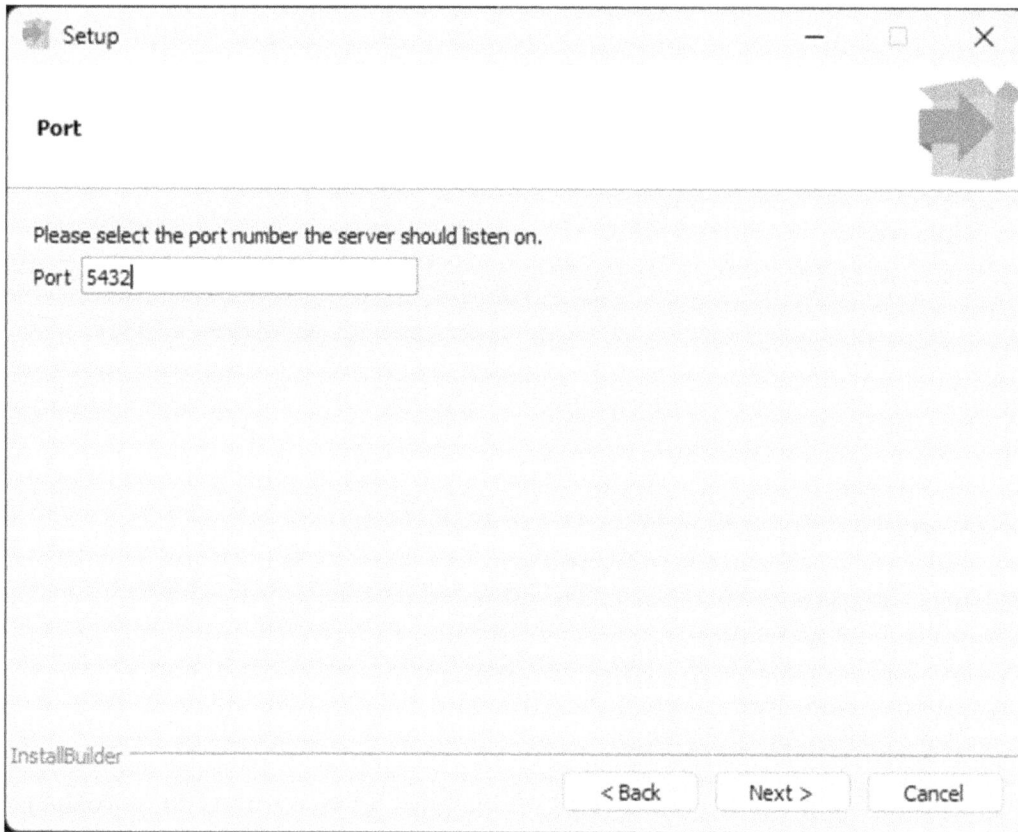

Figure 3-8. Determining the port number

The next step is to set the Locale for PostgreSQL. This determines collation, character sets and more. The default is to set it to the Locale defined within Windows. There is a drop down with all the various locales. For this install, we'll be using the default, [Default locale]. If your installation is localized, you can pick a specific locale. If you're in more of an international setting, a good choice is to use the "C" locale, which effectively means, no locale at all. Figure 3-9 shows the drop down and some of the possible selections:

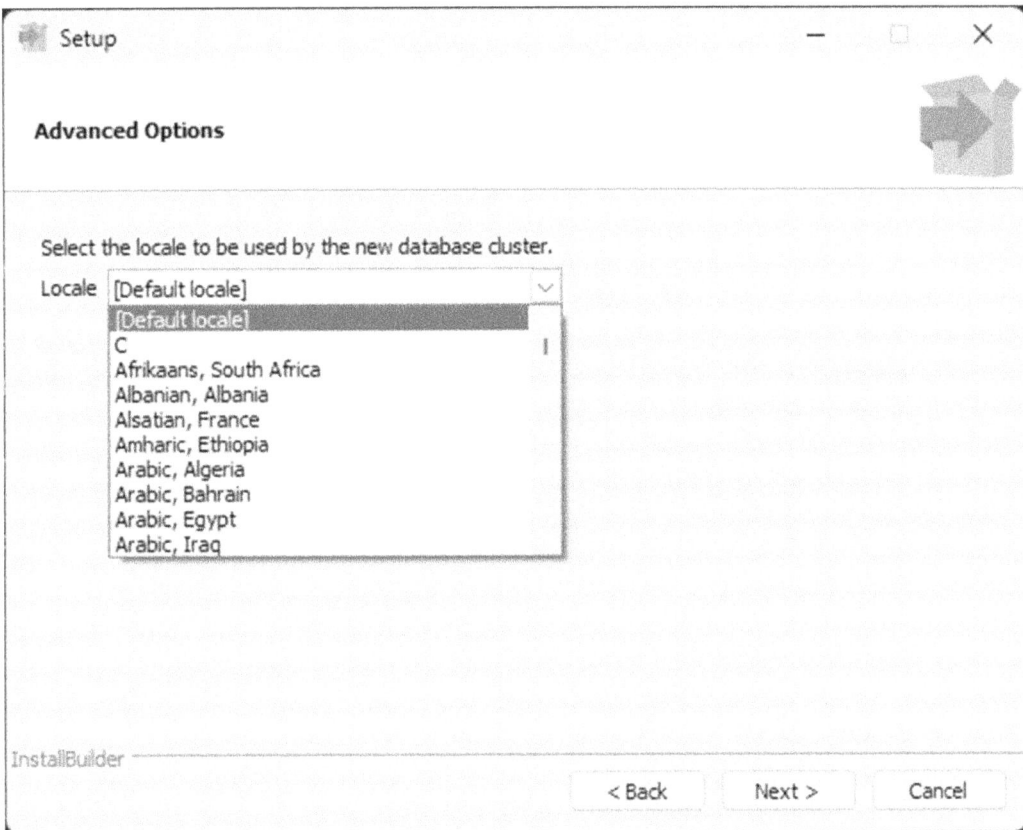

Figure 3-9. Selecting the locale for PostgreSQL

After that there's a screen that shows a summary of your choices and then everything gets installed. We can confirm that things are up and running using several different methods. The first is to just take a look at the services on my Windows machine as seen in Figure 3-10:

Figure 3-10. The PostgreSQL service is running

41

Another way would be to use pgAdmin that was installed along with PostgreSQL. We just have to remember the password we used for the postgres login. After making the connection (details on this in Chapter 4) we can see our cluster:

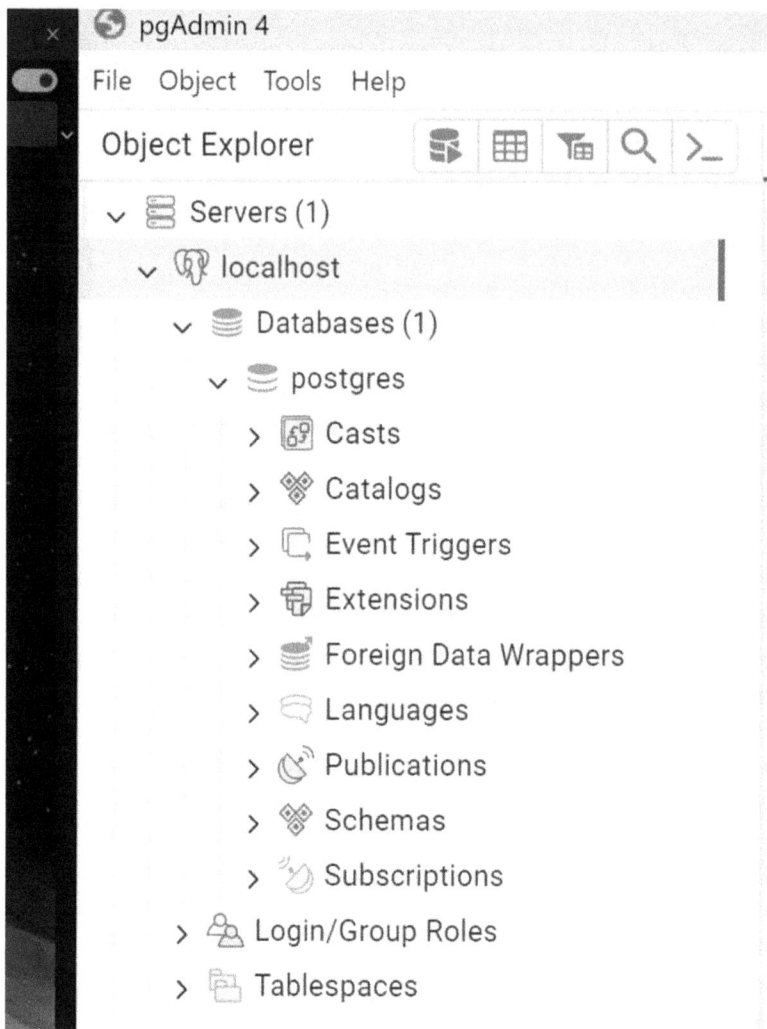

Figure 3-11. PostgreSQL is installed on the local Windows machine

Containers

One other way to get started with PostgreSQL is to use a container. In a lot of ways, this is one of the easiest ways to get your hands on the bits. You will have to have a machine capable of running virtualization (a few operating systems and some hardware won't support it, and some machines may need their BIOS edited in order to enable it. To figure out if your system supports virtualization, you'll need to look up your hardware and operating system).

There are a number of container management systems, but for this book we're going with one of the most widely adopted: Docker. For this example, we have previously installed Docker Desktop on the machine so we can get started creating a PostgreSQL container.

First, we'll have to get the image from Docker Hub. There are a ton of different possible images for PostgreSQL, many of which have a lot of good things going for them. However, here, we're going to focus on the official Docker image located here on the Docker website: http://tinyurl.com/ye8htzet.

To get the latest image of PostgreSQL, we can use the following command:

Listing 3-8.

```
docker pull postgres;
```

You can specify which version of PostgreSQL you're interested in. As of this writing, there are images on Docker Hub going all the way back to version 12.

It takes just a couple of minutes to download the information to the local machine. Once there, we can create a container. There are a few things you must provide. First, you give your container a name. You also have to supply the postgres login password. That's it for the defaults. However, like when we did the install on Linux, we can take more direct control over the container:

Listing 3-9.

```
docker run --name LearningPostgres `
    -e POSTGRES_PASSWORD=*cthulhu1988 `
    -e POSTGRES_USER="grantf" `
    -e POSTGRES_DB="mydb" `
    -p 5433:5432 `
    -d postgres;
```

A lot of listing 3.9 is explained by the description above. What we've added is the name of a Postgres user, "grantf", the name of a database "mydb", and a custom port number.

If you look at "-p 5433:5432" in Listing 3.9, what you see is a mapping between an external port for the Windows system, and an internal port for PostgreSQL. The internal port on this image is running on the default port of 5432. However, since we just installed a cluster on the Windows machine running in the default port of 5432, our container needs to use a different port, hence the mapping of 5433 to 5432 through the line "-p 5433:5432". That maps between the external and internal ports.

We can then connect to this cluster using the following command:

Listing 3-10.

```
psql -h localhost -U grantf -p 5433 -d mydb;
```

When asked to supply a password, give the one defined in Listing 3.9 and we are connected. We can then run the same query as in Listing 3.7 to see that PostgreSQL is indeed up and running.

Conclusion

In this chapter we went over three different ways you can get PostgreSQL installed and running on your local machines. These techniques will work on your laptop, on a server, or inside a virtual machine. You just have to follow the right path for your hardware and operating system and then everything is fine.

We introduced a couple of tools in this chapter. In the next chapter, we'll explore the concept of PostgreSQL tooling in more detail.

4

PostgreSQL Tools

In the previous chapter we installed PostgreSQL and then used `psql` and pgAdmin to verify that the installation went well. In this chapter we're going to explore both of those tools, as well as a couple of others that are commonly used to work with and manage PostgreSQL servers and databases. The majority of the work on PostgreSQL is done inside of the PostgreSQL server. Only a small percentage of the work, such as system configuration (covered in Chapter 5), is done outside the server, so having tools to do the work is vital.

Since automation is one of the keys to a successful implementation of PostgreSQL, we'll start off with the command line tool, `psql`. However, most of us work within a graphical environment such as Linux and Windows desktops, so we'll also cover three graphical tools for working with PostgreSQL: pgAdmin, DBeaver and Azure Data Studio.

psql

In `psql` is the command line driven mechanism for working with and administering your PostgreSQL databases. `Psql` is maintained by the PostgreSQL community as part of the open-source project that maintains the database itself, making it the official interface for working with PostgreSQL. In this section we'll cover getting psql installed, connecting to a server, and some basic functionality.

Installing psql

Generally speaking, every install of PostgreSQL includes the command line tool psql. While it is possible to exclude psql from the install process, in most cases this tool will be available on your server. In addition, since many Linux distributions install PostgreSQL by default, you'll also have a copy of `psql` by default.

However, what about client machines not currently running PostgreSQL? You can install `psql` independently of doing a full server install of PostgreSQL. The Linux install is pretty straightforward:

Listing 4-1.

```
sudo apt install postgresql-client
```

To install on a Windows machine, you use the same installer from Chapter 2 we used to install PostgreSQL. You can choose to only install the client tools, including `psql`.

With the install complete, you can validate that `psql` is available, as well as see the various commands supported by issuing the following command:

Listing 4-2.

```
psql -?
```

The results will look something like Figure 4-1:

```
grant@portege:~$ psql -?
psql is the PostgreSQL interactive terminal.

Usage:
  psql [OPTION]... [DBNAME [USERNAME]]

General options:
  -c, --command=COMMAND    run only single command (SQL or internal) and exit
  -d, --dbname=DBNAME      database name to connect to (default: "grant")
  -f, --file=FILENAME      execute commands from file, then exit
  -l, --list               list available databases, then exit
  -v, --set=, --variable=NAME=VALUE
                           set psql variable NAME to VALUE
                           (e.g., -v ON_ERROR_STOP=1)
  -V, --version            output version information, then exit
  -X, --no-psqlrc          do not read startup file (~/.psqlrc)
  -1 ("one"), --single-transaction
                           execute as a single transaction (if non-interactive)
  -?, --help[=options]     show this help, then exit
      --help=commands      list backslash commands, then exit
      --help=variables     list special variables, then exit

Input and output options:
  -a, --echo-all           echo all input from script
  -b, --echo-errors        echo failed commands
  -e, --echo-queries       echo commands sent to server
  -E, --echo-hidden        display queries that internal commands generate
  -L, --log-file=FILENAME  send session log to file
  -n, --no-readline        disable enhanced command line editing (readline)
  -o, --output=FILENAME    send query results to file (or |pipe)
  -q, --quiet              run quietly (no messages, only query output)
  -s, --single-step        single-step mode (confirm each query)
  -S, --single-line        single-line mode (end of line terminates SQL command)

Output format options:
  -A, --no-align           unaligned table output mode
      --csv                CSV (Comma-Separated Values) table output mode
  -F, --field-separator=STRING
                           field separator for unaligned output (default: "|")
  -H, --html               HTML table output mode
  -P, --pset=VAR[=ARG]     set printing option VAR to ARG (see \pset command)
  -R, --record-separator=STRING
                           record separator for unaligned output (default: newline)
  -t, --tuples-only        print rows only
  -T, --table-attr=TEXT    set HTML table tag attributes (e.g., width, border)
  -x, --expanded           turn on expanded table output
  -z, --field-separator-zero
                           set field separator for unaligned output to zero byte
  -0, --record-separator-zero
                           set record separator for unaligned output to zero byte
```

Figure 4-1. The help command output for psql

This shows the commands available for running psql. For our purposes here, we'll concentrate on some simple examples.

Connecting to PostgreSQL from psql

First, let's connect to our local server. If we configured the security correctly on Ubuntu as in Chapter 2, this command will open up the 'postgres' database in `psql`:

Listing 4-3.

```
psql -d postgres
```

As per the documentation, if you wanted to supply a specific username, you can of course do so:

Listing 4-4.

```
Psql -d postgres -U someuser
```

And of course, if you want to connect to a remote server, you can supply that information either through the server name (if your network is set up correctly), or through the IP address. You may also need to supply a port number if it's not the default:

Listing 4-5.

```
psql -d postgres -U postgres -h 192.168.1.141
```

That gets us connected to a PostgreSQL server running within our local network.

Using psql

Once you're connected, the main purpose of using `psql` is to be able to issue SQL commands to control and query the database. You can do this directly from the command line:

Listing 4-6.

```
psql -d postgres -U postgres -h 192.168.1.141 -c 'SELECT attname FROM
pg_stats'
```

Each of these commands require supplying the correct password for the login used. There are also commands within `psql` that allow us to control the behavior of `psql` and output different kinds of information. For example, to see a list of databases, you type the following:

Listing 4-7.

```
\l
```

The output will look something like Figure 4-2:

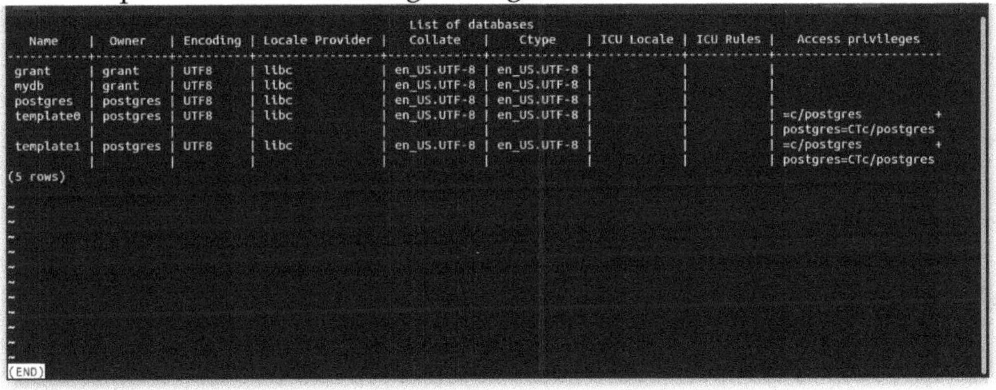

Figure 4-2. A listing of databases inside psql

To exit from the results, simply hit the letter 'q' for quit.

In order to switch the context to one of those listed databases, we can use a command like this:

Listing 4-8.

```
\c mydb
```

Which will result in an output something like Figure 4-3:

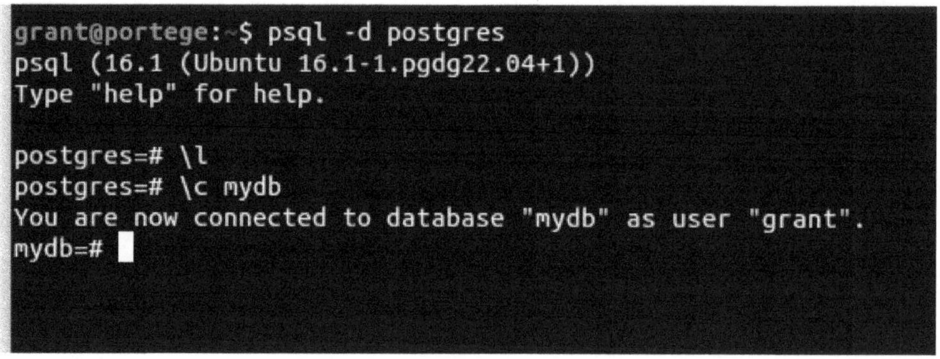

```
grant@portege:~$ psql -d postgres
psql (16.1 (Ubuntu 16.1-1.pgdg22.04+1))
Type "help" for help.

postgres=# \l
postgres=# \c mydb
You are now connected to database "mydb" as user "grant".
mydb=#
```

Figure 4-3. Changing the database context within psql

Once you are in a database, you have all sorts of options for listing tables, functions and other objects, a partial list here:

- \dt – a listing of tables

- \dv – a listing of views

- \df – a listing of functions

- \du – a listing of roles

There are a number of other possible commands. To get a full list, you can issue another command to psql as shown in Listing 4-9:

Listing 4-9.

\?

The partial results of this command are visible here in Figure 4-4:

```
General
  \bind [PARAM]...          set query parameters
  \copyright                show PostgreSQL usage and distribution terms
  \crosstabview [COLUMNS]   execute query and display result in crosstab
  \errverbose               show most recent error message at maximum verbosity
  \g [(OPTIONS)] [FILE]     execute query (and send result to file or |pipe);
                            \g with no arguments is equivalent to a semicolon
  \gdesc                    describe result of query, without executing it
  \gexec                    execute query, then execute each value in its result
  \gset [PREFIX]            execute query and store result in psql variables
  \gx [(OPTIONS)] [FILE]    as \g, but forces expanded output mode
  \q                        quit psql
  \watch [[i=]SEC] [c=N]    execute query every SEC seconds, up to N times

Help
  \? [commands]             show help on backslash commands
  \? options                show help on psql command-line options
  \? variables              show help on special variables
  \h [NAME]                 help on syntax of SQL commands, * for all commands

Query Buffer
  \e [FILE] [LINE]          edit the query buffer (or file) with external editor
  \ef [FUNCNAME [LINE]]     edit function definition with external editor
  \ev [VIEWNAME [LINE]]     edit view definition with external editor
  \p                        show the contents of the query buffer
  \r                        reset (clear) the query buffer
  \s [FILE]                 display history or save it to file
  \w FILE                   write query buffer to file

Input/Output
  \copy ...                 perform SQL COPY with data stream to the client host
  \echo [-n] [STRING]       write string to standard output (-n for no newline)
  \i FILE                   execute commands from file
  \ir FILE                  as \i, but relative to location of current script
  \o [FILE]                 send all query results to file or |pipe
  \qecho [-n] [STRING]      write string to \o output stream (-n for no newline)
:
```

Figure 4-4. A partial listing of psql commands

All of this just scratches the surface of what's possible through psql. You can see a much more comprehensive listing of the commands in the PostgreSQL documentation: http://tinyurl.com/mun6a9uh. It is possible to use nothing but psql when administering PostgreSQL, however, as with most development, there are some advantages to also utilizing graphical tools.

pgAdmin

pgAdmin is the unofficial "official" graphical user interface (GUI) for working with and administering PostgreSQL. Like PostgreSQL, pgAdmin is open source. There is a whole slew of functionality available within pgAdmin, from simply providing a mechanism for running queries, to exploring and managing data structures, to monitoring server activity as well as a vast number of tasks and functions in between. This section will cover getting it installed on Linux and Windows, setting up connections to your server, and some of the basic functionality. For more complete documentation, visit the web site: https://www.pgadmin.org.

Installing pgAdmin

In order to get pgAdmin onto the Ubuntu machine, a number of steps are needed. First, we have to set up access to the public repository where pgAdmin is available. To start with, we'll add the public key and configuration for the repository:

Listing 4-10.

```
curl -fsS https://www.pgadmin.org/static/packages_pgadmin_org.pub | sudo
gpg --dearmor -o /usr/share/keyrings/packages-pgadmin-org.gpg

sudo sh -c 'echo "deb [signed-by=/usr/share/keyrings/packages-pgadmin-
org.gpg]
https://ftp.postgresql.org/pub/pgadmin/pgadmin4/apt/$(lsb_release -cs)
pgadmin4 main" > /etc/apt/sources.list.d/pgadmin4.list && apt update'
```

With that setup out of the way, we can now install pgAdmin. The only decision we have to make is: do we want to install the web version, the desktop version, or both? For demonstration purposes, we'll just install the desktop version:

Listing 4-11.

```
sudo apt install pgadmin4-desktop
```

This will then install the desktop version of pgAdmin. There's no additional steps necessary for the installation. When completed, you'll see an icon, and upon opening it you will get the pgAdmin desktop as shown in Figure 4-5:

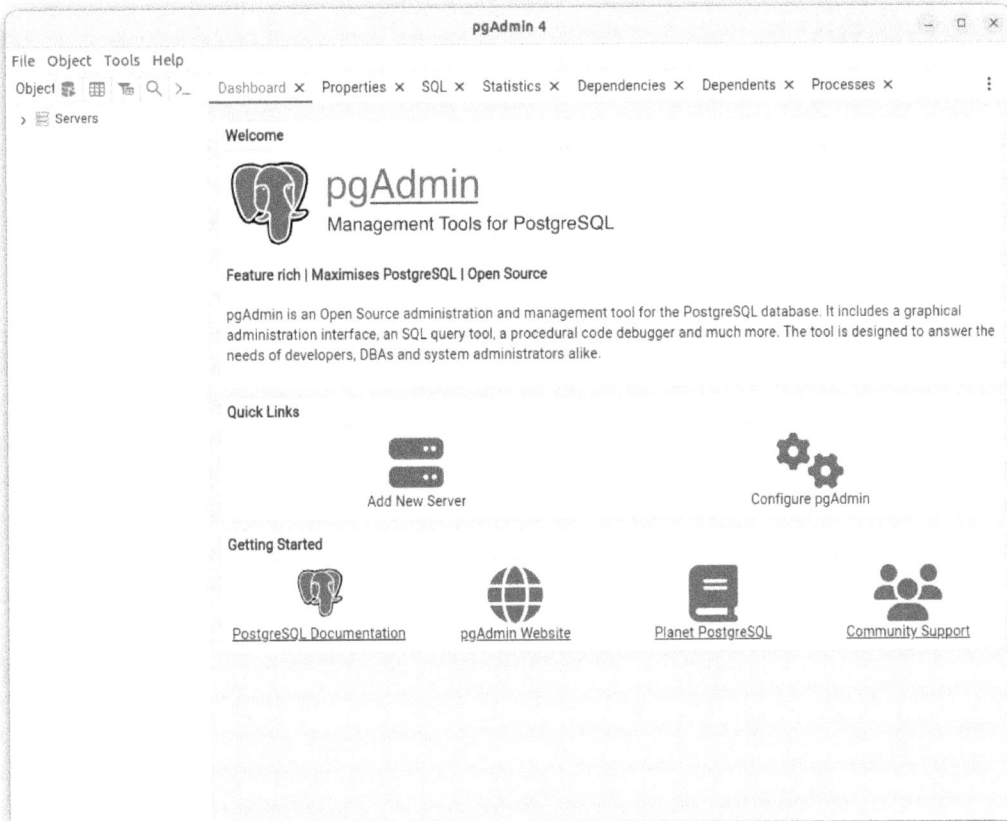

Figure 4-5. Opening screen of the pgAdmin desktop on Ubuntu

For more details, you can see the documentation here: http://tinyurl.com/s4jxp389

To install on a Windows machine, the steps are slightly different. You'll go to the Windows download page: http://tinyurl.com/ya52k2ct. Pick the appropriate version and download the executable. Run the downloaded file, either as Admin, or allowing admin access, and follow the prompts to accept the license agreement and install the tool.

Once completed, again you'll have a new icon in your Start menu and you'll have pgAdmin, looking the same as it did in Figure 4-5 when you launch it.

Using pgAdmin

The beauty of pgAdmin is that it's the same operation, regardless of the operating system you're on. The only clue in the following screenshots as to if this is Windows or Linux is found in the title bar.

To connect to the first server, right click on the Servers list at the top left of the screen. Select "Register" from the context menu. Then select "Server". A window will open requiring details in order to connect to a server. You'll have a prompt informing you that the name cannot be blank. We've decided to name our server connection "LearningPostgreSQL" and have already filled in the first bit of information as shown in Figure 4-8:

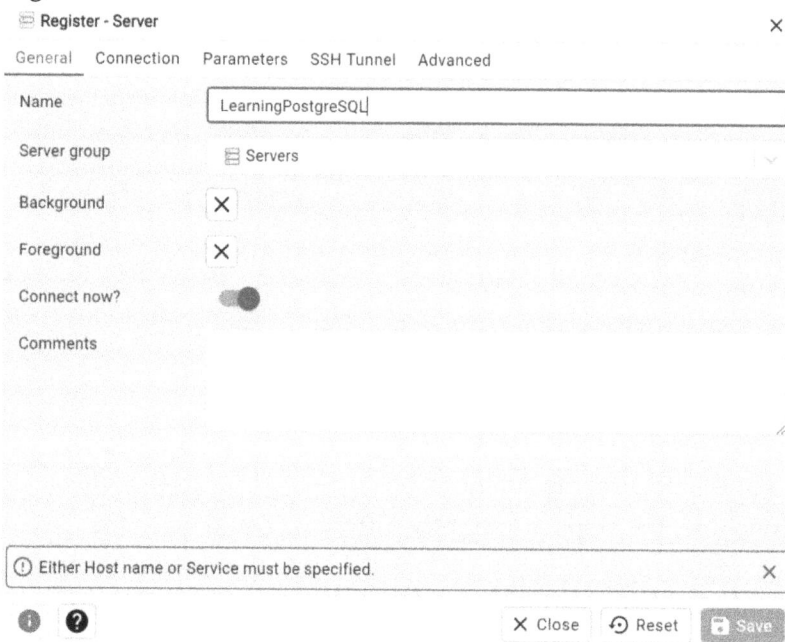

Figure 4-8. The General tab of the server registration in pgAdmin

You can control quite a bit of how pgAdmin is configured from here. You can create groups of servers, control when and how the connections are made to them and more. We're just going to focus on the basics of getting connected.

As prompted, we cannot yet save this connection. Instead, we must define a host name. To do this, select the next tab, Connection. You then have to provide a variety of information. First, you have to supply the host name or the address location of the host. For a local connection, you can simply say "localhost" and be done. Otherwise, you'll need the network name, or the physical network address in order to make the connection.

Next you have to supply the database name that you're going to connect to. The default is the postgres database that is installed on every server. You will be able to change databases after the connection, depending on the permissions of the login used.

Next you have to supply the login name. This is a PostgreSQL defined login that has access to the server in question. The initial login you defined on installation (see Chapter 2) will be your best bet initially. For demonstration purposes here, we're going to use the 'postgres' login.

You have to define whether or not your login is using Kerberos and you may, or may not, supply a password, depending on other choices. There are additional connection options available, but that's the bare minimum involved. You can see our connection settings in Figure 4-9:

Figure 4-9. Connection settings filled out within pgAdmin

From here, just click on Save. By default, the connection will be made and your pgAdmin will change quite a bit as visible in Figure 4-10:

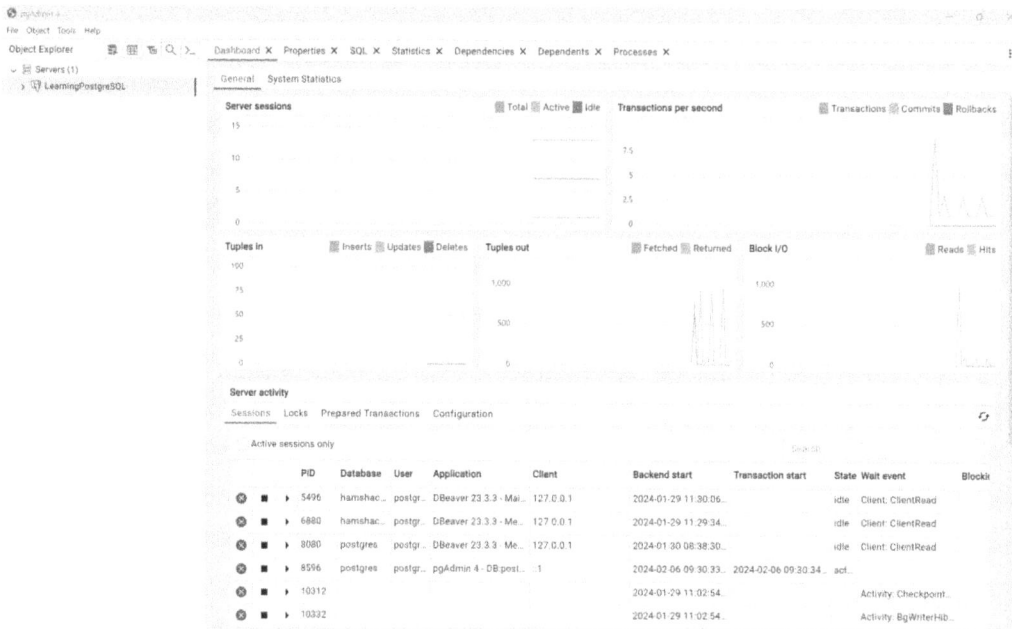

Figure 4-10. *Connected to a server in pgAdmin*

There is a vast amount of functionality now available to you, but we're going to focus on just a couple of points to get started. First, you have the Object Explorer over on the left side of the screen. Clicking on the server we're connected to expands the server, showing a lot more detail in Figure 4-11:

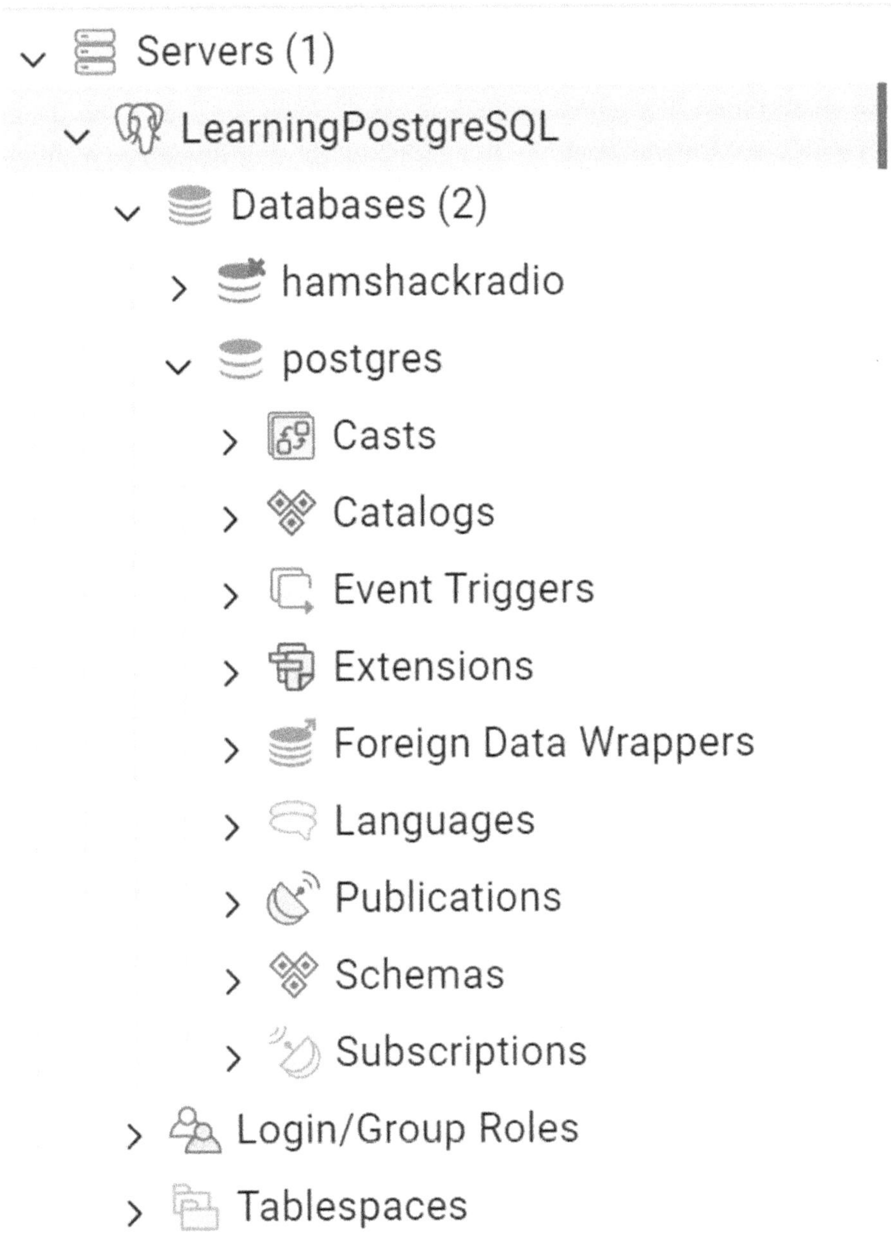

∨ 🗄 Servers (1)

   ∨ 🐘 LearningPostgreSQL

      ∨ 🗃 Databases (2)

         > 🗃 hamshackradio

         ∨ 🗃 postgres

            > 🔲 Casts

            > ◈ Catalogs

            > 🗅 Event Triggers

            > 🎏 Extensions

            > 🗃 Foreign Data Wrappers

            > 💬 Languages

            > 📡 Publications

            > ◈ Schemas

            > 📡 Subscriptions

      > 👥 Login/Group Roles

      > 🗂 Tablespaces

Figure 4-11. The objects within the pgAdmin Object Explorer window

Each of these different choices can be expanded to show more detail and take different kinds of actions on different objects. For example, to see a list of tables, you simply select the "Schemas" drop down and then "Tables".

In order to run queries against the database, we have several options, but if you right click on the server, you can select "Query Tool" from the context menu. You can also get to the Query Tool by clicking the icon in the toolbar just above the servers as shown in Figure 4-12:

Figure 4-12. *The Query Tool is the far-left icon*

With the Query Tool open, you can then run queries and see results. One example of running a query with results is shown here in Figure 4-13:

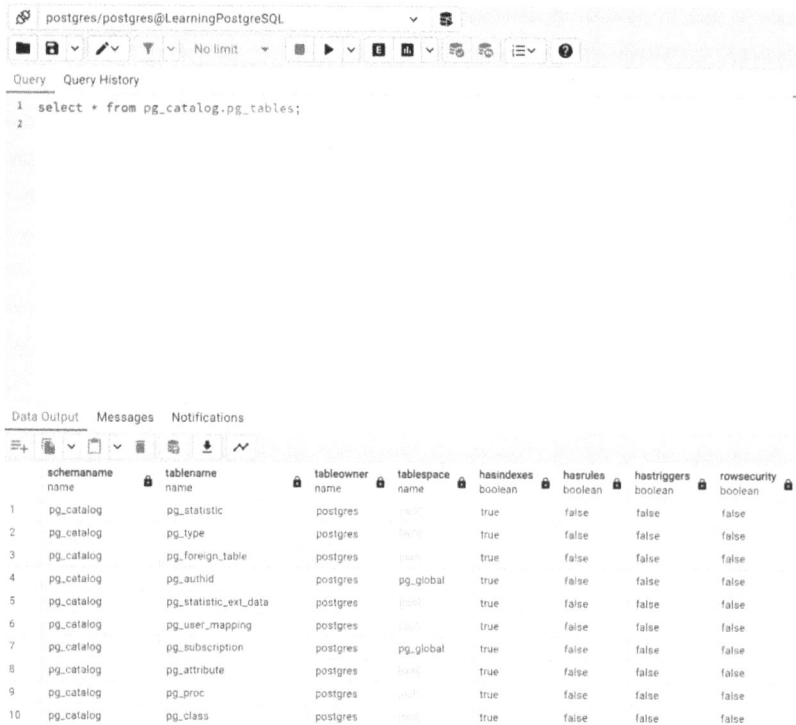

Figure 4-13. *The results of a query in the Query Tool of pgAdmin*

As with many of the tools in this chapter, we're only going to illustrate the starting points for pgAdmin. Follow the links provided to get all the detail on how pgAdmin works.

DBeaver

DBeaver Community is an open source, multi-platform, database management tool that supports more than 80 different database management systems, including PostgreSQL. The functionality within DBeaver, similar to pgAdmin, covers a very broad set of behaviors, from a simple query interface to full management of the objects and processes within your PostgreSQL servers. Because most people do manage more than one data platform, DBeaver has become extremely popular. We are again only going to scratch the surface of the core behaviors of DBeaver in this chapter. You can learn all you need from the DBeaver website: https://dbeaver.io.

Installing DBeaver

Getting DBeaver installed on Linux (specifically in this case, Ubuntu), we're going to use snap as shown in Listing 4-12:

Listing 4-12.

```
snap install dbeaver-ce
```

And that's all there is to it. As with pgAdmin, the interface in DBeaver is the same in Linux and Windows, so before we start to explore the tool, let's go ahead and get the Windows install out of the way.

You download the installer from this page: http://tinyurl.com/2a7r8ed7. Running the executable, you get another wizard that is straightforward to complete. One screen to pay attention to is the "Choose Components" screen. There are a few choices on what it is that you want to install, as you can see in Figure 4-14:

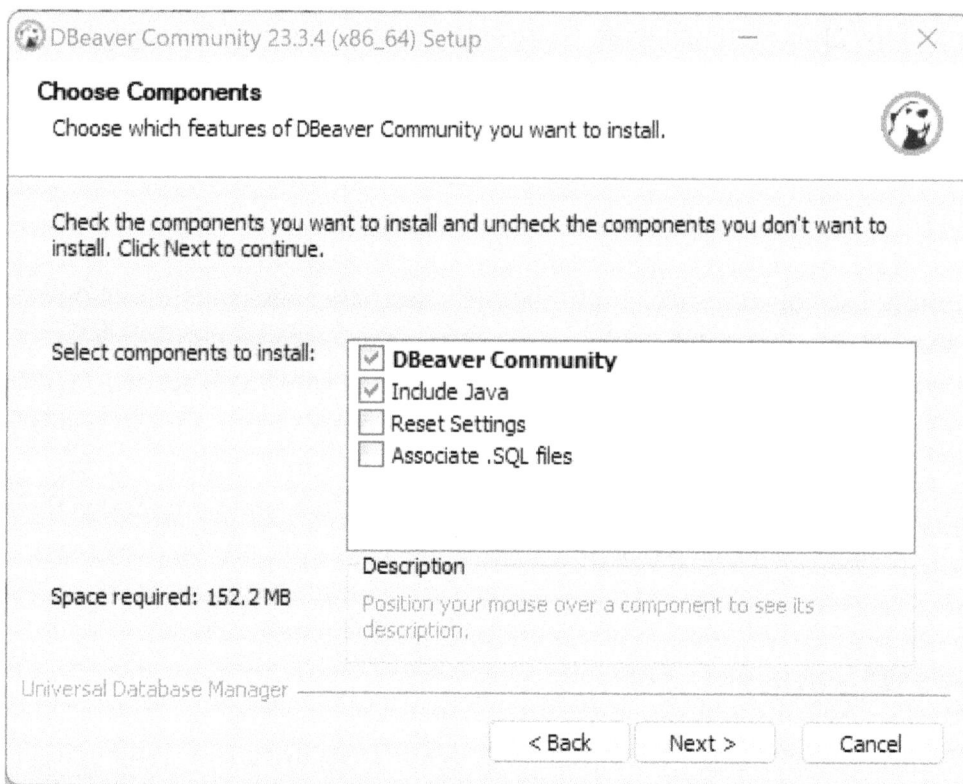

Figure 4-14. *Choosing installation options*

Obviously, if you want to install DBeaver, you do have to select it in the list shown in Figure 4-14. You must have Java installed, but if you maintain it independently, you don't need to rely on this wizard to install it for you. You also have the option to reset your Settings in the event you installed DBeaver previously and would like to go back to the start. Finally, you get the choice to associate .SQL files with DBeaver so that double clicking any .SQL file will open the file within DBeaver.

Using DBeaver

The first time you launch DBeaver, whether in Linux or Windows, it's going to prompt you to create a connection to a server. The list includes a number of different relational database types, but PostgreSQL is right on top as you can see in Figure 4-15:

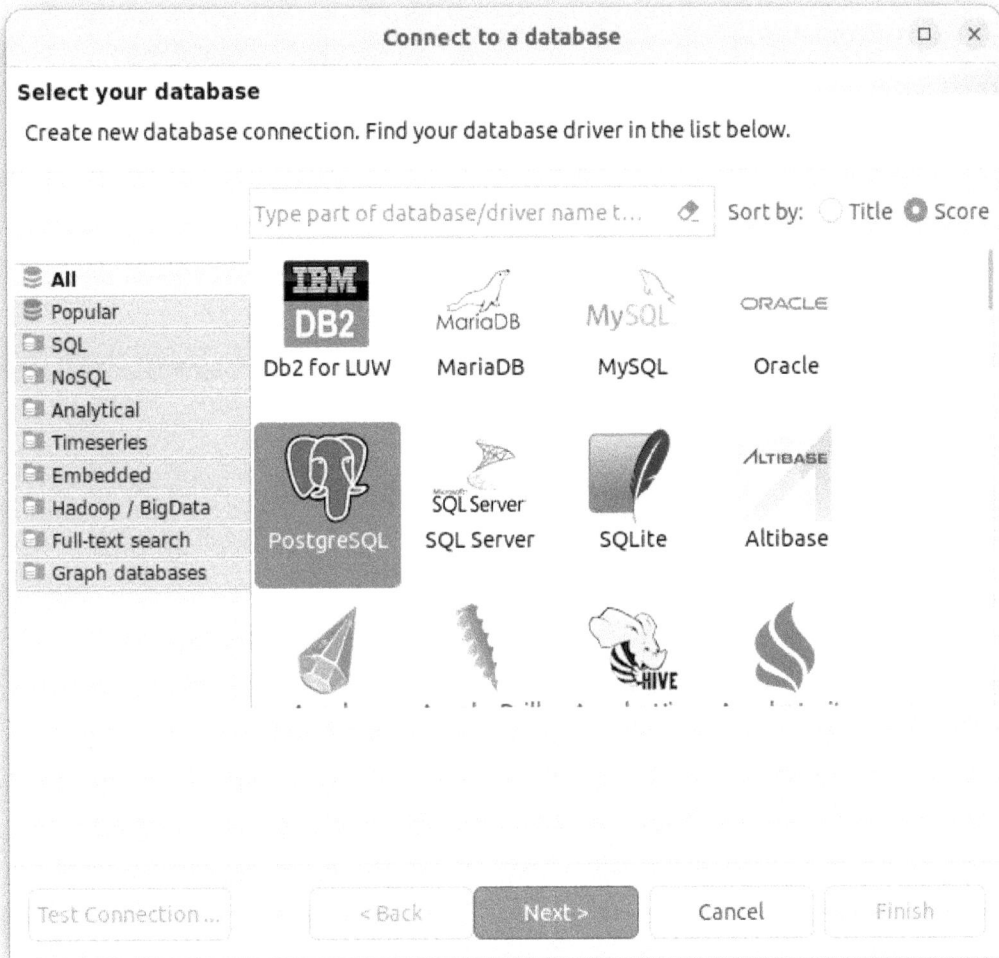

Figure 4-15. *Selecting PostgreSQL for a connection to the server*

After selecting PostgreSQL and clicking on the "Next" button, you'll be presented with the necessary connection settings, very similar to the tools we've already discussed. Figure 4-16 shows the same connection settings I used for pgAdmin, but this time in DBeaver:

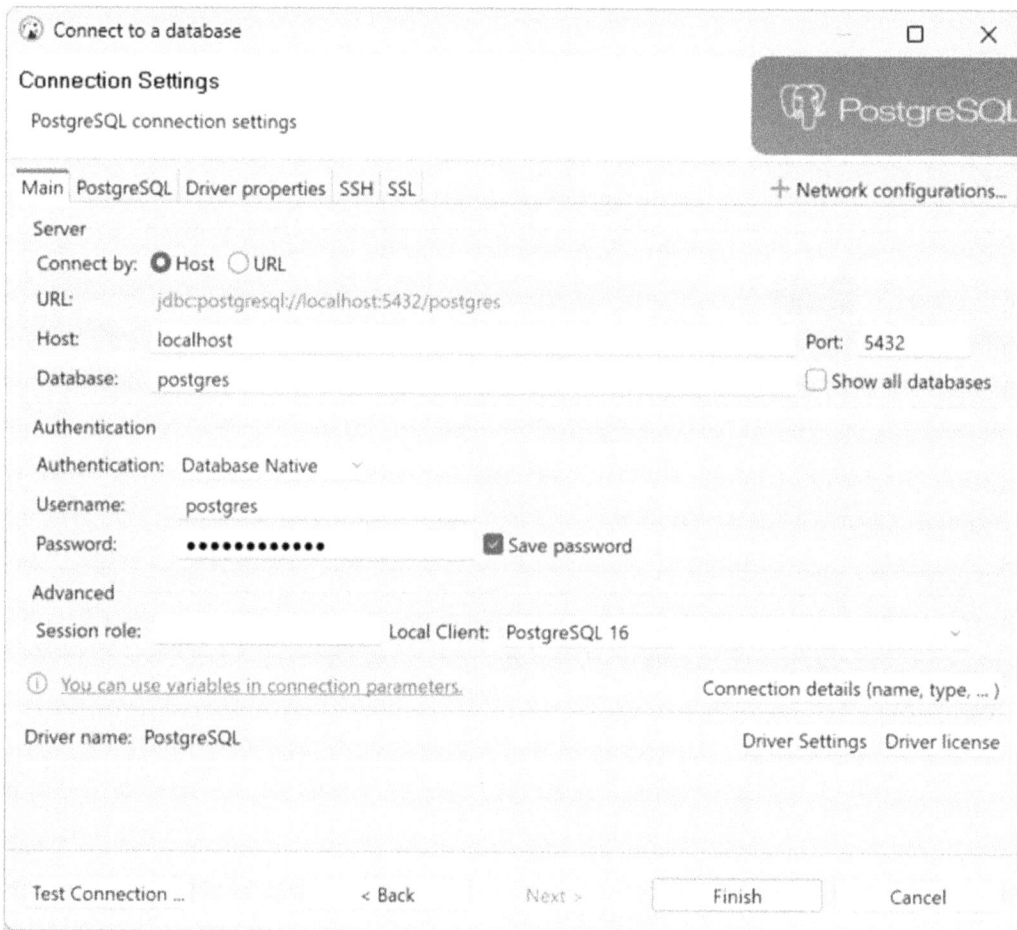

Figure 4-16. Defining the connection properties within DBeaver

The connections can clearly be defined with a lot of different variables. You can get into the details as needed. However, just to get started, the defaults we've used here will suffice, depending on your cluster's location. One helpful tip is to make sure "Show all databases" is checked, otherwise you may not see other databases you have created beyond the one listed in "Database". One bit of functionality that immediately sets DBeaver apart is the ability to test your connection settings without saving them and attempting to connect. Clicking the "Test Connection…" button will validate the connection before you save it back to DBeaver. Figure 4-17 shows the test on this connection:

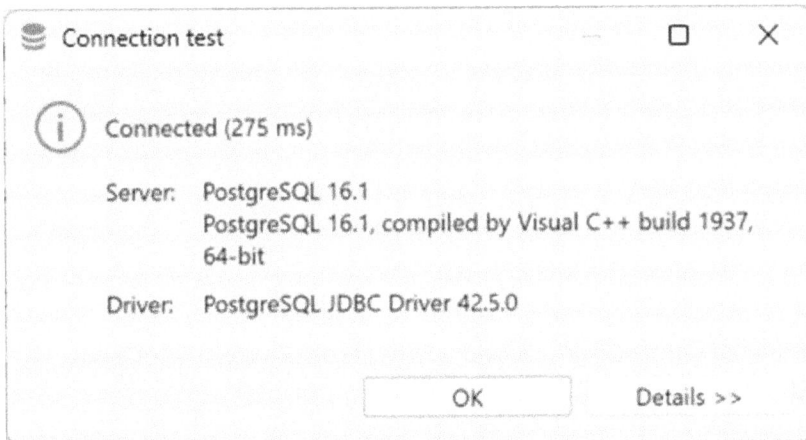

Figure 4-17. *A successful test connection in DBeaver*

Note: You may have to download the appropriate driver when you test the connection.

With a successful test, we can click the "OK" button to clear this window and then click "Finish" to save the connection back to the DBeaver window. I'll now have one connection in the Database Navigator window. I can click on that connection and it will connect to my database, as shown in Figure 4-18:

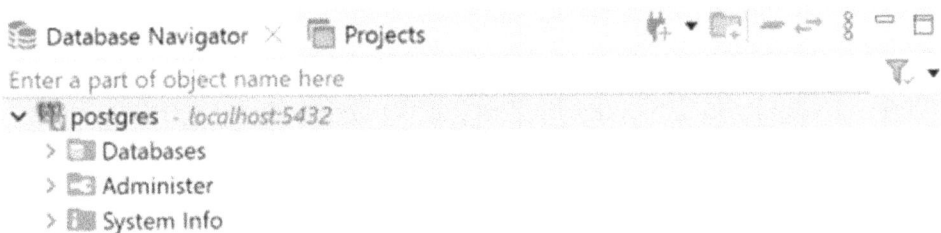

Figure 4-18. *Connected to the localhost in DBeaver*

Each of those headings can be expanded to get more choices. So, if I wanted to see the details of a given database, I can expand the selection to see the databases and Schemas inside the database, visible in Figure 4-19:

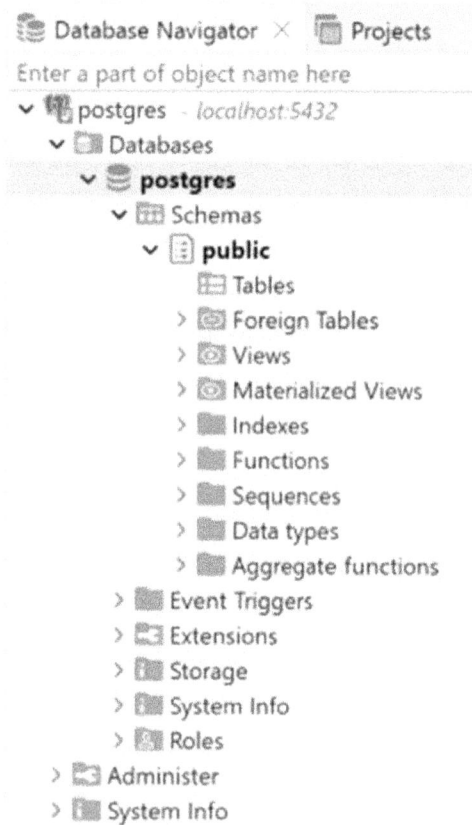

Figure 4-19. Navigating database objects within DBeaver

Within each of these folders you can take different kinds of control and activities with each of the objects in question. We'll be covering DBeaver in more detail throughout the book as this will be the primary GUI we use.

Here, we'll just show how to get to a query editor window and run a query. There is a tool bar just above the Database Navigator window:

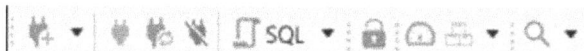

Figure 4-20. The DBeaver tool bar showing the SQL drop down menu

You can click on the SQL drop down menu and select "Open SQL console" from that menu, or you can use the key combination CTL-ALT-ENTER, or you can also right click within the Database Navigator window to get a context menu that includes the same SQL drop down. Regardless of how you choose to open it, once done, you'll get a window in which you can type and run queries as shown in Figure 4-21:

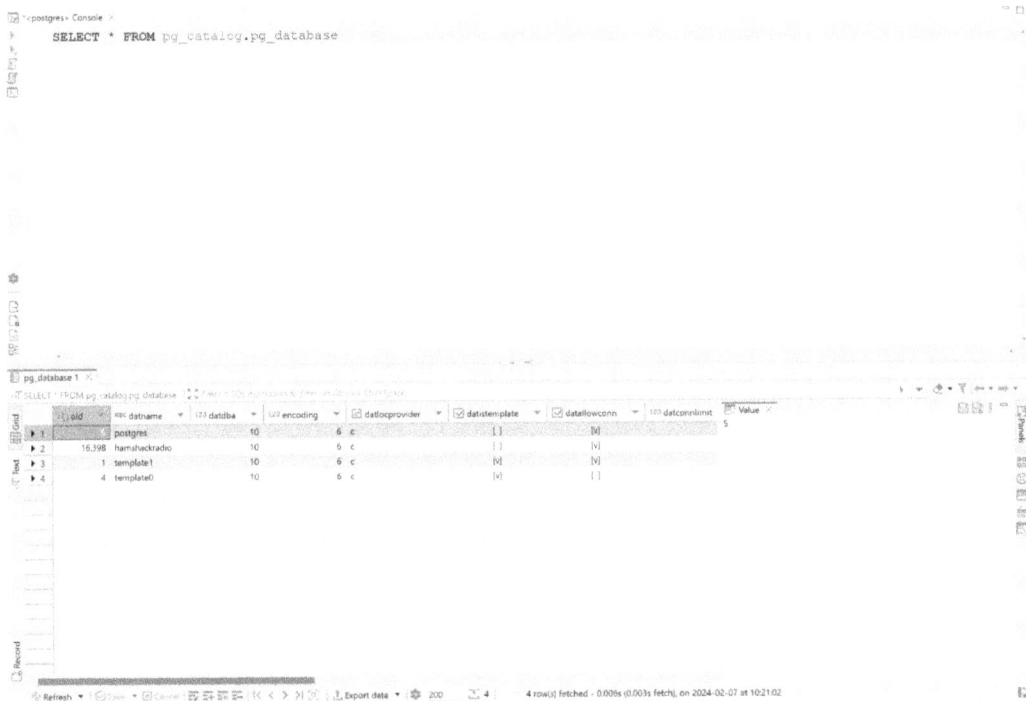

Figure 4-21. The SQL Console window within DBeaver

As we'll be using DBeaver throughout the book, you'll see more of the SQL console window and its functionality. We'll also be covering quite a bit of the rest of the functionality within DBeaver as we go along. You can always read more from the excellent DBeaver documentation: https://dbeaver.io/docs/dbeaver.

Azure Data Studio

Azure Data Studio is a free tool from Microsoft designed for database development, forked from their popular VSCode GUI. Azure Data Studio includes an extension for working with PostgreSQL databases. Since so many people are likely to be maintaining more than one database platform or are migrating between platforms to PostgreSQL, we've included this tool from Microsoft as just one more possible way you can make building and administering your PostgreSQL databases just a little bit easier. One of the big strengths of Azure Data Studio is its ability to work within source control. It does add some power to this tool that is a bit beyond what the others offer.

Installing Azure Data Studio

The install of Azure Data Studio is very similar for both Linux and Windows. You first navigate to the Microsoft download web page: http://tinyurl.com/24hasnmb. From there, you pick the appropriate installation media from the list visible in Figure 4-22:

Download Azure Data Studio

Azure Data Studio 1.47.1 is the latest general availability (GA) version.

- Release number: 1.47.1
- Release date: January 10, 2024

⌂ Expand table

Platform	Type	Download		
Windows	User Installer	x64 ↗	ARM64 ↗	
	System Installer	x64 ↗	ARM64 ↗	
	.zip	x64 ↗	ARM64 ↗	
macOS	.zip	Universal ↗	Intel Chip ↗	Apple Silicon ↗
Linux	.tar.gz	x64 ↗		
	.deb	x64 ↗		
	.rpm[1]	x64 ↗		

Figure 4-22. Downloading Azure Data Studio

Once installation is complete, you need to run Azure Data Studio and the PostgreSQL extension. Open the software and you'll be presented with a window similar to Figure 4-23:

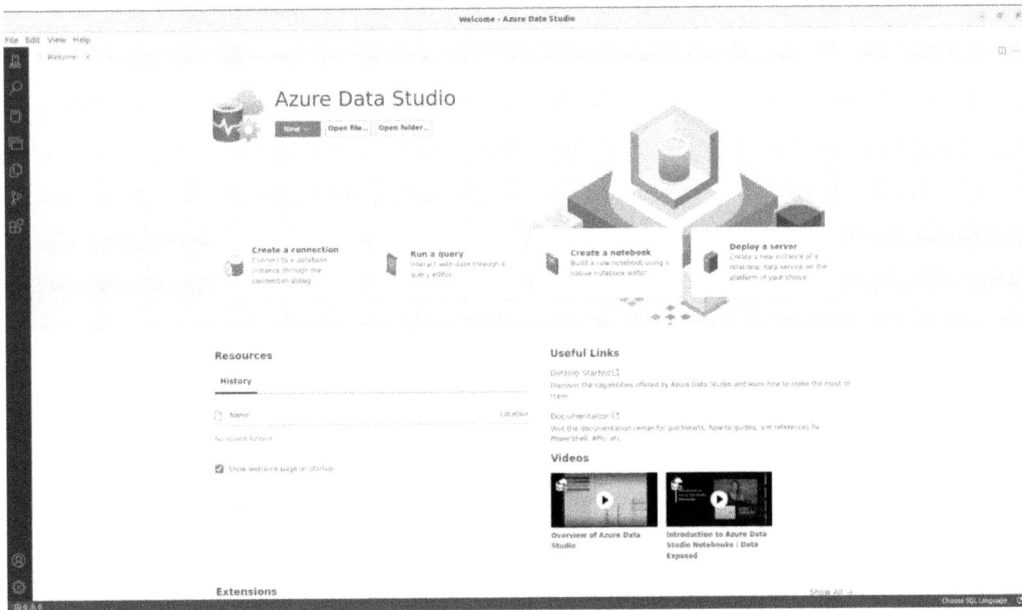

Figure 4-23. Azure Data Studio opening screen

On the left-hand side of the screen, at the very bottom, is the Extensions management tab. Clicking on that will open the Extensions search window. Typing in "postgresql", you'll see the PostgreSQL extension as shown in Figure 4-24:

Figure 4-24. Selecting the PostgreSQL extension to install

Simply click on the Install button next to the PostgreSQL icon. The extension will be installed. The only indication you'll have for this is the change in the buttons next to the

PostgreSQL icon. You'll now see two buttons, Disable and Uninstall. We can now connect to PostgreSQL within Azure Data Studio.

Working With Azure Data Studio

To make a connection to a PostgreSQL database, we need to navigate back to the connection tab. It's the icon at the top of the toolbar on the left. Since there are no existing connections, you'll be prompted for a new one, similar to Figure 4-25:

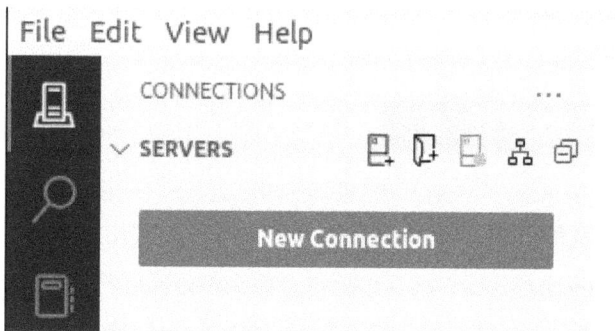

Figure 4-25. *Creating a new connection in Azure Data Studio*

Clicking on the "New Connection" button, you'll open a window with Connection Details:

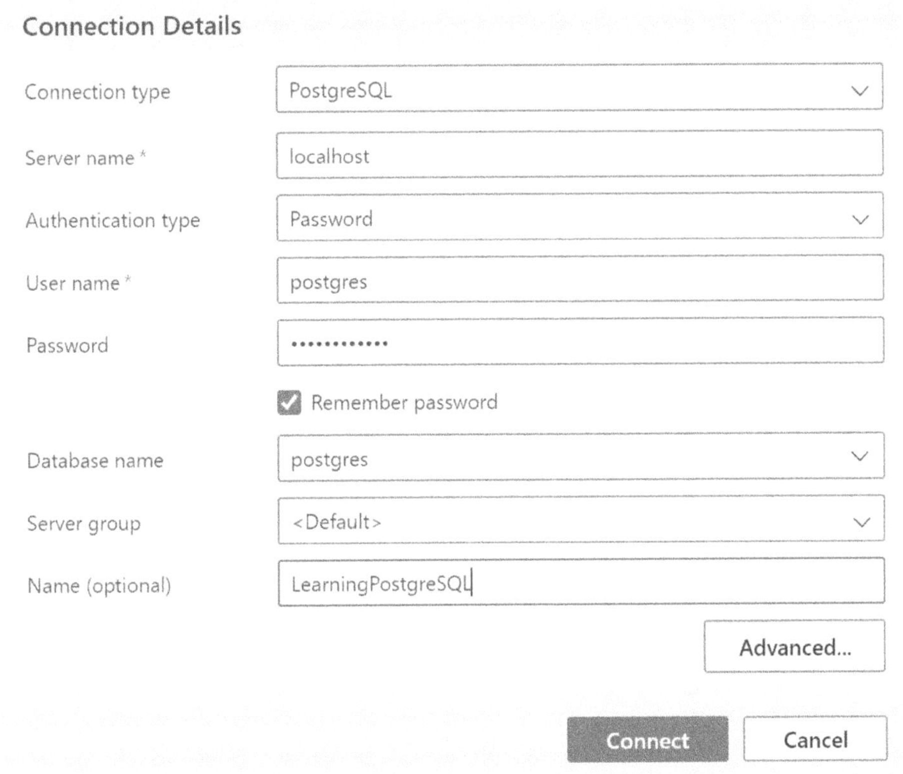

Connection Details

Connection type	PostgreSQL ∨
Server name *	localhost
Authentication type	Password ∨
User name *	postgres
Password	••••••••••••
	☑ Remember password
Database name	postgres ∨
Server group	<Default> ∨
Name (optional)	LearningPostgreSQL

Advanced...

Connect   Cancel

Figure 4-26. Connecting to PostgreSQL within Azure Data Studio

Clicking on the Connect button, a new connection will be saved on the left within the Servers inside the Connections tab. This consists of an explorer type window similar to the other GUI tools we've already looked at in Chapter 3, as shown in Figure 4-27:

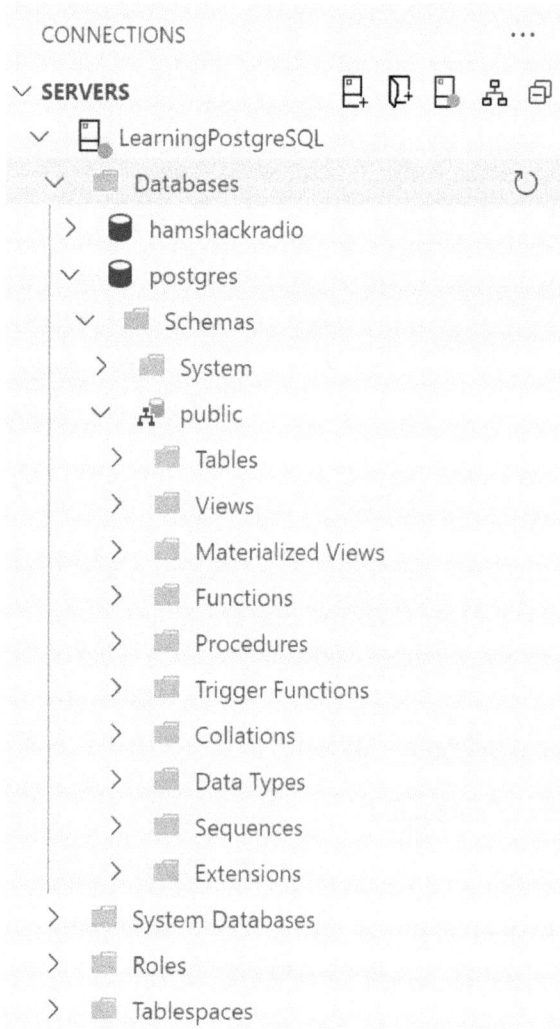

Figure 4-27. Exploring the PostgreSQL database within Azure Data Studio

Similar to the other tools, there is additional functionality available from the explorer window here. However, as with the other tools, we'll simply end on how to run a query against the database.

You can right click on a database within the explorer and there will be a "New Query" context menu. You can also click on the toolbar in the center of the screen. From there, you have a wide-open field in which you can type a query. One example is shown here in Figure 4-28:

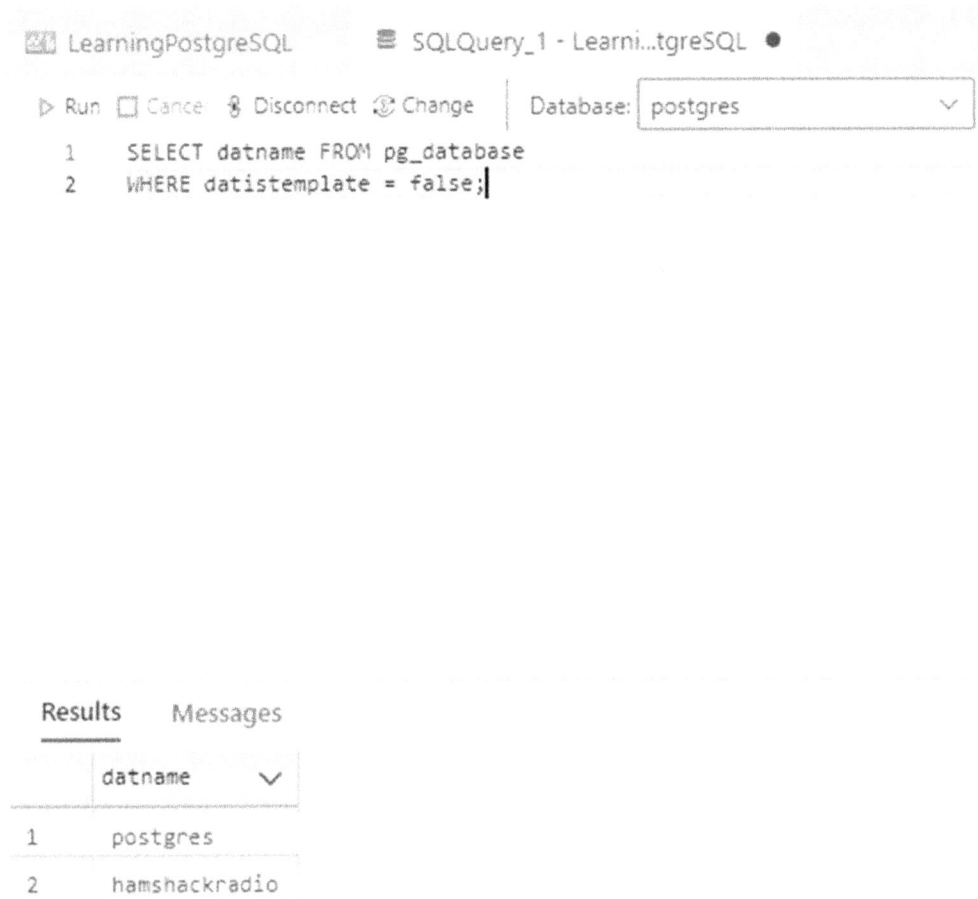

```
LearningPostgreSQL          SQLQuery_1 - Learni...tgreSQL  ●

▷ Run  □ Cance  ⸓ Disconnect  ⸓ Change    Database:  postgres        ∨
  1    SELECT datname FROM pg_database
  2    WHERE datistemplate = false;|
```

```
Results    Messages

   datname      ∨

1    postgres

2    hamshackradio
```

Figure 4-28. Query and results in Azure Data Studio

As with the other tools, there is much more to know about Azure Data Studio. Microsoft maintains extensive documentation here: http://tinyurl.com/y2s93mhc.

Conclusion

As you can see, you have a lot of choices when it comes to the tooling you can use to assist you in creating and managing your servers and databases within PostgreSQL. For the most part, you're likely to focus on only a couple of these tools for most of your work. The obvious choice to use psql for its ability to automate through the command line will likely be one of the tools you use. The others all work, more or less equally well. It's mainly a question of finding the one that works best for you and your environment. Throughout the rest of the book, we'll be using a combination of psql and DBeaver for the majority of our work

5
Server Configuration

As with any database server, knowing about some key configuration settings to check and validate will keep your PostgreSQL server running at peak performance. In fact, PostgreSQL has well over 350 configuration options that can be tuned based on your workload and server resources. This means that you can tune options like how much memory is available to hold cached data pages or adjust many settings that will directly affect how the query planner chooses certain plans. Because many of these tuning options simply aren't available for users to configure in databases like SQL Server, we want to provide you with the background and knowledge of where to start as you begin the journey into PostgreSQL.

As you may be able to guess, the most important settings to start with are all about memory configuration.

Memory Settings

The generally accepted guidance for SQL Server has been to configure the memory as high as possible for a given server because SQL Server will manage and use as much as is available. For the most part, however, SQL Server takes ownership of how that memory is managed. While there are some advanced levers to reserve memory for specific uses, most guidance focuses on the main amount of memory available to a SQL Server instance so that the server can manage what happens dynamically in the background. One of the most important parts of managing how memory is used in SQL Server deals with calculating memory grants for each query to help manage memory resources across connections. As a user, we don't have many options to influence that memory reservation. SQL Server does that work behind the scenes, and while it usually does a good job, sometimes it gets the grant wildly wrong, negatively impacting query and server performance.

With PostgreSQL, however, the way that memory is configured and used requires a bit more hands-on attention. Understanding and initially tweaking the settings covered in this chapter and monitoring their effect over time is essential to having a well performing server and application. If you use a hosted solution like Amazon RDS or Azure Database for PostgreSQL – Flexible Server, most of the settings mentioned here have reasonable starting defaults. Still, be diligent to monitor your database and application because your data, application, and query patterns might not fit well with those default values and it's up to you to configure them accordingly.

As an example, with PostgreSQL, we need to specifically configure the amount of memory that will be used for the shared buffers (i.e. "buffer pool" in SQL Server). However, that is the only memory setting we can effectively hard code an overall limit for at runtime. Other memory usage, like that used to process queries, doesn't reserve memory ahead of time, and if the available memory settings aren't tuned correctly, can significantly slow down query performance. Therefore, knowing how each of these memory settings work in tandem with ongoing server and query processing, is key.

Let's dig in.

Note: Some of the "serverless" PostgreSQL offerings by the major cloud providers have done more extensive work to the PostgreSQL codebase, attempting to dynamically change many of these settings over time and workloads. In some cases, you can't even modify a few of the settings we discuss in this chapter. That may, or may not, work in your favor.

Still, in our opinion, it's important for any PostgreSQL user to understand how these settings impact your PostgreSQL experience.

Modify Configuration Settings in PostgreSQL

The settings discussed in this chapter, and hundreds of others, can be set at the server level in the `postgresql.conf` file. If you're using a hosted solution like AWS or Azure, then many of these values are changed through a CLI or console application.

Additionally, in some cases, settings can be modified for a specific session which can be helpful if a query needs more memory to perform a specific query. If a setting can be set during the session, we've noted it below.

Caching Data Pages

The first setting that needs your attention is `shared_buffers`. This setting is used to determine the amount of memory allocated for caching data in PostgreSQL's shared memory buffers. Unlike SQL Server, we get to tell PostgreSQL how much memory to reserve for frequently accessed data to reduce the need for disk I/O operations.

If your server has a lot of memory and you can allocate enough memory to cache the entire database (or databases), great! PostgreSQL will try to use the memory. However, if you have a limited amount of server memory and your database is many times larger than `shared_buffers`, PostgreSQL will have to do more swapping of data from disk as queries come and go.

There are lots of (generally old) posts and formulas in the wild which talk about how to set this value. Starting at 25% of available server memory is common and reasonable advice. But that's only a starting point.

The best way to tune `shared_buffers` is to track the cache hit ratio as shown in Listing 5-1. This is not a specifically tracked statistic, but one that you can find through a simple query shown below. Unlike SQL Server where page life expectancy (PLE) is often used over cache hit ratio, tracking the cache hit ratio value provides the indicator you need to see if enough buffer memory has been allocated.

Listing 5-1. Example PostgreSQL Hit Cache Ratio query

```
SELECT
sum(heap_blks_read) as heap_read,
sum(heap_blks_hit) as heap_hit,
sum(heap_blks_hit) / (sum(heap_blks_hit) + sum(heap_blks_read)) as ratio
FROM
pg_statio_user_tables;
```

If the ratio is consistently below a reasonable threshold (or drops every time certain jobs run), this indicates that a lot of data is moving between memory and disk to satisfy query results. Ideally you want the cache hit ratio to be as close to 100% as possible under normal operation. Anything less than ~80-85% consistently shows that your application isn't performing as well as it should and increasing `shared_buffers` should be considered.

However, if increasing this setting means more than 35%-40% of your total available PostgreSQL memory, then this is an indication that the server is resource constrained and you should probably invest in a bigger instance if application and data changes don't have a measurable impact.

Query Memory

`work_mem` is the next most important setting to investigate in PostgreSQL because it directly affects query planning and performance. It also works very differently from SQL Server and most of what you know about memory usage during query planning.

When PostgreSQL plans a query, it doesn't pre-allocate memory like SQL Server does. Most of the time SQL Server does a reasonable job requesting a specific memory grant so that the data and query operations can all be held in memory for quick work. If SQL Server requests too much memory, the query might be delayed while it waits for memory to be freed. If it requests too little memory, then we get the dreaded warning icon (⚠) in the query plan and data spills to disk.

In PostgreSQL, the *plan nodes* of the query plan (what SQL Server would call *operators*) can use up to the amount of `work_mem` for their specific operation. If a complex query plan has many sorting or hashing nodes, each node, for each currently running query, can use up to this amount.

By default, work_mem is set to 4MB per node operation. If you execute a query that contains two sorting nodes in the plan, then that query plan could potentially use up to 2x work_mem in memory to process the data (i.e. 8MB with the default value). If any nodes need more than work_mem, that operation will spill the data to disk, and your query will be slower.

The easiest way to see the impact of an undersized work_mem setting is to look at the EXPLAIN ANALYZE plan output for larger, slow queries. Any time the plan contains Sort Method: external {merge|sort} Disk: xxxxkB, the query spilled to disk because it didn't have enough memory to perform the merge or sort operation. Remember, PostgreSQL didn't do anything wrong, it's simply constrained by the work_mem setting. We'll talk more about how to tune this setting for specific queries in Chapter 11.

Assuming you have enough memory in your server, a reasonable value to start with is probably 8MB or 16MB. To tune this value more effectively, my recommendation is to find a monitoring solution that tracks slow queries and grabs the execution plan detail. Look over a representative timeframe for how high (and consistent) the external disk requirement was and consider if this is a reasonable value to set work_mem to globally. For instance, if you see that many queries spill to disk at 5MB or 10MB, then increasing the server config a little higher might be all you need to do.

Be aware that setting the server-wide value too high will probably waste a lot of available memory and quickly cause "out of memory" server crashes if you're not careful. For modern hardware, increasing this to 16MB is probably safe in most cases as a starting value. Another quick back-of-the-napkin check is to ensure that (connection_limit * work_mem) + shared_buffers is less than the total memory available to PostgreSQL.

The potential problem with raising the work_mem setting at the server level is that PostgreSQL won't check if there's enough memory left to run a query. If you set work_mem to 256MB and your server only has 4GB of total RAM, you could easily run out of memory with just a handful of connections running queries simultaneously.

If you can change the application code, one choice is to modify the setting on the fly within the session for queries that need more memory to run quickly and efficiently.

Reporting queries, for instance, often need more memory but may only run a few times a day. Therefore, as part of the query session (or parameters that some frameworks provide), modify the `work_mem` value with the SET command:

```
SET work_mem = '32MB' -- per session value
```

Number of Connections

The third setting to look at is how many connections your PostgreSQL server will allow. By default, PostgreSQL limits the available connections to 100. An active application without a load balancer can quickly exhaust this limit.

However, because each connection uses a process, simply increasing this value isn't the magic fix, either. Remember, every connection could use at least a `work_mem` amount of memory, and more for each sort/hash node. If you don't have enough available memory, or you've increased the server-wide `work_mem` setting, increasing the connection limit could quickly contribute to memory exhaustion.

The correct way to plan for connection overloads is to look at a connection pooler like `pgBouncer` or `pgPool-II`. Some frameworks in popular languages like Python have also begun to implement their own pooling capabilities.

Ongoing Maintenance and Backup/Restores

Like any database, PostgreSQL does background work to maintain the data, schema, statistics, indexes, dump/restore of data, and more. Each of these tasks needs enough memory to efficiently process data, tasks like restoring data, creating a new index, or keeping statistics up to date. However, one of the main reasons it's important to tune the background worker memory is because of something called dead tuples.

PostgreSQL uses Multi-Version Concurrency Control (MVCC) to support transaction isolation and concurrency of data. One of the benefits of the PostgreSQL implementation is that readers (almost) never block writers under normal querying. It also allows cool features like transactional DDL statements.

However, there are trade-offs to how PostgreSQL manages this process. In SQL Server, when you UPDATE or DELETE a row, the old "version" of the row is written to a transaction log, where it is stored in case it is needed later for rollback or recovery. PostgreSQL, on the other hand, leaves these old "versions" in place within the table, and marks them to be cleaned up later. These leftover rows are often referred to as dead tuples. To reclaim that space (and do some other necessary stuff in the background), PostgreSQL must run a process called VACUUM on a regular basis to keep data clean and the database in tiptop shape!

MVCC and VACUUM are important concepts in PostgreSQL, something we'll cover in Chapter 13. But simply knowing that the process exists is helpful so that we can briefly talk about `maintenance_work_mem`.

The background jobs that keep your database in shape need enough memory to free the space of dead tuples, update table statistics, create and maintain indexes, and more. In our experience, if the memory settings are reasonable for your workload, you probably won't think about VACUUM for 95% of your tables. It "just works."

But, under load, or with databases that have heavily updated tables, VACUUM can fall behind and you end up with table bloat (at least), indexes that take too long to create or update, outdated statistics, and other potential problems that will cause the cluster to go into read-only mode until the VACUUM process is caught up. With versions of PostgreSQL over the last many years, however, issues like this are rare, especially if you tune it appropriately.

By default, PostgreSQL sets `maintenance_work_mem` at 64MB, 16X the value of the default 4MB `work_mem` setting. Background processes only run one at a time per process type, so a higher memory setting won't impact server load as much as increasing `work_mem` (which is multiplied by every connection).

If you have 16GB of RAM or more, consider increasing this to at least 256MB and see how things improve. One suggestion from a reputable PostgreSQL consultant is `(available RAM) * 0.05`. However, setting this beyond a few hundred MBs, that calculation starts to break down a bit, too. If you're having issues with jobs keeping up, our recommendation is to increase the amount by 32MB or 64MB and see if things improve. If not, increase it again.

Unless you have 32GB of RAM or more, you should be very cautious of going above 1GB. It might work and be what you need but reserving that memory will have an impact on other memory that's available to PostgreSQL.

Query Plan Settings

Unlike SQL Server, there are many cluster level settings that can be modified which influence the query planner. Some are sledgehammer-like settings that try to turn off specific query operations (like table scans). Most of these should never be turned off at the server level, so we won't discuss them here. It might be helpful at times to disable some of these settings for individual sessions to test various query optimizations, but otherwise they should be left untouched.

There are a few settings, however, which you should check and adjust for your workload.

Random Page Cost

PostgreSQL table storage is heap-based. There is no guaranteed order of rows on disk, which means that for many queries PostgreSQL will favor sequential scans (table scans in SQL Server) rather than needing to do random page access to selectively get pages of data. This also means that index-based table access won't be prioritized in these cases, covering indexes excluded.

Before modern hardware and fast SSD disk access, this general principle made sense. When data was stored on spinning disks, sequentially scanning pages was more efficient than random access. The default PostgreSQL settings still assume that random page access is 4X slower than reading the pages sequentially. Therefore, when the query planner believes it will need to access a percentage of table pages over some meaningful threshold, it will almost always choose to do the sequential scan rather than use a lookup index.

Obviously, most of us are not using spinning disks today in our environments, at least not our production environments. Therefore, the general guidance for SSD or faster burstable storage with cloud vendors, is to set `random_page_cost = 1.1`. This isn't an exact science, so some experimentation with troublesome query plans is probably necessary.

As with many settings in PostgreSQL, this can be set for the connection or a specific role. More likely, you should just configure this at the instance level so that all database connections inherit the settings and try to make more efficient query plans.

Effective Cache Size

The query planner in PostgreSQL doesn't assume that cached data is only in `shared_buffers`. It assumes that some data is also cached by the filesystem outside of the core PostgreSQL memory allocated for recent data pages.

If the planner is told that there is likely to be more RAM available for cached data than just the shared buffers, the planner will tend to consider index scans more often than sequential scans. In most cases, this is a good thing.

Most recommendations recommend a good starting point is to set `effective_cache_size` to approximately half of the total RAM available to the server and includes memory already set aside for shared buffers. Essentially, we're giving a hint to the planner to expect more cached pages to be available than what's in the shared buffers, meaning it may not have to pull data from disk, and therefore, index scans will be more efficient. Generally, the higher the value, the more likely PostgreSQL will choose an index scan.

There are two more things to note about this setting.

First, it does not actually allocate RAM for caching. Only the `shared_buffers` setting does that. Again, we're trying to help the planner figure out how much actual memory cache is available between PostgreSQL and the filesystem cache.

Second, this setting *can* be used to trick a smaller PostgreSQL server into selecting query plans that match larger production systems. Be aware, there's a bit of hackery using this setting for such a purpose. However, if you have a testing server with a backup of your data and less RAM than the production environment, setting this value to match the bigger server can trick PostgreSQL to choose the same plans given that other statistics data matches. Remember, this doesn't actually allocate that amount of memory.

Just-In-Time Compilation

PostgreSQL introduced JIT compilation beginning with PostgreSQL 11. The idea is that some parts of a query plan can be compiled into expressions natively to execute separately on the CPU, yielding a speedup for some operations. JIT in PostgreSQL currently targets two main processes: expression evaluation and tuple deforming, the process of transforming an on-disk tuple into its in-memory representation.

The impact of performing JIT compilation on a query plan is displayed in the output of EXPLAIN if it was utilized. For CPU-bound queries, JIT is likely to be a helpful enhancement. Otherwise, it may simply add overhead that ultimately slows down the process.

JIT is enabled by default in all supported versions of PostgreSQL. If you notice that problematic queries are always performing JIT compilation and it's just adding overhead, this setting can be turned off for the entire instance (`jit = off`). While YMMV, many queries probably won't be improved significantly by JIT in its current implementation, and you can always target queries that would benefit by setting this property for a specific query or connection.

Conclusion

As with any technology, knowing how to configure that technology to your hardware and your needs correctly, is essential to using it well. PostgreSQL has hundreds of potential settings that can be changed, but in this chapter, we've focused on eight that should start to show immediate results as they're tuned for your server load and available resources.

6
Roles and Privileges

PostgreSQL roles are an important and required part of a functioning database cluster. The relationship between the cluster, roles, privileges, and database objects is essential to understand to effectively manage and secure your PostgreSQL cluster. To understand how these pieces fit together, we need to start by understanding the relationships between roles and the cluster.

Host-based Authentication

Recall that the running instance of a PostgreSQL server is called a *cluster*. Multiple clusters (instances) can be running on a host server or VM, but each cluster must use a different port as shown in Figure 6-1.

Each cluster also requires a separate host-based authentication (hba) file named `pg_hba.conf`, which defines connection-level authorization, ie. *which hosts and roles can connect to which databases, using which connection protocols.* The rules defined in the `pg_hba.conf` are read when the cluster is started and stored in memory for fast access later. Then, for every connection we attempt to make to the cluster, the rules are checked top-down to find a match.

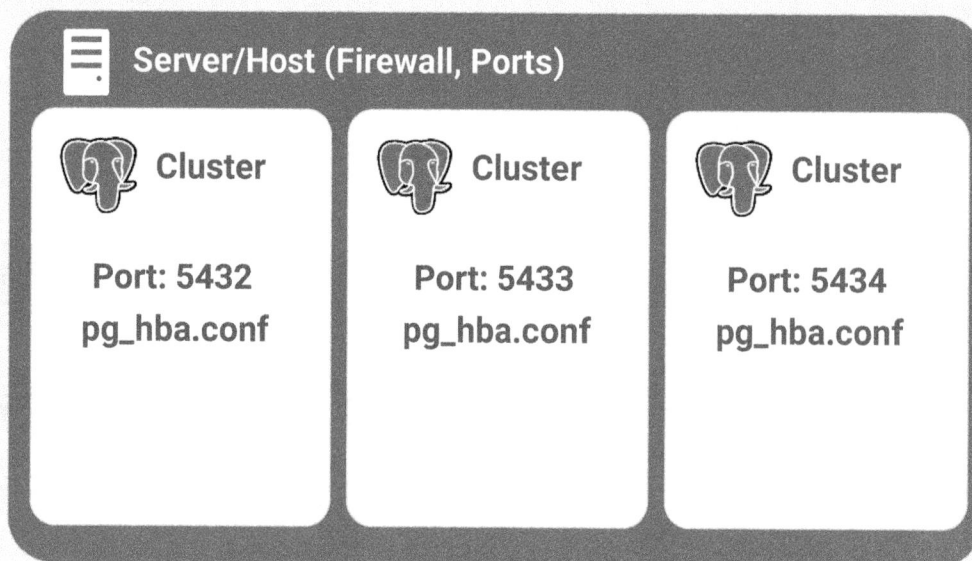

Figure 6-1. *Multiple PostgreSQL clusters running on different ports.*

At this point in the connection process no authentication has taken place yet. The cluster first needs to ensure that the properties of the connection (host, address, role, method) are allowed to try and connect to a database.

The first rule that matches the specified authentication properties determines if the connection can then attempt to authenticate with the cluster and database. If no matching rule is found, the connection is refused, and no further authentication is attempted.

The rules in a pg_hba.conf file consist of five (or six) parts:

> **Connection Type:** how is the connection identified, typically local or host. When the type is host (or one of its variants), the address field must be defined.

> **Database:** the database(s) that this connection is authorized to connect to if authentication is successful.

> **User:** which role(s) this rule applies to. A value of all will authenticate any user where other properties match.

Address: a specific IP address, IP range with netmask, or hostname, that a connection is allowed to originate from.

Method: the authentication method that will be used if all identifying properties are matched. There are many possible methods, but most clusters use `scram-sha-256` for password-based login or `gss/sspi` with a central authentication server like Kerberos or Active Directory. `trust` should never be used in production environments and is only suitable for local (sandboxed) development clusters. Even then, using `trust` is highly discouraged by the community. (`trust` means that anyone who has access to the server can access using any user role name they specify that exists, even superusers.)

To get an idea of what the `pg_hba.conf` file format looks like, the PostgreSQL documentation provides a good sample with comments explaining each example rule. A portion of that example is shown in Listing 6-1.

Listing 6-1. A sample pg_hba.conf file

```
# See https://www.postgresql.org/docs/current/auth-pg-hba-conf.html for
# more details and examples.
#
# Allow any user on the local system to connect to any database with
# any database user name using Unix-domain sockets (the default for local
# connections).
#
# TYPE   DATABASE          USER              ADDRESS               METHOD
local    all               all                                     trust

# The same using local loopback TCP/IP connections.
#
# TYPE   DATABASE          USER              ADDRESS               METHOD
host     all               all               127.0.0.1/32          trust

# The same over IPv6.
#
# TYPE   DATABASE          USER              ADDRESS               METHOD
host     all               all               ::1/128               trust
```

```
# The same using a host name (would typically cover both IPv4 and IPv6).
#
# TYPE   DATABASE          USER          ADDRESS              METHOD
host     all               all           localhost            trust

# The same using a regular expression for DATABASE, that allows
# connection to the database db1, db2 and any databases with a name
# beginning with "db" and finishing with a number using two to four
# digits (like "db1234" or "db12").
#
# TYPE   DATABASE                USER        ADDRESS          METHOD
local    db1,"/^db\d{2,4}$",db2  all         localhost        trust

# Allow any user from any host with IP address 192.168.93.x to connect
# to database "postgres"
#
# TYPE   DATABASE          USER     ADDRESS             METHOD
host     postgres          all      192.168.93.0/24     scram-sha-256

# Allow any user from host 192.168.12.10 to connect to database
# "appdb" if the user's password is correctly supplied.
#
# TYPE   DATABASE          USER     ADDRESS             METHOD
host     appdb             all      192.168.12.10/32    scram-sha-256
```

Most cloud hosted Database as a Service (DBaaS) solutions manage the pg_hba.conf file and user-defined modifications are performed through a UI or command line. However, if you run PostgreSQL on your own, even as a container, you need to have a basic understanding of how the pg_hba.conf file works.

Cluster, Databases, and Roles

Notice again that the connection rules define which database(s) a matching connection can connect to. Unlike some database servers that initiate a connection to the server first independent of a specific database, every PostgreSQL connection is created directly to a database. This means that the database used in a connection must exist and that the authenticating role is allowed to connect. Otherwise, the connection is refused even if the other connection properties (user, password, host) are correct.

Note: If your primary experience has been with SQL Server, you may have noticed that PostgreSQL doesn't have a way to switch databases within a script, something like USE mydb. Because the connection is always tied to a database, switching databases requires that the connection be reset.

Roles

Now that we've explained the relationship between the PostgreSQL cluster and the properties of host-based authentication that permit connections to a database, it's time to begin talking about the most important piece of this connection process and overall workings of the database: *roles.*

First and foremost, roles are the authentication principal for managing database access permissions. Although early versions of PostgreSQL had separate principal types for users and groups, these were replaced in PostgreSQL 8.2 (December 2006) with a single principal type called role, in an effort to bring PostgreSQL in line with the SQL standard. Roles in PostgreSQL can be used as users, groups, or a combination of both.

Roles own databases, schemas, and most object types within a database (e.g. tables, functions, views, types, etc.). They are assigned cluster-level privileges called *attributes*, are granted privileges to other databases and objects they don't own, and if they have the right attribute, can grant privileges to other roles. In short, properly managed roles are the backbone of a healthy database and cluster.

Users and Groups

As we mentioned earlier, roles can act as users, groups, or a combination of both. By convention, roles that are assigned the LOGIN attribute are thought of as users, and roles that are assigned the NOLOGIN attribute are thought of as groups, as illustrated in Listing 6-2.

Listing 6-2. *Create "user" and "group" roles*

```
-- User role
CREATE ROLE dev1 WITH LOGIN PASSWORD 'abc123';

-- Group role
CREATE ROLE developers WITH NOLOGIN;
```

Aside from this convention, however, there is nothing semantically different about these roles. Any role, regardless of intent, can own database objects and have any role attributes assigned or not.

Note: PostgreSQL has retained the CREATE USER and CREATE GROUP commands, but they are simply aliases to the CREATE ROLE command. The only difference is that CREATE USER explicitly sets the LOGIN attribute for the role.

Role Attributes

Role attributes are cluster-level privileges or settings assigned to a role. These can be assigned during role creation or modified later by altering the role. They are shown, and typically written in all caps because they are keywords for the CREATE ROLE command. However, there is no requirement that they be entered in caps. For many of the attributes, there is a corresponding "NO..." keyword which unsets that privilege. Keywords in **bold** are the default for that attribute if not otherwise stated.

LOGIN | **NOLOGIN** – Can the role login to the cluster. LOGIN implies the role is a user, NOLOGIN implies a group role.

INHERIT | NOINHERIT – When granted membership in another role, does this role inherit the privileges of the parent role.

SUPERUSER | **NOSUPERUSER** – Does this role have superuser access (discussed later in the chapter)

CREATEROLE | **NOCREATEROLE** – Can the role create, alter, or drop other roles.

CREATEDB | **NOCREATEDB** – Can this role create new databases on this cluster.

REPLICATION | **NOREPLICATION** – This attribute is required for roles that are used to manage replication connections or slots.

BYPASSRLS | **NOBYPASSRLS** – Can this role bypass row-level security policies.

PASSWORD – Sets the role's password. Can be omitted if roles will not be using password authentication methods.

CONNECTION LIMIT – how many concurrent connections this role can make. Unlimited (-1) by default.

If no attributes are specified when a role is created, then it will not be able to login, will inherit privileges from other roles it has membership in, and have unlimited connections to the database.

Note: It's also possible to ALTER roles and set PostgreSQL configuration settings that will be automatically applied for that role every time it connects. Almost any setting that isn't reserved for superusers and can be configured using the SET command directly in SQL, can be applied to the role.

This could be useful for increasing the `work_mem` settings for a nightly reporting user, for instance, or to turn off a setting like Just-in-time (JIT) plan compilation.

```
ALTER ROLE user1 SET jit TO off;
```

To reset the configuration setting for the role, use the RESET command while altering the role.

```
ALTER ROLE user1 RESET jit;
```

The Superuser Role

To effectively manage the PostgreSQL cluster, at least one role must exist with the SUPERUSER attribute because some commands can only be performed by superusers, and the initial database user must have permission to create roles and databases.

Superusers are very powerful within a cluster because they bypass all security checks once they successfully authenticate to the database. These roles are analogous the sa account in SQL Server or root in Linux, and have authority to perform any task on the cluster or database.

Every time a PostgreSQL database cluster is initiated, a default database and superuser are created. In most clusters, both the superuser and database are named postgres. Interestingly, this isn't hardcoded into the cluster initiation process, although nearly all documentation and online demos expect both the database and role to exist.

Fun fact: By default, the initial superuser is named after whichever system user owns the running PostgreSQL process when the cluster is initiated. Since all common PostgreSQL installations create a system user named postgres, essentially all installations have this as the first superuser role that is created.

Because the superuser role is so powerful and could cause problems if not used carefully, the prevailing guidance for running PostgreSQL is to create at least one "superuser-like" role (Listing 6-3) that can create new databases and roles without having the power to alter, delete, or in other ways modify the database without restraint.

Listing 6-3. Create a super-like role

```
-- superuser-like administration role
CREATE ROLE cluster_admin WITH LOGIN CREATEROLE CREATEDB
PASSWORD 'abc123';
```

Once this role is created, one last security related modification is recommended in production (or production like) environments that can decrease the risk of unfettered database change by a superuser account.

First, using the superuser, grant membership of this new role into the superuser role. Then, the superuser can set the NOLOGIN attribute on itself which would prevent any active connections from blindly logging in as a superuser and potentially causing harm to objects and data.

However, now that the superuser-like role (we created as `cluster_admin` in Listing 6-3) is a member of the superuser role, it can always assume the superuser role when needed to perform superuser-only tasks. In a Linux environment, this would be analogous to using the `su` or `sudo` command to temporarily assume the privileges of the root user. We'll discuss in more detail how to grant membership in roles and how to temporarily assume a role that you have membership in.

Finally, if you use a cloud managed PostgreSQL database, you will not get access to the superuser role because it has too much power within the infrastructure of the database environment. Instead, whatever role you are initially given by the provide will most likely be "superuser-like".

Role Privileges

Now that we understand what roles are and how to assign attributes to them for cluster-level privileges (attributes), it's time to talk about database-level privileges. After all, this is what most DBA's and security professionals are really concerned with, and end-users care when they can't perform their job effectively because of misconfigured permissions. Just like Goldilocks and the Three Bears, we want to create roles that have just enough privilege to do everything required of them, but nothing more.

Below we show a brief overview of each privilege. For a more detailed description of each privilege and how it affects the role's ability to perform specific tasks, see the PostgreSQL documentation. (https://www.postgresql.org/docs/current/ddl-priv.html)

SELECT – allows selecting from tables, views, and other table-like objects, including the use of the COPY TO command. Required for UPDATE, DELETE, or MERGE privileges to work.

INSERT – allows the insert of new rows into a table, view, etc. Required to use the COPY FROM command.

UPDATE – allows updates to any column of a table, view, etc.

DELETE – allows deletion of a row from a table, view, etc.

TRUNCATE – allows the truncation of a table.

REFERENCES – allows the creation of foreign key constraints.

TRIGGER – allows the creation of a trigger.

CREATE – depending on the parent object type, allows the creation of related child objects. For databases, creation of schemas among other things. For schemas, the creation of objects like tables, view, functions, etc.

CONNECT – allows the role to connect to the database (in combination with the host-based authentication checks)

USAGE – the role can use the object type. Most importantly, this role can access schema objects if other privileges for that object type allow it. Without USAGE on the schema, roles may still see the names of objects like tables and functions, but they can't access them even if the SELECT privilege (for instance) was granted. Usage and access privileges must both be set.

TEMPORARY – the role can create temporary tables within the database.

EXECUTE – the role can call functions and procedures.

With these privilege definitions in mind, we'll now turn to the actual process of granting privileges to roles.

GRANT and REVOKE

There are two forms of the GRANT and REVOKE command that are similar but affect different object types.

The first form is used to grant or revoke privileges to objects in a database to a given role (e.g. SELECT on tables, CREATE on schemas, etc.). The second form is used to grant or revoke a role membership to another role. This is most often used to manage privileges through group roles (those with NOLOGIN set) and granting user roles membership.

Granting Privileges to Database Objects

To GRANT or REVOKE privileges to database objects, you must either be a superuser, the owner of the objects to which privileges are being applied, or a role that has been given the GRANT privilege for an object that they don't own.

Granting privileges to objects is applied separately within each database. For example, granting the CREATE privilege on a schema to a role in one database does not transfer that privilege to another database that contains the same schema name.

Many of the different database objects each have a slightly different set of options when granting privileges to a role. For a complete set of examples, please see the GRANT documentation (https://www.postgresql.org/docs/current/sql-grant.html) which clearly outlines each specific type.

The basic form of the GRANT command is shown in Listing 6-4.

Listing 6-4: Basic GRANT statement format

```
GRANT { comma separated list of privileges for object type }
ON { object type } TO { role name }
```

While there are additional properties and commands you can add to each object type, this form will generally work for most needs.

To demonstrate how to grant privileges to database roles, we're going to assume the following roles have already been created in our database.

Group Roles (NOLOGIN)

`app_users:` assigned minimal privileges to all roles

`app_developers:` assigned higher-level privileges to developers

`app_admins:` assigned create privileges to admin roles

User Roles (LOGIN)

`app_read_only:` used by the application to only select data

`app_dev_jr:` a role with elevated privileges to modify data and use most objects

`app_dev_sr:` a role with elevated privileges to create objects within the database including new schemas

With these roles created, we'll show how to grant privileges to the three common object types: databases, schemas, and tables. Although you're likely to need to apply privileges to other object types, starting with these three should help you understand the basic principles.

Database Privileges

Roles can be granted three different privileges to a database; CREATE, CONNECT, and TEMPORARY/TEMP. Given the snippet of the documentation for granting database privileges in Listing 6-5, we want to ensure that all roles can connect to the database, but only admin users can create schemas within the database (Listing 6-6).

Listing 6-5: PostgreSQL documentation sample for database privileges

```
GRANT { { CREATE | CONNECT | TEMPORARY | TEMP } [, ...] | ALL [
PRIVILEGES ] }
    ON DATABASE database_name [, ...]
    TO role_specification [, ...] [ WITH GRANT OPTION ]
    [ GRANTED BY role_specification ]
```

Listing 6-6: GRANT privileges on the database

```
GRANT CONNECT, TEMP ON DATABASE app_db TO app_users;
GRANT CREATE ON DATABASE app_db TO app_admins;
```

Schema Privileges

Even though a role can connect to a database, they won't be able to do anything else unless they have the USAGE privilege. For database admins, we need to grant them the privileges to CREATE objects in this schema. (Listing 6-7 and 6-8)

Listing 6-7: PostgreSQL documentation sample for schema privileges

```
GRANT { { CREATE | USAGE } [, ...] | ALL [ PRIVILEGES ] }
    ON SCHEMA schema_name [, ...]
    TO role_specification [, ...] [ WITH GRANT OPTION ]
    [ GRANTED BY role_specification ]
```

Listing 6-8: GRANT schema privileges to the appropriate group roles

```
GRANT CREATE ON SCHEMA app_schema TO app_admins;
GRANT USAGE ON SCHEMA app_schema TO app_users;
```

Table Privileges

Finally, we need each role to have the right set of table privileges to perform their required tasks. (Listing 6-9 and 6-10)

Listing 6-9: PostgreSQL documentation sample for table privileges

```
GRANT { { SELECT | INSERT | UPDATE | DELETE | TRUNCATE | REFERENCES |
TRIGGER }
    [, ...] | ALL [ PRIVILEGES ] }
    ON { [ TABLE ] table_name [, ...]
        | ALL TABLES IN SCHEMA schema_name [, ...] }
    TO role_specification [, ...] [ WITH GRANT OPTION ]
    [ GRANTED BY role_specification ]
```

Listing 6-10: GRANT table access privileges to each group role

```
GRANT SELECT ON ALL TABLES IN SCHEMA app_schema TO app_users;

GRANT INSERT, UPDATE, DELETE, TRUNCATE
  ON ALL TABLES IN SCHEMA app_schema TO app_developers;

GRANT ALL PRIVILEGES ON ALL TABLES IN SCHEMA app_schema
  TO app_admins;
```

Granting Membership to Another Role

The second form of GRANT and REVOKE deals with granting membership in other roles. As we just discussed, all roles (user or group) are granted membership to the PUBLIC role. Likewise, any role can grant membership to into that role if they have the privilege to do so.

This is most common with group roles. Because they cannot login, they are used to assign privileges and then user roles are granted membership to these roles. Membership in other roles confers their privileges to all members. This is the most effective way to manage database privileges at scale.

In the previous section we outlined three group roles and assigned them privileges based on their intent: read-only users, developers, and administrators. Once those roles are created and configured, we can then grant membership to user roles (Listing 6-11) which will acquire their privileges, even across multiple group roles.

Listing 6-11: Granting membership to other roles

```
GRANT app_users TO app_read_only, app_dev_jr, app_dev_sr;

GRANT app_developers TO app_dev_jr, app_dev_sr;

GRANT app_admins TO app_dev_sr;
```

With all the roles set up, all roles can use the database and select table data; all developers can perform database manipulation on all tables; and senior developers can create schemas and objects and have all privileges on tables (Figure 6-2).

Unlike executing a GRANT statement on objects in a database, which only modifies objects in existence at the time, modifying privileges on a role applies to all members, regardless of when they were added as a member of the parent role.

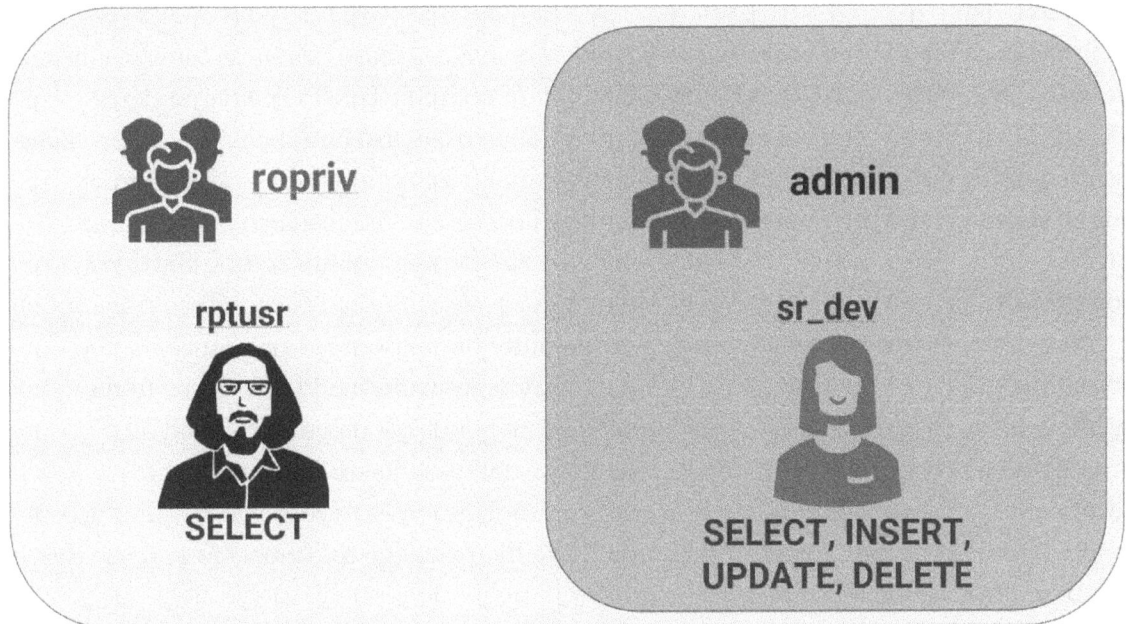

Figure 6-2. Role privilege inheritance

The PUBLIC Role

Now that we've talked about role membership and how privileges are inherited, we need to discuss the special PUBLIC role.

Every PostgreSQL database has a group role called PUBLIC and all roles have membership in this role. The PUBLIC role cannot be dropped, and roles cannot be removed from it. Likewise, every database has a default schema called `public` which members of the PUBLIC role has privileges to. While it can be dropped, most databases retain it and simply reset the privileges to be more restrictive.

The initial purpose of the PUBLIC role is to provide the necessary privileges to all roles that allows them to connect to and use a database. Recall that having the CONNECT and USAGE privilege in the database doesn't imply any further privileges to query or manipulate the schema or data. To query data (DML) or modify the schema (DDL), additional privileges must exist for the PUBLIC role or another role which the session role has membership in.

By default, the PUBLIC role in every newly created database has these four privileges assigned to it for the `public` schema: CONNECT, USAGE, TEMPORARY, and EXECUTE. In PostgreSQL 14 and below, the PUBLIC role also had the CREATE privilege granted to the `public` schema, which meant that all roles could create objects in the public schema if the privileges weren't modified otherwise. For security reasons, the CREATE privilege was removed from the PUBLIC role as a default setting starting with PostgreSQL 15.

Knowing that this possible security vulnerability has existed for several years, the prevailing guidance has been to REVOKE all privileges from the PUBLIC role to the public schema in all databases. Additionally, some resources recommend that all privileges be revoked for the PUBLIC role on the database itself. This forces the administrator to explicitly grant the necessary privileges to each role that requires access to the database or schema, rather than inheriting the privilege to connect to and use the database through the PUBLIC role.

However you decide to implement security on the PUBLIC role and schema, it's valuable to understand the importance of why it exists. The goal is to be intentional in your decisions to apply privileges and know which roles can create and manage objects within the database.

Object Ownership

Understanding roles and privileges is essential to effectively, and safely, using PostgreSQL. In many ways, however, everything we've discussed so far is a necessary precursor to understanding the importance of roles and object ownership.

If you're coming to PostgreSQL with experience in another platform like SQL Server, the differences of how roles and ownership work together can be hard to navigate given your existing knowledge. To bridge the gap, you need a good foundation in how PostgreSQL object ownership impacts schema management and object privileges. Otherwise, you're likely to become frustrated as projects get larger, and more developers are involved.

Objects in PostgreSQL generally refer to anything created with a DDL command, like tables, functions, stored procedures, schemas, and others. As with any database, objects must be owned by a role and access to that object is managed in various ways depending on the platform.

In PostgreSQL, all objects are initially owned by the role that created them. While that might not seem surprising, the implications this has for managing those objects are important to understand.

First, only the owner of an object (or a superuser) can modify the object in any way. For example, any modification to a table like adding, dropping, or renaming columns, changing datatypes, or modifying constraints is limited to the owner of the table. Regardless of how many privileges another role has in a particular database, unless they are a superuser, they will not be able to modify an object that another role owns. Hold on to that for a minute.

Second, all objects are initially created without any privileges granted to other roles. For other roles to access data or use functions, for example, the owner of the object must specifically grant those privileges. As we noted above with object ownership and DDL modifications, no number of standard privileges will automatically give other roles access to the object unless they are explicitly granted, or the accessing role is a superuser.

In essence, it's easiest to think of the object owner as a superuser *of that object*. Much like there are no restrictions in the database for a real superuser role, an object owner has no restrictions on the objects they create. They can limit their object privileges after creation, but they can always expand privileges again because, you guessed it, they are like a superuser for the objects they own.

Herein lies the challenge for many new users to PostgreSQL. They rarely experience these restrictions because they only use one role or they are always connected as the initial superuser role, `postgres`. Therefore, as an individual user, it often feels like there are few, if any, restrictions on creating or accessing data because that role owns all the user objects and has full access.

In a real application, we want to have more control over who can create and own objects, what roles can modify them, and what roles can modify or query data using those objects. Let's look at three ways to make managing object privileges easier.

Granting Privileges Manually

Earlier in this chapter we talked about how to grant privileges to individual objects. Although tedious to maintain, this is the most straightforward way to manage role privileges to objects.

But let us remind you again that any time you manually grant privileges to objects, it will only affect the objects that currently exist. For example, if we look at the earlier example where we granted the `app_users` role SELECT on all tables, only the tables in existence would have their privileges updated. If we create a new table, the correct privileges need to be assigned or the `app_users` role will not be able to select from it. (Listing 6-12)

Listing 6-12: Create a new table and manually grant privileges to it

```
/*
 * As app_dev_sr role, create a new table
 */
CREATE TABLE app_schema.category (
    category_id integer GENERATED ALWAYS AS IDENTITY NOT NULL,
    name text NOT NULL,
    last_update timestamp with time zone DEFAULT now() NOT NULL
);

GRANT SELECT ON TABLE app_schema.category TO app_users;
```

Alternatively, we could just grant SELECT on all tables again, which would leave the existing table privileges unmodified while updating the new table to allow SELECT for this group role. (Listing 6-13)

Listing 6-13: Grant SELECT access on all tables

```
GRANT SELECT ON ALL TABLES IN SCHEMA app_schema TO app_users;
```

Either way, the privileges would be updated and the `app_users` role will be able to select data from the new table.

On a large scale, however, this can often prove to be tedious to maintain. Schema migration tools can help, but it still requires diligence to ensure that as roles are added and the schema is changed, that the correct permissions are applied each time.

Create Default Privileges

Rather than manage privileges object by object, PostgreSQL provides a mechanism, called DEFAULT PRIVILEGES, to apply the desired privileges to objects as they are created.

Default privileges are created and managed by each role that will create objects. Because we know that the role that creates an object is the initial owner, PostgreSQL will look to see if that role has any default privilege rules which need to be applied to the object for other roles as it is created. This means that individual GRANT statements can be created ahead of time to ensure that each role receives proper access to the object.

Creating a default privilege is straightforward. We need to identify the type of object we are creating a default privilege for, the role(s) the privilege applies to, and what privileges need to be applied. For the example shown in Listing 6-14, we'll connect as the app_dev_sr role and create rules for both app_users and app_developers to be applied for every object the app_dev_sr role creates.

Listing 6-14: Create default privileges for tables which are applied to newly created tables

```
/*
 * For every table this role creates, apply these privileges
 * to other roles as specified
 */
ALTER DEFAULT PRIVILEGES IN SCHEMA app_schema
   GRANT SELECT ON TABLES TO app_users;

ALTER DEFAULT PRIVILEGES IN SCHEMA app_schema
   GRANT INSERT,UPDATE,DELETE ON TABLES TO app_developers;

/*
 * Create a table without manual GRANT statements and the
 * roles specified above will still have the appropriate access
 */
```

```
CREATE TABLE app_schema.states (
    state_id integer DEFAULT AS IDENTITY NOT NULL,
    name text NOT NULL,
    abbreviation text NOT NULL,
    last_update timestamp with time zone DEFAULT now() NOT NULL
);
```

After creation, this table will allow members of app_users to select data, and members of app_developers to insert and modify data without manually executing additional grants.

To undo default privileges, or to remove a privilege generally granted to a role like PULIC, you can REVOKE the default privilege as necessary. Listing 6-15 demonstrates how to remove the DELETE default privilege to app_developers and the EXECUTE privilege on newly created functions to the PUBLIC role.

Listing 6-15: Modify default privileges to remove a privilege granted previously

```
/*
 * Modify a previously created default privilege
 */
ALTER DEFAULT PRIVILEGES IN SCHEMA app_schema
    REVOKE DELETE ON TABLES FROM app_developers;

/*
 * Remove the EXECUTE privilege on new functions for PUBLIC
 */
ALTER DEFAULT PRIVILEGES FOR ROLE app_sr_dev
    REVOKE EXECUTE ON FUNCTIONS FROM PUBLIC;
```

Using default privileges streamlines object privilege management and helps to ensure each role can use and access the required schema, data, functions, etc. However, default privileges are only applied based on the role that creates the object. If multiple roles can create schemas, tables, and more, each of them needs to create the correct set of default privileges to ensure proper access to all other roles. Even then, only the owner of each object can modify it, which might lead to more frustration down the road.

A Sustainable Approach to Default Privileges

Managing privileges in a real application that is constantly growing and changing is challenging if there is no centralized owner of all database objects. Therefore, it is generally considered a best practice to create one group role that is used to create all database objects, and with that role, create and maintain all default privileges for other roles. This will ensure privileges are applied consistently over the life of the application.

In the example shown in Listing 6-16, we'll create a new group role, `app_ddl_admin` and grant membership to `app_admins`. Then we'll create the same default privileges from Listing 6-14 to demonstrate using this group role to create a table object with the correctly applied privileges.

Listing 6-16: Using a newly created group role to manage default privileges for all objects

```
/*
 * Create a new superuser-like group role with and grant
 * membership to all app_admins.
 */
CREATE ROLE app_ddl_admin WITH NOLOGIN;
GRANT USAGE, CREATE
    ON SCHEMA app_schema TO app_ddl_admin;

/*
 * Grant membership to all app_admins, which includes
 * app_dev_sr currently.
 */
GRANT app_ddl_admin TO app_admins;

/*
 * With the role created and membership granted to app_admins,
 * connected as any app_admin role, assume the app_ddl_admin
 * role and create default privileges.
 */

-- During a session, roles can always "SET ROLE" to any role
-- they are a member of.
SET ROLE app_ddl_admin;
```

```
ALTER DEFAULT PRIVILEGES IN SCHEMA app_schema
   GRANT SELECT ON TABLES TO app_users;

ALTER DEFAULT PRIVILEGES IN SCHEMA app_schema
   GRANT INSERT,UPDATE,DELETE ON TABLES TO app_developers;

/*
 * While the connection is currently set to app_ddl_admin role
 * create the a new table object.
 */
CREATE TABLE app_schema.city (
    city_id integer DEFAULT AS IDENTITY NOT NULL,
    state_id integer NOT NULL,
    name text NOT NULL,
    last_update timestamp with time zone DEFAULT now() NOT NULL
);
-- Reset the connection back to the role that initially
-- established the session. In this example, app_dev_sr.
SET ROLE NONE;

INSERT INTO app_schema.city (state_id, name) VALUES
   (10,'Albany');
```

The example in Listing 6-16 is limited to managing default privileges for table objects. More thought is needed to identify and create the correct set of default privileges for your specific application. But if you use one centralized role to create the objects (preferably one that cannot login), you can build a template which ensures access privileges are applied consistently throughout the life of the database.

Predefined Roles

There is one final option for more easily managing privileges to database objects. Beginning with PostgreSQL 14, new predefined roles were added which provide commonly requested privileges without the need to create and maintain grants across the entire database (e.g. read-only access). Be aware, however, that predefined roles are applied at the cluster level. This means that when the predefined role provides access to database-level functionality, it is granted across all databases in the cluster.

For instance, we could grant membership into the `pg_read_all_data` predefined role to allow read-only access to all data as shown in Listing 6-17. However, this access would apply to any database that the role has access to. Therefore, to limit data access, we would want to revoke the USAGE permission to databases that the role should not be able to query.

Listing 6-17: Grant read access to all tables, views, and sequences with predefined role

```
/*
 * Grant membership into the pg_read_all_data predefined role
 */
GRANT pg_read_all_data TO app_read_only;
```

Likewise, if we created a role that should have the privilege to insert and modify data in any table, it could be granted membership into the `pg_write_all_data` predefined role. (Listing 6-18)

Listing 6-18: Grant write access to all tables, views, and sequences with predefined role

```
/*
 * Grant membership into the pg_read_all_data predefined role
 */
GRANT pg_write_all_data TO app_developers;
```

However, let us caution you one more time. Granting membership into any role with sweeping database privileges needs to be done with great care. In the case of `pg_read_all_data` and `pg_write_all_data`, all other privileges currently granted or revoked for tables, views, and sequences are ignored. That may be perfectly acceptable for the assigned role, but it still requires an understanding of how the role will be used.

Conclusion

Managing role, privileges, and security in PostgreSQL can be complicated to do well. Because there is a lot of flexibility in how privileges can be granted or revoked for many database objects, managing them requires an understanding of object ownership and a well thought out plan. That said, simpler is often better. Using principles from the examples in this chapter, particularly the use of group roles and default privileges, take some time to think about how your application database will be used now and into the future, and then start using these techniques to your advantage.

7
Creating Databases

In the earlier chapters of the book, we have installed PostgreSQL, looked at tools, configured our server and started establishing security. In this chapter, we'll start working with the fundamental construct for managing data within PostgreSQL, the database. Most of your work developing and maintaining PostgreSQL will take place within a database. However, to get there, we first must be able to create a database. In this chapter we'll cover:

- What is a database?
- Database templates
- Creating a database
- Working with tablespaces
- Altering a database
- Dropping a database

What Is a Database

A database within PostgreSQL is primarily a means of organizing the data and other objects necessary to store and maintain your information. Inside of a database is where tables are created. Functions, views, and other code objects are all defined within a database. Then, those databases are backed up, restored and generally maintained as a unit.

In general, a database is used to delineate one set of information from another. For example, an organization stores all customer information in one database, separate from its inventory management information. This is because these two data sets, while they may interact in some ways, have different functional requirements, varying security requirements, and are accessed by different applications in different ways. The database acts to organize and isolate these requirements.

When you create a PostgreSQL server, you automatically get three databases, postgres, template0 and template1. We'll discuss the template databases in the next section.

Because connecting to PostgreSQL requires a database to be specified, the "postgres" database is created during installation as an initial database to get you started. Like other databases you will create, this database has access to global information about your PostgreSQL server, often referred to as metadata, data about data. The information is stored internally but is exposed through system catalogs. These act like tables or views (covered in later chapters) in that you can query them to get information about your server, the databases in the server, and the objects defined within those databases.

The databases themselves are stored as groups of files in the operating systems file structure in the specified data directory. The files themselves consist of pages of information, a page being 8kb in size (by default, although this can be changed). The information about your database and the information in your database, are both stored in the database on these page structures. This can get quite complex quickly since different objects within the database may store their information within the pages in slightly different ways, depending on if we're talking about a table, an index or other objects. For the moment, just knowing that storage within the database is managed through these 8kb pages by default is enough. The complexity is managed behind the scenes by the PostgreSQL engine.

You can query information about your databases. Listing 7-1 shows how to get a list of databases from the system catalog:

Listing 7-1. Querying pg_database to see a list of databases on a server.

```
SELECT
      pd.datname,
      pd.datistemplate
FROM
      pg_database AS pd;
```

The results from a brand-new server without any user created databases is shown in Figure 7-1:

ABC datname	datistemplate
1	postgres	[ ]
2	template1	[v]
3	template0	[v]

Figure 7-1. List of databases on a new server

You can see the three default databases in the list in Figure 7-1. You can also see that two are marked as templates. From here, let's create a database to get started testing.

Creating a Database

The initial syntax for creating a new database is extremely straight forward:

Listing 7-2. Creating a database using defaults

```
CREATE DATABASE hamshackradio;
```

Connecting to the server through the postgres database and running this SQL will create a new database. We can confirm this by running the SQL from Listing 7-1 again and we'll now see results like Figure 7-2:

	ABC datname ▼	☑ datistemplate ▼
1	postgres	[ ]
2	template1	[v]
3	template0	[v]
4	hamshackradio	[ ]

Figure 7-2. List of databases after creating a new one

To see the files that were created by this command, we need to know the default tablespace. We will cover this in more detail later in this chapter, but a tablespace refers to the various locations where data is stored. There are several mechanisms for finding this. Listing 7-3 shows how to query the pg_settings system table:

Listing 7-3. Getting the data directory

```
SELECT
      setting
FROM
      pg_catalog.pg_settings AS ps
WHERE
      ps."name" = 'data_directory';
```

On my system, the output is in Figure 7-3. Your system may be different, which is why knowing this information is useful:

	ABC setting ▼
1	/var/lib/postgresql/data

Figure 7-3. The file system location of the data directory

The files themselves are in a directory below this: /base/<oid>. The oid value stands for Object ID. We can modify our listing from 7-1 to look more like 7-4 to get the oid value for our databases:

Listing 7-4. Listing the databases along with the oid values

```
SELECT
       pd.oid,
       pd.datname,
       pd.datistemplate
FROM
       pg_database AS pd;
```

On the system we are working on for this demo, the output looks like Figure 7-4:

	123 oid	ABC datname	☑ datistemplate
1	5	postgres	[ ]
2	1	template1	[v]
3	4	template0	[v]
4	17,982	hamshackradio	[ ]

Figure 7-4. Databases along with the oid value

Our new database has an oid value of 17,7982. We can navigate to the data directory in the operating system to see the folder structure shown in Figure 7-5:

```
root@d9311ebb6f5a:/var/lib/postgresql/data/base# ls
1   17982   4   5
```

Figure 7-5. Contents of the base directory

You can see directories for all the databases listed above, including the one for hamshackradio. Figure 7-6 displays the contents of the 17982 folder:

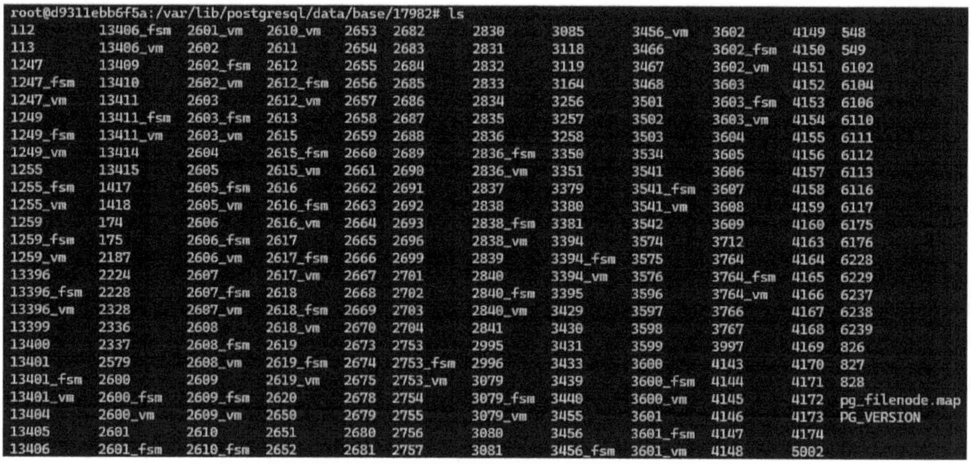

Figure 7-6. *The files and folders that store the hamshackradio database*

As you can see, our database isn't stored as a single file, let alone as something human manageable. This series of files and folders are defined and managed by the PostgreSQL database system, and this is where all the database objects and data will be kept.

There are several options available to use in the CREATE DATABASE command. The full description of the command is available here: https://tinyurl.com/3k8y4wst. By default, when nothing is specified, the owner of the database is the role (also called user) that created the database. Some of the other defaults include the tablespace is the default data directory, template1 is used automatically, and the collation is adopted from the settings on the server, just to name a few.

Before we go on, we're going to create a new role in the hamshackradio database. We'll use this for several other examples in this chapter. Roles and security were covered in more detail in Chapter 6.

Listing 7-5. *Creating the hamshackadmin role*

```
CREATE ROLE hamshackadmin;
```

Now, if we wanted to, for example, set the database owner to a different role, we'd change the CREATE DATABASE code to something like Listing 7-6:

Listing 7-6. *Designating the owner of the database*

```
CREATE DATABASE roletest OWNER hamshackadmin;
```

This would create a new database named roletest that would be owned by the hamshackadmin role. We'll cover controlling several other settings in the rest of the chapter.

Another way to create a database within PostgreSQL is to use the createdb client application, documented here: https://tinyurl.com/2pmxyf9r. The createdb application is just a wrapper around the CREATE DATABASE SQL command, and so the syntax will be similar. Listing 7-7 is an example:

Listing 7-7. *Using the client application createdb*

```
createdb –U postgres clientappdemo
```

That's how we create a database within PostgreSQL. Now, let's see how we can modify an already created database.

Modifying a Database

You may find after you've created a database that you need to make some changes to that database. PostgreSQL answers this need with the ALTER DATABASE command. For example, we need to change the owner of the hamshackradio database from the postgres user that created it, to the hamshackadmin role. The syntax would look like Listing 7-8:

Listing 7-8. *Using ALTER DATABASE to change owner*

```
ALTER DATABASE hamshackradio OWNER TO hamshackadmin;
```

If you're not currently connected to a given database, you can use the ALTER DATABASE command to rename that database:

Listing 7-9. *Changing a database name*

```
ALTER DATABASE roletest RENAME TO renametest;
```

Running Listing 7-4 again we'll see the renamed database:

	oid	datname	datistemplate
1	5	postgres	[ ]
2	1	template1	[v]
3	4	template0	[v]
4	17,982	hamshackradio	[ ]
5	17,985	renametest	[ ]
6	17,986	clientappdemo	[ ]

Figure 7-7. *Database has been renamed*

You can also make changes to the database to adjust settings so that they're not the same as the system defaults. For example, we can run the query in Listing 7-10 to see that the default date style for my system is 'MDY', the default for many countries outside the EU:

Listing 7-10. *Getting the Date Style for the server*

```
SELECT
      setting
FROM
      pg_catalog.pg_settings
WHERE
      name = 'DateStyle';
```

If we want to modify my database so that it's formatting the dates like our friends in the UK prefer, we can run the code in Listing 7-11:

Listing 7-11. *Changing the Date Style for a database*

```
ALTER DATABASE hamshackradio SET
datestyle = "Postgres, DMY";
```

Now, when dates are retrieved from the hamshackradio database, they'll be in the format of Day, then Month, then Year, rather than the system setting of Month/Day/Year. We can even verify this worked by querying the pg_db_role_settings table from out database:

Listing 7-12. *Checking settings on the hamshackradio database*

```
SELECT
        pd.datname,
        pg_catalog.array_to_string(pdrs.setconfig,
        E'\n') AS settings
FROM
        pg_catalog.pg_db_role_setting AS pdrs
JOIN pg_catalog.pg_database AS pd
ON
        pdrs.setdatabase = pd.oid;
```

The output is visible in Figure 7-8:

ᴬᴮᶜ datname	ᴬᴮᶜ settings
1 hamshackradio	DateStyle=Postgres, DMY

Figure 7-8. DateStyle is different for one database

While there are several configuration values you can change for the database, some are only available at the server level. For example, we could try to change the port for our hamshackradio database as shown in Listing 7-13:

Listing 7-13. Attempting to change the port

```
ALTER DATABASE hamshackradio SET
port = 4444;
```

Instead of modifying the port for one database, which isn't possible, an error is generated:

```
SQL Error [55P02]: ERROR: parameter "port" cannot be changed without
restarting the server
```

You can read more about the possibilities of the SET statement here: https://tinyurl.com/4cny95px. For more details on ALTER DATABASE: https://tinyurl.com/2p8d7t9u.

Before continuing, we're going to use one more ALTER DATABASE command to remove the settings that have been changed:

Listing 7-14. Resetting the hamshackradio database

```
ALTER DATABASE hamshackradio RESET ALL;
```

This will remove all setting configuration changes made. You can also specify specific settings that you want to reset by replacing the keyword ALL with the desired setting name Listing 7-14.

Removing a Database

We've seen how to create databases and change their settings. It's time to learn how to get rid of them entirely. The core syntax to the DROP DATABASE command is straight forward as you can see in Listing 7-15:

Listing 7-15. Dropping the clientappdemo database

```
DROP DATABASE clientappdemo;
```

Running that will immediately remove the database. Not only does it remove the database, but it removes all the folders and files that defined the database within the OS. You can't run this command from within the database you're trying to drop. Also, there can't be connections to the database you're dropping (more on that in a moment). If we were to run Listing 7-14 a second time, we'd get the following error:

```
SQL Error [3D000]: ERROR: database "clientappdemo" does not exist
```

Because of this, a safer way to run the DROP command is shown in Listing 7-16:

Listing 7-16. *Dropping only if the database is there*

```
DROP DATABASE IF EXISTS clientappdemo;
```

If the database is there, it'll be dropped. If it's not there, you don't get an error. Instead, nothing happens. You won't see an error, but you will get a message:

```
database "clientappdemo" does not exist, skipping
```

You do have one additional option when it comes to dropping databases when there are users connected to them. Listing 7-17 shows how we could try to DROP a database with active connections:

Listing 7-17. *Drop using WITH FORCE*

```
DROP DATABASE IF EXISTS renametest WITH (FORCE);
```

This will try to terminate any connections to the database. Some connections, such as replication connections, can't be terminated. Also, you have to have permission to terminate connections. Generally speaking, this is a rather unsafe way to go about dropping databases. If there are existing connections on a database, maybe it shouldn't be dropped.

For more detail on the DROP DATABASE command: https://tinyurl.com/y3wmurkd.

Database Templates

When you create a database in PostgreSQL, by default, the template database template1 is used as a source for the new database. All the examples so far have used this template.

The template contains all the system tables, functions and views that define the database. They will all be copied to the default file location as defined by your PostgreSQL settings. Any necessary information about your database, data about it, or meta data, will be added and stored too. Otherwise, it will be an empty database, ready for you to use for all the information you wish to manage there.

There are several database settings that can be changed after a database is created (as we went over in the ALTER DATABASE section). Some of these are likely to be individualized for a given database. However, it's entirely possible that you'd like to have a setting on all your databases configured in a particular way. To ensure that all databases automatically receive this setting, you can make the change to the template1 database. Then, any database created will have that same setting.

Further, you can add objects to the template1 database that will then be automatically created in any other database. If we connect directly to the template1 database, we can run the following command:

Listing 7-18. Creating a logging table in template1

```
CREATE TABLE updatelog(updateby varchar(50),
updatedate timestamp);
```

We'll be covering CREATE TABLE commands in more detail in Chapter 9. In the meantime, this creates a simple table that could be used to log changes inside of a database. You must disconnect from template1 before you try to create another database, or you will hit an error. Once disconnected, running Listing 7-19 creates a new database:

Listing 7-19. Create the existingtable database

```
CREATE DATABASE existingtable;
```

And finally, to see this in action, we'll connect to the existingtable database and run a query to see if the table is there:

Listing 7-20. Pulling from the updatelog table

```
SELECT * FROM updatelog AS ul;
```

While no data exists, the query doesn't cause an error because that user table, now a part of template1, is also now a part of our new database, existingtable.

Before we go further, we're going to connect back to the template1 database and remove the table, so that it's not a part of the template1 database anymore:

Listing 7-21. Dropping the updatelog table

```
DROP TABLE updatelog;
```

We're not limited to the two defined template databases either. We can turn an existing database into a template database. Listing 7-22 shows how:

Listing 7-22. Altering the existingtable database

```
ALTER DATABASE existingtable WITH IS_TEMPLATE = TRUE;
```

If we now go back and rerun the query from Listing 7-4 to see the list of databases, we get the following:

	123 oid	ABC datname	☑ datistemplate
1	5	postgres	[ ]
2	1	template1	[v]
3	4	template0	[v]
4	17,982	hamshackradio	[ ]
5	17,993	existingtable	[v]

Figure 7-9. A new template database

The existingtable database is now a template and can be used to create new databases. Listing 7-23 shows how to change the CREATE DATABASE syntax to pick a template:

Listing 7-23. Picking a template in CREATE DATABASE

```
CREATE DATABASE fromnewtemplate WITH TEMPLATE = existingtable;
```

This will create a new database, fromnewtemplate, that will include the user table, updatelog. You can confirm this by connecting to fromnewtemplate and running the query from Listing 7-20. The table will be there.

You can also define a template when you create a database if you use the IS_TEMPLATE = TRUE option in the CREATE DATABASE command.

The only thing you should always do though is leave template0 as is. It's meant to provide a guaranteed standard template for PostgreSQL.

Tablespace

In creating the databases throughout this chapter, we've been manipulating quite a few settings for those databases. What we have yet to talk about is the ability to store your data in more than one location. You're not limited to the default storage location. You can create what are called tablespaces. These are a way to expand the way you can store your data. You can create tablespaces for whole databases, or just small subsets of a database. This allows you to bring in more drives and drive controllers to enhance performance and reliability.

A tablespace can be defined for individual objects within a database such as a table or an index. You can also define a database as having a default tablespace. While every database created will have some metadata within the original data directory, you can create a database into a defined tablespace, or you can change the default tablespace for an existing database.

To create a new tablespace, we use the syntax defined in Listing 7-24:

Listing 7-24. Defining new storage locations for databases

```
CREATE TABLESPACE extrastorage LOCATION '/usr/xstore';
```

In this example, we're just using a folder on the same drive. In a real environment, this would typically be a separate drive, SAN, or some other storage location. The location must be owned by the service account that is running PostgreSQL. However, once done, that tablespace is now ready to use.

To create a new database using the extrastorage tablespace as a storage location, we'll use the syntax shown in Listing 7-25:

Listing 7-25. Another modification of CREATE DATABASE for a Tablespace

```
CREATE DATABASE newstorage TABLESPACE extrastorage;
```

If we then navigate to the specific location, /usr/xstore, we see the following:

```
root@d9311ebb6f5a:/usr/xstore# ls
PG_16_202307071
root@d9311ebb6f5a:/usr/xstore#
```

Figure 7-10. A new storage space in a new location

That is the tablespace, but not the database. Drilling into that location we see this:

```
root@d9311ebb6f5a:/usr/xstore/PG_16_202307071# ls
26174
root@d9311ebb6f5a:/usr/xstore/PG_16_202307071#
```

Figure 7-11. A new database in our new tablespace

When we run the query from Listing 7-4 the oid for our new database is indeed 26174. If we look into that folder, we see the files and folders that define a PostgreSQL database, just like at the beginning of the chapter:

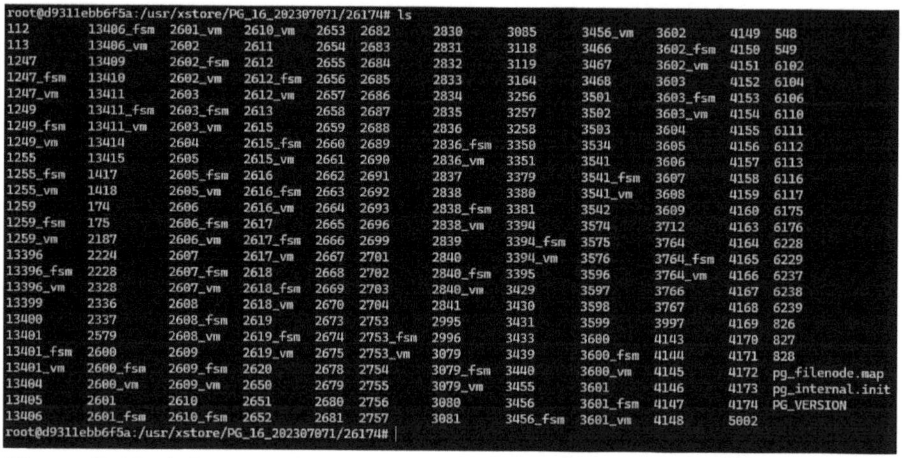

Figure 7-12. A PostgreSQL tables and other objects

We can take advantage of the ALTER TABLE command to change the default storage of a database:

Listing 7-26. Changing the default storage for a database

```
ALTER DATABASE fromnewtemplate SET
TABLESPACE extrastorage;
```

Any new tables, indexes, sequences, etc., will be created in the new tablespace. Existing objects could be moved to that tablespace as well.

Conclusion

The basics for creating a database are indeed quite simple. However, as you dig into the details, there are quite a few options to ensure that you create a database just the way you need it. Since you can easily alter databases as well, you can do what's necessary to build out and maintain your systems appropriately. And, of course, you can drop databases, just be extremely cautious about this because organizations tend to value their data quite a lot. Finally, with the addition of templates and tablespaces, you have even more control, at a granular level, about what gets deployed when you create a database and where the information gets stored.

8
Extensions

Near the end of Chapter 1 we shared our opinions on why PostgreSQL has seen so much growth in recent years. While the very permissive open-source license is certainly a driving factor, the extensibility of PostgreSQL is certainly a close second. To fully understand the power and potential available to you as a database developer with PostgreSQL, it will be helpful to understand what they are, how they work, and some specific nuances to be aware of as you begin utilizing extensions within your database.

The History of Extensions

PostgreSQL has been an open-source database for nearly 30 years. In that time, numerous projects have forked the code repository and modified portions of code to implement new features or derive completely independent variants of PostgreSQL. Doing so, however, is not for the faint of heart. Because PostgreSQL has a consistent track record of yearly major releases and four minor releases each year, keeping a separate fork in sync with all the updates and changes can be overwhelmingly time consuming. The alternative would entail submitting patches directly to the core product which can often take months for the global developer community to discuss, verify, and include, and that is assuming there is agreement those changes belong in PostgreSQL.

As we mentioned in Chapter 1, one of the goals of the original POSTGRES project at Berkely was to create a database that allowed for the creation of custom data types, operators, and other objects, in order to provide a level of extensibility not available in other relational databases. As an open-source project, this extensibility really came into its own, with open-source contributors able to make new packages and modules for other database users independent of the core PostgreSQL product.

While this did provide challenges for distribution, with some projects requiring users to compile source code and sort through different shared libraries, the overall utility of this process was undeniable, and for years some of the best contributions were distributed along with PostgreSQL, affectionately known as "contrib modules". Eventually the ecosystem around these PostgreSQL add-ons became so significant (and complicated) that a number of developers, led by Dimitri Fontaine, began a project to create a more formalized way of managing how these external projects would interact with PostgreSQL.

In version 9.1 (September 2011), after several years of development, the ability to add functionality through extensions was released. For the first time, users had a well-defined way to package up their own code to perform specific functionality. It might be as simple as a versioned set of SQL maintenance functions used within a DBA team across all their PostgreSQL servers, or it could be a full-fledged, compiled set of code that implements new indexes, query plan nodes, or even modify how data is stored. And, in the true spirit of open source, these extensions could be made available for others to use.

It's hard to know if the team really understood what a pivotal shift this would be in the growth and adoption of PostgreSQL, but it has driven significant development and innovation that wouldn't be possible through the normal patching process.

What Are Extensions?

Now that we understand how extensions came to be in PostgreSQL, we need to dive into what they are and what they can do. This is where the fun really begins.

First and foremost, extensions are a way to package code that can be installed (made available) from within a database. An extension can be written purely in SQL or pl/pgsql, however, when advanced features are needed or performance is a concern, writing the extension in C is usually necessary. In the last couple of years, the Rust extension framework *pgrx* has been popular with many developers to more easily write powerful extensions which are then compiled to a PostgreSQL compatible C binary.

Extensions are also versioned. This means that updates can be made to the package (new code, updated functions, etc.) and installed as an updated version. Because PostgreSQL tracks what version is currently installed in a particular database, it's easy to find databases that have not been updated when functionality is added or modified.

And finally, extensions can perform a wide range of functionality. At the simple end of the scale, an extension might just create new pl/pgsql functions. These simpler extensions don't register for any specific kind of runtime behavior that can add more elaborate features or control over PostgreSQL. Utilizing extensions in this way is often a great way for a DBA team to package up functions or procedures that they use in managed databases to help with specific tasks or maintenance activity. By grouping everything as an extension, you can always see if the functions are installed in managed databases and if they are updated to the correct version.

At the other, more complex end of the scale, extensions can create functions and runtime code using helpers from the PostgreSQL C code and register with various *hooks*, places in the runtime code that allow extensions to inspect database state, react to events, and even alter how PostgreSQL internals work.

There are about 30 hooks currently available in PostgreSQL that cover security, query planning, query execution, and specific pl/pgsql events. Utilizing hooks allows for some truly unique, creative, and powerful extensions that can compress/decompress data on the fly, transform PostgreSQL into a world-class geospatial database, and even allow you to create "hypothetical" indexes to test if they would improve a query before using the resources to create and maintain the index itself. There are so many interesting use cases, and we'll do our best to highlight some of the most popular ones later in this chapter.

Regardless of what the extension does or the features it provides, they are always installed inside of the database where you want to use them. The package itself is installed into a specific location on the filesystem to make it available, but the extension doesn't become "active" and available to use until it is created within a database using the CREATE EXTENSION command, something we'll cover in just a bit.

This means that if you manage multiple databases on the same PostgreSQL cluster, each of them would need to have the needed extensions created in the database before sessions connected to a database can use it. This creates a bit of a maintenance problem with backup and restores which we'll address a bit later.

Available Extensions

At this point we think we've established that extensions are a big deal in PostgreSQL and so, as you might expect, there is a simple way to discover the extensions that are available on the cluster to be installed within a database. As shown in Listing 8-1, there is a standard PostgreSQL view that returns the list of extensions that are currently available in the cluster. A partial output of the view is shown in Figure 8-1. We always recommend ordering the result so that you can easily scan for specific extensions.

Listing 8-1: *Discovering available extensions*

```
SELECT * FROM pg_available_extensions
ORDER BY name;
```

	name	default_version	installed_version	comment
1	address_standardizer	3.4.0	[NULL]	Used to parse an address into constitu
2	address_standardizer-3	3.4.0	[NULL]	Used to parse an address into constitu
3	address_standardizer_data_us	3.4.0	[NULL]	Address Standardizer US dataset exam
4	address_standardizer_data_us-3	3.4.0	[NULL]	Address Standardizer US dataset exam
5	adminpack	2.1	[NULL]	administrative functions for PostgreSQ
6	amcheck	1.3	[NULL]	functions for verifying relation integrity
7	autoinc	1.0	[NULL]	functions for autoincrementing fields
8	bloom	1.0	[NULL]	bloom access method - signature file b
9	btree_gin	1.3	[NULL]	support for indexing common datatype
10	btree_gist	1.7	[NULL]	support for indexing common datatype
11	citext	1.6	[NULL]	data type for case-insensitive characte
12	cube	1.5	[NULL]	data type for multidimensional cubes
13	dblink	1.2	[NULL]	connect to other PostgreSQL database
14	dict_int	1.0	[NULL]	text search dictionary template for inte
15	dict_xsyn	1.0	[NULL]	text search dictionary template for ext
16	earthdistance	1.1	[NULL]	calculate great-circle distances on the
17	file_fdw	1.0	[NULL]	foreign-data wrapper for flat file acces
18	fuzzystrmatch	1.2	1.2	determine similarities and distance bet

Figure 8-1: *A partial listing of extensions available on cluster*

There are two things that you should notice and pay attention to. First, each extension shows what version would be installed if you do not specify a specific version, displayed in the `default_version` column. Second, if an extension is installed in the database for this session, the `installed_version` column will show which version is currently installed. For example, Figure 8-1 shows that version 1.2 of the *fuzzystrmatch* extension installed in the current database.

Many extensions, however, will make multiple versions available at one time. This is helpful when upgrading from one extension version to the next, by allowing you to stage newer versions before performing the extension upgrade. To see all the versions that are available for each extension, you can query another view (Listing 8-2).

Listing 8-2: Query all available extension versions

```
SELECT * FROM pg_available_extension_versions
ORDER BY name;
```

The columns that are returned are different than the first view (Figure 8-2).

name	version	installed	superuser	trusted	relocatable	schema	requires	comment
· 101 pg_hint_plan	1.5	[ ]	[v]	[ ]	[ ]	hint_plan	NULL	
· 102 pg_hint_plan	1.5.1	[ ]	[v]	[ ]	[ ]	hint_plan	NULL	
· 103 pg_hint_plan	1.6.0	[ ]	[v]	[ ]	[ ]	hint_plan	NULL	
· 104 pg_prewarm	1.1	[ ]	[v]	[ ]	[v]	[NULL]	NULL	prewarm relation data
· 105 pg_prewarm	1.2	[ ]	[v]	[ ]	[v]	[NULL]	NULL	prewarm relation data
· 106 pg_show_plans	2.0	[ ]	[v]	[ ]	[v]	[NULL]	NULL	show query plans of all
· 107 pg_stat_statements	1.10	[v]	[v]	[ ]	[v]	[NULL]	NULL	track planning and exe
· 108 pg_stat_statements	1.4	[ ]	[v]	[ ]	[v]	[NULL]	NULL	track planning and exe
· 109 pg_stat_statements	1.5	[ ]	[v]	[ ]	[v]	[NULL]	NULL	track planning and exe
· 110 pg_stat_statements	1.6	[ ]	[v]	[ ]	[v]	[NULL]	NULL	track planning and exe
· 111 pg_stat_statements	1.7	[ ]	[v]	[ ]	[v]	[NULL]	NULL	track planning and exe
· 112 pg_stat_statements	1.8	[ ]	[v]	[ ]	[v]	[NULL]	NULL	track planning and exe
· 113 pg_stat_statements	1.9	[ ]	[v]	[ ]	[v]	[NULL]	NULL	track planning and exe
· 114 pg_surgery	1.0	[ ]	[v]	[ ]	[v]	[NULL]	NULL	extension to perform s
· 115 pg_trgm	1.3	[ ]	[v]	[v]	[v]	[NULL]	NULL	text similarity measurer
· 116 pg_trgm	1.4	[ ]	[v]	[v]	[v]	[NULL]	NULL	text similarity measurer
· 117 pg_trgm	1.5	[ ]	[v]	[v]	[v]	[NULL]	NULL	text similarity measurer

Figure 8-2: Listing all available extension versions

Aside from the extension versions and showing which one is installed, the superuser and trusted columns are important to consider. In the example output above, we can see that all of these extensions require a superuser to install them. Thinking back to Chapter 6 about roles and privileges, we know that acting as the superuser has some inherent dangers. Therefore, many extensions also mark the extension as trusted, so that roles with the CREATE privilege on the database can install them. From the documentation:

For many extensions this means superuser privileges are needed. However, if the extension is marked trusted in its control file, then it can be installed by any user who has CREATE privilege on the current database. In this case the extension object itself will be owned by the calling user, but the contained objects will be owned by the bootstrap superuser (unless the extension's script explicitly assigns them to the calling user). This configuration gives the calling user the right to drop the extension, but not to modify individual objects within it.

Looking at the result shown in Figure 8-2 again, we can see that the `pg_stat_statements` extension, version 1.10, is installed and that a superuser had to install it. However, all the available versions of the `pg_trgm` extension can be installed by any user that has the CREATE privilege on the database.

This is particularly relevant with cloud hosted DBaaS solutions. Just because an extension shows as being available, you may not be able to install it if you don't have superuser access (which you often don't in hosted offerings). Each provider will list the extensions that are available to install and if they require membership in a specific role to install them.

A general rule of thumb is that if you installed and support the PostgreSQL cluster yourself (bare metal or even in a cloud hosted VM instance), you have a lot of flexibility to use pretty much any extension if you install it on the cluster host. However, if you are using a DBaaS service like RDS PostgreSQL or a flavor of Azure PostgreSQL, you'll need to look in your cloud provider's documentation for the list of extensions you can install.

Installing Extensions

Once you have identified an extension that you want to use in your database, the next step is to install it. In PostgreSQL, this is done with the CREATE command (not to be confused with the CREATE privilege). Since we talk about `pg_stat_statements` in this book, and the community in general recommends this extension for every database, we'll use that for our examples.

Listing 8-3 shows how to install the default extension version (Figure 8-1) into the database you're connected to, and Listing 8-4 shows how to specify the specific version you want to use.

Listing 8-3: Installing the default version of an extension

```
CREATE EXTENSION IF NOT EXISTS pg_stat_statements;
```

Listing 8-4: Installing a specific version of an extension

```
CREATE EXTENSION IF NOT EXISTS pg_stat_statements VERSION '1.10';
```

While we agree that Listing 8-3 is simpler and doesn't require you to figure out which version you want to install, we always recommend specifying the version of the extension. This is particularly important when you provision new database clusters or upgrade an extension, expecting a specific version to be available. If the version you specify is not available on the cluster, PostgreSQL will produce an error, which quickly tells you that there is work to be done on the cluster before it can be installed.

Tip: In Chapter 7, we discussed how to create databases and the use of database templates. Because 'template1' is the default template used when creating new databases, if you install an extension in that database, all newly created databases will also have the extension installed and ready for use.

Updating an Extension

Once an extension is installed, there will often be new versions released over time, either to add new functionality or address bugs. Once the updated version of the extension is installed in the cluster and available to install, the ALTER EXTENSION command shown in Listing 8-5 will execute the appropriate scripts included with the new version of the extension to upgrade it.

Listing 8-5: *Update an extension to a specific version*

```
ALTER EXTENSION pg_stat_statements UPDATE TO '1.11';
```

In this case, the version that you are updating to must be listed. Not only is this a requirement, but it's also a benefit for the same reason we discussed when installing an extension. If the version you are trying to update to is not available on the cluster, PostgreSQL will produce an error, alerting you that the specific version is not available (and therefore needs to be installed on the cluster).

Dropping an Extension

There are times where dropping an extension is necessary, either to remove unused extensions, or possibly to "reset" an extension by dropping it and starting fresh. This is accomplished using the DROP EXTENSION command, shown in Listing 8-6.

Listing 8-6: *Dropping an extension*

```
DROP EXTENSION IF EXISTS pg_stat_statements;
```

By default, this will drop all objects that are associated with the extension but fail (RESTRICT) if other objects rely on anything created by the extension.

Making Extensions Available for Use

It might seem like this section is out of place. Why would we talk about making extensions available to install *after* we talk about installing them in a database? The main reason is that most PostgreSQL users today don't have much control over the set of extensions that they can use. As we mentioned earlier, nearly all managed database services dictate the extensions that you can install with their service. They have vetted the code, ensured they don't pose any high-level security risks to their environments, and they often provide some level of support or documentation for extensions that are not included as part of PostgreSQL core. Because these are the environments that most new PostgreSQL users are using, it made more sense to talk about how to install and manage extensions first.

However, if you have the opportunity to manage your own PostgreSQL database, either locally or via a container service like Docker, it's good to know some of the ways that you can install and manage extensions.

Extension Registries

As the extension landscape has grown over the years, a few community members have tried to tackle the problem of surfacing which extensions are available for others to use and providing an easy way to install them. These extension repositories are analogous to PyPi for Python or npm for Node.js. Creators of PostgreSQL extensions can upload their packages, and then other users can install them using a command line tool which does the work of installing the code in the correct place.

PostgreSQL Extension Network (PGXN)

This is one of the original repositories for PostgreSQL extensions. Several members of the community saw the need for a central registry and created both the command line tool and the website (pgxn.org) to host extension packages. The command line tool is written in Python and available through PyPi using the pip installation command. Please note that while the pgxn command line tool will allow you to install extensions on Windows, support for some extensions might be limited or non-existent, depending on the extension in question. This is another of the many reasons we don't recommend running production PostgreSQL clusters on Windows.

To install the PGXN client, you'll need to have Python 3 installed and the pip tool available. Listing 8-7 shows the pip command.

Listing 8-7: Installing the PGXN command line client

```
$ sudo pip install pgxnclient
```

Once the client is installed, you can find available extensions through the PGXN website. To be clear, there are more extensions available in the wild than are listed at PGXN, but the extensions that you are likely looking for and have a lot of community support will often be uploaded and available at PGXN.

For our example, we went to the website and looked for the extension by a long-time community member Stefanie Janine Stölting called `pgsql_tweaks`. This is a package that contains many different functions and views for retrieving information about the database, object ownership, schema details, and more.

Listing 8-8: Installing the latest stable version using the pgxn client

```
$ pgxn install pgsql_tweaks
```

Listing 8-9: Installing a specific version using the pgxn client

```
$ pgxn install 'pgsql_tweaks=0.10.5'
```

Once the extension is installed in the filesystem, it will be available to any database in the cluster and will show up in `pg_available_extensions`. To install it into a specific database, you simply execute the CREATE EXTENSION command.

Listing 8-10: Installing the newly added pgsql_tweaks extension into the database

```
CREATE EXTENSION IF NOT EXISTS pgsql_tweaks;
```

Trunk Extension Registry

Trunk (pgt.dev) is a recent addition to the extension registry landscape. Created and supported by Tembo (tembo.io), the aim is to be a more modern registry that pulls from the wider PostgreSQL community, which has grown significantly since the creation of PGXN. Interestingly, one of the original creators of PGXN, David Wheeler, was hired by Tembo in 2024 to try and coalesce the community around a better approach for managing and distributing extensions.

Much like PGXN, there is a command line tool that pulls packages from the registry and installs them.

Pre-made Docker Containers

Many PostgreSQL developers use Docker containers regularly, something we discussed in Chapter 3. Aside from the main PostgreSQL image that is maintained by the Docker team (https://hub.docker.com/_/postgres), there are a plethora of other containers that build upon the open-source base image. Using one of these images can help you get started quickly with a host of useful extensions. A few that we've either used before or are well loved by the community include:

PostGIS (https://hub.docker.com/r/postgis/postgis)
An extension for adding a complete, world-class geospatial database.

postgres.ai (https://github.com/postgres-ai/custom-images)
A custom image maintained by the team at postgres.ai with many standard and useful extensions installed and ready to use.

Timescale (https://hub.docker.com/r/timescale/timescaledb)
A PostgreSQL time-series database with many advanced features for large amounts of data.

Supabase (https://hub.docker.com/r/supabase/postgres)
A community PostgreSQL image with a common set of extensions.

There are plenty of others, but if you want to get started with PostgreSQL quickly and still have access to some of the most common extensions, give one of these a try first.

Linux Package Managers

If you are managing your own installation of PostgreSQL on a Linux host, odds are that your package manager lists many of the most popular extensions in their registry. There are a few community members that faithfully maintain PostgreSQL installation packages and at least a few dozen extension packages. For instance, to install the `pg_cron` extension on Debian and Ubuntu hosts, use an `apt-get` command similar to:

```
$ sudo apt-get -y install postgresql-16-cron
```

Note that other operating systems also provide some support for PostgreSQL extensions on their systems. These include the Ports system in BSD, Homebrew on OSX, and Chocolatey on Windows, just to name a few. While these tools can be useful, in practice their support tends to be narrower than the other options we have mentioned above.

Cloud-Hosted Databases

At the beginning of this chapter, we mentioned that when you use cloud-hosted databases, you usually will not be able to manage the extension packages or install new extensions. All vendors will have a set list of extensions that you are permitted to use with their service. And, unfortunately, these lists rarely match one-for-one between cloud vendors. That said, a majority of the most popular and regularly used extensions will be available across providers. Extensions like pg_stat_statements, pg_partman, or pg_cron, will usually be available no matter where you host the database.

On the other hand, in the new world of AI and vector databases, at least three popular cloud providers (as of 2024) provide different extensions for working with vectors and LLM searches. Many of them will eventually coalesce around one or two, but just be aware of which extensions each provider makes available in case you need to change providers at some point in the future.

Two Words of Caution

We love extensions and believe that they are a superpower of PostgreSQL. Hopefully, we've made that abundantly clear throughout this book. However, there are two administration issues that often catch inexperienced users by surprise especially when they manage their own PostgreSQL clusters. Being aware of these things ahead of time will prevent some headaches later.

Extensions Across Environments

When we discussed how to install or update extensions, we strongly encouraged you to always reference the specific version of the extension you're expecting to use. The main reason for this is because you aren't guaranteed that each environment you manage will have the exact same extensions and versions installed on disk to be available for use. For instance, if you have different maintenance windows for your development, staging, testing, and production clusters, one of them may not get updated before you release updated application code that uses new functions in an extension. When this happens, the application may start to throw errors.

Therefore, it is essential that you always know which extensions and versions are installed across environments. Otherwise, if something gets out of sync, it will likely end up causing some problems until the correct version is in place. Always specify the extension version and you'll never get stuck with a bad release.

Extension Backup and Restore

The second thing to consider when you administer PostgreSQL extensions is that the dump files or schema-only backup scripts do not specify which version of the extension was installed, only *that* the extension was installed in this database. This makes the earlier caution even more imperative. We see this most often when restoring a database dump to a developer environment or when creating a new cluster as part of a PostgreSQL upgrade.

Let's say that you stand up a new PostgreSQL cluster in preparation for upgrading your databases to the newest release. When you create a database dump from the old cluster, it doesn't save the specific version of the extension that's currently installed. It just dumps the generic CREATE EXTENSION command without a version. On restore, the script will try to install (CREATE) each extension even if it's not the correct version, because the backup file didn't specify it. This can certainly cause unexpected application behavior.

Always keep track of the extensions and versions that you use and ensure each of your environments matches to avoid unexpected problems. Utilize the `pg_available_extensions` and `pg_available_extension_versions` views to verify that your systems have the same extensions and versions in preparation for an planned dump and restores.

Extensions to Try

There is no magic number of extensions to try, and you can easily find dozens of posts online which claim to show the top 10 or 20 most popular extensions. Feel free to check them out and experiment with the extensions they list. For our purposes, however, we wanted to highlight a few go-to extensions that nearly everyone uses, and a couple that are gaining a lot of attention (as of November 2024) because they deal with AI and vector datatypes.

Keep in mind that there is one promise we can make about this list of popular or "try first" extensions, even in the first edition of the book: it will change as time goes by. PostgreSQL extensions are developing at such a fast pace that it's impossible to know what the future holds.

Alright. Let's talk extensions!

For some of the extensions we list next, you will see an image of the PostgreSQL mascot, Slonik, next to the extension name.

This indicates that the extension is one of the "contrib modules" that we discussed earlier and available, the theory, on any PostgreSQL installation. No external install process with an extension registry or package repository is needed.

That said, there may still be some of these which are not permitted to install by a cloud provider, so always check the listings in their respective documentation.

---

pg_stat_statements

`pg_stat_statements` is an extension that allows PostgreSQL to metrics about parameterized versions of queries to help you identify performance bottlenecks and various other counters like how many times a query has been executed. Since we spend some time talking about the extension in Chapter 15, we won't say more here. However, our advice about this specific extension is simple. Install it. Always. In every database. Full stop.

postgis

PostGIS is the leading open-source geospatial database, all made possible by extending PostgreSQL with support for storing, indexing, and querying geospatial data. It includes new geo-specific datatypes, a myriad of functions for calculating distances between points, measuring area, overlaps in geometries, performing geocoding, and supporting integration with other mapping and GIS tools. It's an amazingly powerful extension that adds powerful new ways to query and analyze data in relation to the physical world.

The PostGIS team maintains consistent releases and is quick to ensure compatibility with each release of PostgreSQL. The Bluebox sample database includes geospatial data for both the store locations and customers. Using the PostGIS extension, this geospatial data is used to find stores near a customer for both rentals and returns.

pg_hint_plan

In Chapter 2 we briefly mentioned a few things that users of SQL Server or Oracle may expect to be available which are not natively supported by PostgreSQL. Query hints is one of those things.

The developers that have contributed to and largely maintain the query planner code within PostgreSQL continue to believe that, primarily, if hinting a plan is necessary, that it usually points to a limitation in the query planner that should be improved. Therefore, native support for query hints is not directly supported.

The pg_hint_plan extension provides a mechanism for applying Oracle-like query hints to the query planner. It does this by implementing some of the query planner hooks that we briefly mentioned earlier, adjusting the cost of different possible plan nodes (Chapter 11), which essentially forces the planner to select the one you are expecting. From the documentation on Github, a basic example of adjusting a plan is shown in Listing 8-11. This would cause the planner to use a hash join between `table_a` and `table_b`, with a sequential scan on `table_a`.

Listing 8-11: A sample query hint using pg_hint_plan

```
-- Query hints shown using pretend tables
=# /*+
    HashJoin(a b)
    SeqScan(a)
  */
  EXPLAIN SELECT *
    FROM table_b b
    JOIN table_a a ON b.id = a.id
    ORDER BY a.id;
```

There are a lot of hints available in the extension which allow you to change scan methods, join methods and order, and even the number of parallel workers for a query. Of course, the same two cautions apply as with any other database that supports query hints:

1. With great power comes great responsibility.
2. Regularly review your query hints to verify if they are still required over time.

pg_cron

PostgreSQL does not have a native mechanism to create and manage periodic jobs or activities. For many years, developers and DBAs would typically use an external manager like cron on Linux to simply execute scripts using psql or a shell of their choice. While that certainly works, it doesn't usually result in a database accessible log to ensure script success or failure.

pg_cron was developed to provide that mechanism and use a cron-like syntax for creating and managing jobs within a PostgreSQL cluster. For example, if you wanted to run ANALYZE on a nightly basis for a particular database, you might create a job as shown in Listing 8-12.

Listing 8-12: *Scheduling a daily ANALYZE for "database_a"*

```
-- ANALYZE every Sunday at 2:00am (GMT) in a database other
-- than the one pg_cron is installed in
SELECT cron.schedule_in_database('daily-analyze', '0 2 * * 0', 'ANALYZE',
'database_a');
```

You can replace the command with any valid SQL, function, or stored procedure available in the database. Using functions in our sample Bluebox database, we can use pg_cron to regularly create new movie rentals for more realistic data.

Listing 8-13: *Create new movie rentals every five minutes in the Bluebox database*

```
-- Create new movie rentals every 5 minutes for all locations
SELECT cron.schedule_in_database('generate-rentals', '5 * * * *', 'CALL
generate_new_rental()', 'bluebox');
```

You'll notice that we're specifically using the cron.schedule_in_database() function in these two examples. The one nuance with pg_cron is that it can only be installed (CREATE EXTENSION) in one database within a cluster. That database can then be used execute SQL in the local database, or on other databases within the cluster. You'll have to keep that in mind as you consider if pg_cron is the right tool for you.

Finally, pg_cron isn't the only extension or external program that's specifically built for managing periodic jobs within PostgreSQL. However, it is currently installed and available on most major cloud providers that support PostgreSQL, so it's a compelling choice to learn if your databases are primarily hosted in the cloud.

postgres_fdw

PostgreSQL doesn't support querying multiple databases within one connection. There is no way to reference another database within the cluster in a query like you may be used in a platform like SQL Server. This stems, as we mentioned earlier in the book, from the fact that PostgreSQL connections are always to a specific database, not to the cluster itself. Therefore, the current connection can only see one database when executing SQL, functions, stored procedures, etc.

One of the ways to do this is with Foreign Data Wrappers, a framework for creating access methods to different databases and data formats to make them accessible through SQL as foreign tables. With the postgres_fdw extension, you can query tables in another database as long as you can connect to it, whether that be on the same cluster or a different PostgreSQL instance. And because it's made available as a contrib module, any PostgreSQL database should be able to install the extension and create foreign tables to query.

Because it's a framework, similar to the GiST and GIN indexing frameworks we talked about in Chapter 9, there are FDW extensions available for all kinds of data sources. The one for PostgreSQL just happens to ship with the core product and is widely available to use. Check out the documentation for your cloud provider or through registries like PGXN to find other foreign data wrappers that allow you to access other databases, file types like Parquet, or even block storage systems like Amazon S3. Browse the list of dozens of FDW extensions on the PostgreSQL Wiki (https://wiki.postgresql.org/wiki/Foreign_data_wrappers).

pg_partman

PostgreSQL has supported table partitioning for many years. Originally, this was accomplished through table inheritance, but since PostgreSQL 10, native declarative partitioning has been the recommended method and where all new development is happening.

Note: Table inheritance, as defined in the SQL:1999 standard, can be a useful tool for database designers and is still available in PostgreSQL. However, because of how table inheritance works in PostgreSQL, folks figured out many years ago that it could also be used as a method for doing table partitioning and was a "supported" use case in documentation.

Because of some ongoing limitations with inheritance, however, declarative partitioning was added to PostgreSQL to allow for ongoing support and feature development that could specifically target partitioning use cases more accurately.

One nuance with native PostgreSQL partitioning is that all partition maintenance is a manual process, including creating partitions, archiving data, and cleaning up data in the default partition. If partitions don't exist for data before it arrives, particularly with time-series RANGE partitions, then the inserts will fail unless there is a default partition, which creates a different kind of maintenance overhead.

In years past, the solution was to create a set of cron jobs or similar mechanisms to periodically check the database and create enough partitions into the future before data arrived. `pg_partman` is an extension that helps manage the creation and maintenance of partitions in a PostgreSQL database. And because it's been around for many years, it's available and supported on most cloud platforms.

pg_trgm

In Chapter 9, we'll discuss numerous built-in indexes that ship with PostgreSQL core. Two of those index types, GiST and GIN, are frameworks that allow others to create new index types to support specific data needs. `pg_trgm` is an example of how versatile these frameworks are by adding an index on the trigrams found within each string and allowing fast, arbitrary string search and similarity matches. But why would you want a unique index type for strings when we can search for patterns with the LIKE operator? Indexes.

When we write SQL to search for arbitrary text, we only have access to the LIKE/ILIKE operator or, in PostgreSQL, additional regular expression searches. However, traditional B-Tree indexes can't be used when the search starts with a wildcard instead of specifying the first letter of the string. This causes a table scan which is slower and creates more I/O when compared with using an index.

Trigrams are one solution to efficiently perform arbitrary string searches. This is accomplished by breaking up a string into a three letter groups from beginning to end. For instance, the phrase "PostgreSQL is powerful" would be broken up into multiple three-letter groups containing: "Pos","ost","stg","tgr","gre","reS","eSQ","SQL","SL ","L i"," is", etc. These groups are then indexed using the GIN framework which allows quick and efficient arbitrary searches and similarity comparisons.

It is worth noting that the specific index is larger when compared to a B-Tree index, sometimes significantly larger, which does add additional I/O and index maintenance.

However, for the right use case, the pg_trgm extension can provide powerful ways of searching for relevant string values.

hypopg

Query tuning is an essential responsibility for database developers and DBAs, and many times, creating indexes is one tool for improving query performance. There is one problem, however, with creating indexes as part of your query tuning process. To see if the index will have the desired, positive impact, it needs to be created and tested. Depending on the size of the indexed table, the datatype, and the index type, testing indexes can create additional problems.

This is where creating hypothetical indexes using the hypopg extension can help. Once installed, you can test the effect an index will have on queries without actually creating the index. It's a quick operation regardless of the table size, and once the hypothetical index is created, running an EXPLAIN plan will show you if the index will be used as intended. It's a quick way to iterate on potential indexes to help in one aspect of query tuning.

Vector and AI Extensions

To finish out this chapter, we need to at least acknowledge that as of November 2024, while we're writing this, AI and Vector databases are all the rage. From large language models (LLMs) to retrieval-augmented generation (RAG) applications, the data we store, and query has a lot of potential to bring new value propositions to the database layer. And PostgreSQL, with such powerful extension capabilities, is well positioned to be a leading alternative for storing vector data and getting operational value from it.

That said, this is still a rapidly growing field and even more so with PostgreSQL because of how extensions allow multiple approaches to be developed independently while still benefiting from unique PostgreSQL features (i.e. new index types). Over the next couple of years, we believe the community will likely coalesce around one or two primary extensions for building these kinds of data applications with PostgreSQL. And while a lot of effort and education is focused on a couple of extensions right now, the clear "winner" is yet to be seen. Therefore, it's a bit premature to dig into these extensions much, but you can easily find numerous recorded conference presentations and tutorials with a simple search in your favorite search engine or AI assistant.

For now, we'll simply highlight a few extensions to know about within this space and hope that a future edition of this book will go into more detail and likely even focus a chapter on AI users in PostgreSQL.

pgvector

By far the most popular extension that is currently used and developed is pg_vector. This extension adds a new vector datatype for creating embeddings of the data, indexes that utilize specific features of vector data, and numerous functions to help query your data using this new information.

The development is community driven, developed using the permissive PostgreSQL license, and available in all major cloud providers. The current release version is 0.7.0 at the time of writing, which demonstrates that the contributing developers believe there is still more work to do before officially releasing the first major version.

pgai

Timescale released the pgai extension in the summer of 2024 to utilize features of pgvector while adding additional features to assist in scalability of vector data and queries. Installing pgai in turn installs the pgvector, pgvectorscale, and pgai extensions together, using the vector datatype while adding additional indexing and search capabilities.

With this extension, you can also more easily integrate with LLMs like OpenAI GPT4, Claude Sonnet, and Ollama, and others, which helps create more powerful RAG applications. Like we said at the beginning of this section, the features and long-term viability for pgai and other AI extensions remains to be seen.

However, since these extensions utilize the permissive PostgreSQL license, there should be more collaboration over time to help build powerful AI apps.

azure_ai

Finally, there are going to be vendor specific offerings that integrate with their specific AI applications. azure_ai is an example of this kind of extension currently available within the PostgreSQL offerings in Azure. This extension adds functions to create embeddings of your data and functions to call Azure specific AI functions like sentiment analysis and text summarization.

If your primary PostgreSQL environment is hosted in Azure and the overall Microsoft ecosystem, it's definitely worth looking at the azure_ai extension. Because the extension is currently proprietary, there is a chance that data portability could become a problem if you were to switch where the database is hosted, so just keep that in mind.

Conclusion

In this chapter we talked in more detail about what PostgreSQL extensions are, how they are developed and installed, and finished by pointing out a few extensions that we think are worth investigating further. But to be honest, we've just scratched the surface.

Extensions really are a major reason for the versatility of PostgreSQL, which has contributed to the rise in popularity. Be curious and experiment with extensions that may be helpful and keep an eye on what extensions cloud vendors and the community routinely support for some guidance on which ones are providing consistent value in various use cases. We think that it won't be long until you experience the power and excitement behind this important aspect of PostgreSQL.

9

Core Object Types in PostgreSQL

PostgreSQL is a very versatile relational database that supports many different types of database objects. It also allows a significant amount of customization through the use of extensions, which can create additional object types. In this chapter, we'll explore the main object types that are included "out of the box" with PostgreSQL.

SQL Examples

In the sections that follow, we may provide some example SQL code, however, the PostgreSQL documentation on creating, altering, or dropping specific object types is very thorough and almost every command will have additional clauses and settings that we will not cover. To dig in further to any of the objects, head over to the SQL Commands section of the documentation.

https://www.postgresql.org/docs/current/sql-commands.html

Object Ownership

Before we dive in and discuss many of the core objects in PostgreSQL, it's important to repeat the conclusion of Chapter 6; object ownership is very important in PostgreSQL. Only the owner of an object, or a superuser, can alter or drop an object. Even if other roles have the create privilege within a database, they cannot modify objects that don't belong to them.

As you read through this chapter and consider the various objects, even some that might be new to you, keep the ownership and privileges learnings from Chapter 6 in mind.

Core Object Types

The rest of this chapter isn't an exhaustive list of every single object type in PostgreSQL. We are highlighting what we believe are the most important to discuss and point to differences that are worth knowing about.

The specific role privilege required to create, alter, or drop a specific object is noted in parenthesis for each object. Although we do not recommend using a superuser for day-to-day work, remember that a superuser can create, alter, or drop any object in any database that they have access to, so use with extreme caution.

Let's get to it!

Databases

As you would expect, a database is the primary core object in PostgreSQL. They contain (group) all other objects , and all connections to a PostgreSQL cluster are directly to a database, not just the server, and so without a database there's not much to be done. No surprise there, right?

As explained in Chapter 7, by default, all PostgreSQL clusters are created with a user database (typically named `postgres`) and two template databases called `template0` and `template1`. Unless otherwise specified as part of the CREATE DATABASE command, `template1` will be copied to create the new database. This means that any standard roles privileges, extensions, schemas, etc. that should be included in each of your databases can be added to the `template1` database.

The `template0` database is intended to be an untouched, pristine template of what a standard PostgreSQL would look like with a new instance. You can always specify that a database be created using `template0`, or in rare cases, the `template1` database could be dropped and recreated using `template0` if things have gotten out of hand. And, of course, it's possible to create multiple template databases of your own for PostgreSQL to use if specified at database creation.

To create databases, a role must have the CREATEDB role attribute applied.

Schema

Schemas are effectively namespaces that are used to group objects within a database. And, as we saw in Chapter 6, it's good practice to use schemas to organize related application objects into namespaces and to manage privileges and usage of those objects effectively.

Once a role authenticates and connects to a database, schema privileges can be the first line of defense for what a specific role can see and do with objects in the schema. Recall from Chapter 6 that the PUBLIC role always exists and cannot be dropped, and by default, all databases have a public schema. Because all roles are granted membership in the PUBLIC role, they can connect to the database and list objects in the public schema. Prior to PostgreSQL 15, all roles could also create objects in the public schema, which can be a security concern.

Most modern PostgreSQL recommendations suggest that all create privileges be revoked from the PUBLIC role and that all application objects reside in a specific, named schema so that there is no ambiguity on user objects and system objects.

To create a schema, a role must have the CREATE privilege for the database.

Tables

Without tables, a database wouldn't be worth much, right? There are very few surprises on how typical tables are created or altered in PostgreSQL compared to the database you are familiar with. However, there are a few notable differences that we'd like to highlight here.

To discuss some of the differences, Listing 9-1 shows the standard SQL code to create the rental table from our sample database. We'll only discuss a few differences, however, so please consider reading the CREATE TABLE documentation that can be found in the PostgreSQL documentation link at the beginning of the chapter.

Listing 9-1: Basic Table Creation

```
CREATE TABLE public.rental (
    rental_id bigint PRIMARY KEY NOT NULL,
    rental_period tstzrange,
    inventory_id integer NOT NULL
REFERENCES inventory (inventory_id) ON DELETE RESTRICT,
    customer_id integer NOT NULL
REFERENCES customer (customer_id) ON DELETE RESTRICT,
    staff_id integer NOT NULL,
    last_update timestamp with time zone DEFAULT now() NOT NULL
);
```

This is all pretty standard, aside from a datatype like `tstzrange` that you might not be familiar with. That said, let's look at a few differences that are good to know about with table objects in PostgreSQL.

To create a table, a role must have the USAGE and CREATE privilege on the assigned schema.

Identity Columns

One of the first things you may notice is that we haven't specified an identity column which would be auto incremented as data is inserted. From the earliest days of PostgreSQL this has been accomplished by creating a SERIAL/BIGSERIAL column which functioned like an identity. A separate object, called a sequence, was created automatically and the appropriate constraints put in place so that inserting new rows would retrieve the next sequence value and use that for the corresponding column. Listing 9-2 shows how to create a serial column.

Listing 9-2: Creating a serial column in a PostgreSQL table

```
CREATE TABLE public.rental (
    rental_id BIGSERIAL PRIMARY KEY NOT NULL,
    ...
);
```

However, sequences are not identities. Therefore, there is no constraint that prevents inserting directly into the column or modifying the value later. In modern versions of PostgreSQL, **we do not recommend using serial columns directly** because the intent is ambiguous and could result in unexpected usage.

Starting in PostgreSQL 11, identity column support was added with a flexibility that we don't see in SQL Server. Regardless of which form you choose when creating an identity column for a table, a sequence is still created under the covers, but how PostgreSQL interacts with the column and sequence is different. When creating an identity column in PostgreSQL, we must choose how the identity value is created and treated.

The first option, shown in Listing 9-3, is to specify that the value should be generated only if it's not provided with the insert statement. This is essentially like using a serial column, but with a more explicit intent shown in the DDL.

Listing 9-3: Creating an identity column with generated default value if not provided

```
CREATE TABLE public.rental (
    rental_id bigint GENERATED BY DEFAULT AS IDENTITY
PRIMARY KEY NOT NULL,
    ...
);
```

Alternatively, using the form shown in Listing 9-4, an identity column is created and DML is not allowed to insert or update the value without additional effort. Using it this way functions most similarly to SQL Server identity columns.

Listing 9-4: Creating an identity column that is always generated and no values may be inserted otherwise

```
CREATE TABLE public.rental (
    rental_id bigint GENERATED ALWAYS AS IDENTITY
PRIMARY KEY NOT NULL,
    ...
);
```

There is no concept in PostgreSQL like SET INSERT_IDENTITY=ON. Instead, to insert an explicit value into an identity column that is generated always, an insert statement must add the OVERRIDING SYSTEM VALUE clause explicitly.

Copying a Table Schema

There are many times, specifically in development and testing, when the ability to quickly copy the schema and properties of another table can be tremendously helpful. This is also helpful when creating a temporary table in a function or procedure to store data during processing, as part of a larger transformation process.

PostgreSQL provides this functionality through SQL without the need to generate a DDL script for the copied table first and execute it manually. Using this method also provides options for what table constraints are copied into the new table.

Given the rental table shown in Listing 9-1, we could create a copy of the schema, constraints, statistics, indexes, etc. using the SQL command in Listing 9-5.

Listing 9-5: Creating a new table based on an existing table including all properties

```
CREATE TABLE bluebox.rental_new
(LIKE bluebox.rental INCLUDING ALL);
```

If we wanted to create a copy but exclude indexes for some reason (or any other property of the table) we could instead use the command in Listing 9-6.

Listing 9-6: Create a new table based on another with all objects except indexes

```
CREATE TABLE bluebox.rental_new
(LIKE bluebox.rental INCLUDING ALL EXCLUDING INDEXES);
```

Partitioning

While PostgreSQL has always allowed users to manually create partitions using table-inheritance features, native table partitioning similar to other database systems has been included since PostgreSQL 10. There is no difficult setup of partitioning functions or TABLESPACE (i.e. "filegroups" in SQL Server) before creating a partitioned table. You can specify a different schema or table space for a particular partition at creation time, but it's not required.

The parameters for distributing data need to be specified at creation time, which means that existing tables cannot be partitioned directly. To partition existing tables, you will need to implement the "expand/contract" method which would create a new partitioned table, copy the old data into it, and then drop/rename the old and new tables.

PostgreSQL supports three types of native partitioning: RANGE, HASH, and LIST. Listing 9-7 demonstrates how to create a partitioned version of the payment table (the parent shell which doesn't hold data) and then, in Listing 9-8, we create a few monthly partitions for specific ranges of date values.

It's worth pointing out that if you have a primary key on the table, the partitioning key must be included as part of the primary key if one exists. Below, the primary key is made up of both payment_date and payment_id.

Listing 9-7: Create a partitioned table by date range on the payment date column

```
CREATE TABLE bluebox.payment (
      payment_id serial4 NOT NULL,
      customer_id int4 NOT NULL,
      rental_id int4 NOT NULL,
      amount numeric(5, 2) NOT NULL,
      payment_date timestamptz NOT NULL,
      CONSTRAINT payment_bak_pkey PRIMARY KEY (payment_date, payment_id)
) PARTITION BY RANGE (payment_date);
```

Once the parent table is created, individual partitions need to be created for each partition range before data arrives as shown in Listing 9-8.

Listing 9-8: Create individual partitions to hold data based on the partitioned column

```
CREATE TABLE bluebox.payment_y2024m01
      PARTITION OF bluebox.payment FOR VALUES
FROM ('2024-01-01') TO ('2024-02-01');

CREATE TABLE bluebox.payment_y2024m02
      PARTITION OF bluebox.payment FOR VALUES
FROM ('2024-02-01') TO ('2024-03-01');

CREATE TABLE bluebox.payment_y2024m03
      PARTITION OF bluebox.payment FOR VALUES
FROM ('2024-03-01') TO ('2024-04-01');
```

And that's it. There are other properties and parameters that can be defined, but this simple setup will create a partitioned table, and all partition management will occur through the parent table.

Sequences

Sequences are automatic number generators that are guaranteed to return unique integers in incrementing order. While you can technically create a sequence to use for your own purposes, generally they are only used as identity value generators. Any column defined as a SERIAL/BIGSERAL or IDENTITY will result in the automatic creation of a sequence which is then attached as the value generator of the column. Internally, sequences are like a single row table that stores configuration and value data.

Accessing sequence values are done through the `nextval` and `currval` functions. Like sequence values in SQL Server, sequences in PostgreSQL can be reset or set to a specific value if needed, using the `setval` function.

To create a sequence, a role must have USAGE and CREATE privilege on the schema. To actually use the sequence with a column in a table, the role must be the owner of the table.

Indexes

Indexes are obviously an essential component to having a performant database and application. Both PostgreSQL and SQL Server default to creating B-Tree indexes if not otherwise specified. However, PostgreSQL natively ships with at least six (6) different index types that help the query planner to effectively locate data of various, complex data types. Additionally, numerous extensions are available to add index types beyond what ship standard with the core PostgreSQL engine.

PostgreSQL B-Tree, GiST, GIN, and BRIN indexes all support multi-column indexes, while, B-Tree, GiST, and SP-GiST indexes support included columns for more efficient data retrieval where beneficial.

One other notable feature of PostgreSQL indexes is that you can specify to create (and drop) indexes CONCURRENTLY, a feature that would require a more expensive license in most proprietary databases.

There are many good articles and videos that dive into the various index types in PostgreSQL, so we'll just highlight what they are and when they are worth considering for a given workload or datatype.

To add indexes to a table, a role must be the owner of the table.

B-Tree

Listing 9-9: *Creating a one-column B-Tree index*

```
CREATE INDEX rental_inventory_id_idx
  ON bluebox.rental USING btree (inventory_id);
```

As mentioned above, many of the features that you already understand about B-Tree indexes hold true with PostgreSQL, and in most cases, this is the type of index you'll be using.

However, one of the most unique features of B-Tree indexes available in PostgreSQL 13+ is index deduplication. Enabled by default in available versions, this unique feature essentially uses an array datatype under the covers to consolidate rows in the index that reference the same indexed value.

Consider an index based on `film_id` column in the `inventory` table in our sample database. The same `film_id` is referenced hundreds of times among different inventory entries. Rather than a traditional B-Tree index that has one row in the index per inventory entry (ordered by `film_id`), PostgreSQL 13+ will create one or more rows in the index that contain an array of pointers to the appropriate pages. This reduces the storage overhead in many cases. And generally, the smaller the index, the more efficient it is to scan and utilize.

HASH

Listing 9-10: *Creating a HASH index*

```
CREATE INDEX rental_inventory_id_idx
  ON bluebox.rental USING hash (inventory_id);
```

Hash indexes compute the 4-byte hash value for the indexed key column and then divide the hashed values into "buckets", the equivalent of leaf pages in a B-Tree index. PostgreSQL has a set of hashing functions that allow any datatype to be hashed into a 4-byte. The number of buckets used for an index is dynamic and will change over time as more unique indexed values are added.

Like a traditional (not deduplicated) B-Tree index, there is one index row for each row in the indexed table. In most cases, however, the hashed value of an index key is smaller than the key itself. This means that hash indexes are typically very small compared to a B-Tree index of the same column.

In most cases, this also means that there is also less I/O when scanning a HASH index compared to a B-Tree index. Rather than having to descend through a tree to get to the leaf pages, using a HASH index provides direct access to the bucket page with the probing hash value. As such, HASH indexes only support equality comparisons.

GiST

Listing 9-11: Creating a GiST index for a timestamp range column

```
CREATE INDEX rental_rental_period_idx
  ON bluebox.rental USING gist (rental_period)
```

GiST stands for Generalize Search Tree, and ultimately produces a balanced tree structure like B-Tree indexes. However, a GiST index isn't just one type of index for a specific data type. Instead, it's a framework for the creation of new tree indexes that can be specifically tailored to different data types, including custom types. GiST indexes also provide for more comparison operators than a standard B-Tree index.

But what does this really mean?

Consider the range type in PostgreSQL. It has a lower value and an upper value and supports integer, numeric, date, and timestamp values (i.e. ['2024-01-01','2024-02-01']). Creating a B-Tree index over this multi-part data type wouldn't be possible. Instead, PostgreSQL ships with a GiST index type that specifically knows how to index range types so that we can query across ranges more effectively.

With a GiST index in place for our example range type, we can filter data in some interesting ways that don't exist when using a B-Tree index. For example, a few common ways that ranges are queried using the index include:

- Which ranges contain a specific value?

- Which ranges overlap a specific range?

- Is a range to the left or right of another range?

For other data types like geometric, a GiST index can be used to find overlapping shapes and nearest neighbor points. The possibilities are only limited by the datatype and the value that a GiST index could assist with. One theoretical example I often hear mentioned when discussing GiST indexes is image data. If a GiST index were created to process images and catalog various properties of the image (i.e. "overexposed", "blurred background", "contains dogs"), then a predicate on that column could potentially use the index in some way. Pretty cool, right?

Out of the box, PostgreSQL ships with GiST index support for geometry, range/multirange, inet, and full text search types. The core project also ships with a handful of extensions that can add even more unique kinds of GiST indexes for specific data types.

Also be aware that because GiST indexes can often search for entries in ways beyond the typical set of B-Tree comparisons (equal, greater than, less than, etc.), each datatype often supports additional comparison operators to indicate different searches like "contains", "overlaps", "to the left/right of", and more.

SP-GiST

Listing 9-12: *Creating a SP-GiST index*

```
CREATE INDEX customer_phone_idx
  ON bluebox.customer USING spgist (phone);
```

As you can probably guess, this index type is a variation of the GiST index access method, but the search tree is space partitioned, which will typically become unbalanced as time goes on, and that's a feature of the index. Suitable for complex datatypes like geometric data, it is intended to perform well for data that might have clustering near the top of the tree, but fan out unevenly further down the structure towards the leaf nodes.

GIN

Listing 9-13: *Creating a GIN index for full text search*

```
CREATE INDEX film_fulltext_idx
  ON bluebox.film USING gin (fulltext)
```

The Generalized Inverted Index (GIN) access method is designed to index composite values like arrays or complex text searches. The inverted nature of the index means that each row of the index stores the key (value) from the composite type and then a list of pointers to rows where that key can be found. Keys will only be stored once in the index, even if that key is included in multiple values.

Like GiST indexes, the GIN access methods allow the creation of indexes over new types of composite indexes if created. Currently, GIN indexes are available for arrays, JSON and JSONB, and tsvector for full text search. Additionally, the core PostgreSQL package ships with the `pg_trgm` extension to support trigram text searches, and the `hstore` extension to support key/value datatypes.

BRIN

Listing 9-14: *Creating a BRIN index the start of a rental period*

```
CREATE INDEX idx_rental_rental_date_brin
  ON bluebox.rental USING brin (lower(rental_period))
```

The Block Range Index (BRIN) is a newer addition to PostgreSQL in comparison to other standard index types. The concept is very simple and powerful under the right conditions.

BRIN indexes work on physical blocks (pages) on disk. Depending on what the range value is set to (128 pages by default), this index will scan adjacent pages and determine the low and high range of values within those pages. If the query asks for a value within that range, then all 128 pages will be returned and scanned by the query executor. However, if the value isn't contained in the range for those pages, the planner knows it can skip them all and not do any processing.

When the column that you're indexing has some inherent ordering in pages on disk, a BRIN index can be very efficient with significant space savings. Time-series data is often a good candidate for BRIN indexes because data is often append-only and is naturally inserted in relative time order on disk. Therefore, instead of saving one index row for each data row, the BRIN index stores one row for the range of pages, significantly reducing the index size and often helping the planner access the necessary pages of data very quickly.

There are some caveats to using BRIN indexes, but under the right circumstances it is a unique, and helpful index type to utilize.

Functions

User created functions are generally used more heavily in PostgreSQL than SQL Server. The are both practical and historical reasons for this difference.

First, as we've seen in previous chapters, doing ad hoc procedural programming is accomplished with anonymous code blocks which are often cumbersome and have limited functionality compared to what SQL Server provides directly in T-SQL. Therefore, functions are readily created to perform these repetitive tasks.

Second, PostgreSQL didn't support stored procedures until PostgreSQL 11. This means that where SQL Server users would typically use stored procedures for maintenance tasks (EXEC sp_fixMyData;), PostgreSQL has always used functions instead (SELECT fix_my_data();). This definitely takes some getting used to.

The basic creation of a function in PostgreSQL is broadly similar to other platforms like SQL Server. You must specify the name, any input and output parameters, and the return type of the function. They can also be written in any supported language. Beyond that, however, there are several differences to be aware of.

To create a function, the role must have the USAGE and CREATE privileges on the schema. To use a function, the role must have the EXECUTE privilege for the function. This is granted by default to all functions in the public schema through membership in the PUBLIC role, unless those privileges have been modified.

Return Types

Functions can return data four ways, broadly speaking: a single value, a table of data, a set of data, or nothing.

When returning a set of data, the type of data must be specified. This can be a table if the function will return all columns of the table appropriately, a composite type defined elsewhere in the database, or even a generic record type that is defined by the output parameters.

If you want to return an arbitrary table of data that does not correspond to an existing type, then use the return type TABLE, along with a list of column definitions.

Variables

When writing functions in a procedural language like pl/pgsql, variables not initiated as parameters must be declared before the function body using one DECLARE block. They cannot be declared inline.

Variables are also case sensitive and require no special prefix (like the "@" symbol) in code.

And finally, variables themselves can be defined as any available data type, a row or column type from a table schema, or a generic record (undefined schema).

Planner Cost and Row Hints

One of the more unique aspects of PostgreSQL functions is the ability to provide unique cost and row estimate values for the function.

Cost estimates default to 100 units for a single value return, or 100 units per returned row, for sets. Higher values will cause the planner to try and avoid calling the function frequently if possible.

Closely related to the cost estimate is the declared number of rows the assume the function will return. In other database systems, the row estimate is static and unchanging. By default, PostgreSQL plans for 1,000 rows to be returned (multiplied by the cost value). Raising or lowering this value may influence the type of join that will be performed when the function is used in a query.

Procedures

Stored procedures were introduced in PostgreSQL 11, and in many ways are implemented like functions with some limitations and a few unique features. In fact, when you read the documentation for procedures, there are still references to function creation to avoid duplicate explanation. Like functions, procedures can be written in any supported language.

There are a couple of unique differences to how procedures were implemented in PostgreSQL that you should be aware of compared to other databases like SQL Server.

Like functions, to create a procedure, the role must have the USAGE and CREATE privileges on the schema. To use a procedure, the role must have the EXECUTE privilege for the procedure. This is granted by default to all procedures in the public schema through membership in the PUBLIC role, unless those privileges have been modified.

Return Values

Procedures in PostgreSQL cannot return query results directly. If OUT or INOUT parameters are defined, then those will be returned as a single row at the end of the procedure execution, but not a full result set. If you need to return a dataset, then you should use a function instead.

Subtransactions

Subtransactions are exactly what they sound like, additional transactions that start inside of an outer transaction. While that might not sound very special (we can begin new transactions in SQL Server procedures, too), subtransactions in PostgreSQL can commit or abort without effecting the parent transaction. In SQL Server, if an inner transaction fails, the entire chain fails and gets rolled back.

Having the ability to start smaller transactions in a larger scope can make error handling easier and allow processed data to be committed in smaller increments without losing work up to the point of failure.

We've found this particularly helpful when using a procedure to process and transform a large table of data in some way. If we process the data a few thousand rows at a time, committing after each batch saves our work even if later transaction fails.

To run a stored procedure, use the CALL keyword.

View

A view defines a query that is executed each time the view is referenced in a query. Although there are some PostgreSQL specific parameters that can be specified at view creation time, generally they work the same as in other databases.

Regardless of the permissions a role has to select data from tables in the defined query, views can only be modified by the owner or a superuser.

To create a view, a role must have USAGE and CREATE privileges on the schema.

Materialized View

A materialized view in PostgreSQL is similar to an indexed view in SQL Server. The defined query is executed and the results are materialized and stored to disk. They are especially useful for frequently used aggregated queries that take a long time to process. Computing and storing the values ahead of time can significantly improve query speed.

Materialized views can have additional indexes applied like a table and the view can be refreshed at any time using the `REFRESH MATERIALIZED VIEW` command.

To create a materialized view, a role must have USAGE and CREATE privileges on the schema.

Foreign Table

Modern applications often require the ability to query data from multiple sources, some of which might not be databases at all (e.g. a folder full of CSV files). But with *foreign tables*, you can create a table schema to represent the data outside of your PostgreSQL database and then interact with the data like a regular table through SQL.

The ability to access the data is accomplished in PostgreSQL through the concept of Foreign Data Wrappers (FDW), access methods that can be defined which allow querying other data sources with SQL. Almost like the GiST index we discussed earlier, the FDW framework defines the access methods that must exist to query alternative data sources. PostgreSQL doesn't care where the data is coming from, only that the access methods allow PostgreSQL to interact with the data like a table.

Foreign tables make use of FDWs, which are extensions that define how Postgres will interact with a given data source, similar to how database drivers work. In modern versions of PostgreSQL, you can query text files, online object storage, and even other databases using the appropriate foreign data wrapper.

There has been a significant amount of work done over the last many years on the FDW framework around predicate pushdown, filtering, sorting, and more. Additionally, PostgreSQL can retain table statistics about the foreign table locally to assist in better query planning. However, maintaining this data on large foreign tables efficiently can become a bottleneck and should be used with caution.

To create a foreign table, a role must have USAGE and CREATE privileges on the schema.

Trigger

Love them or hate them, triggers still play an essential role in nearly all database architectures. As mentioned earlier, PostgreSQL developers generally don't shy away from using functions in database work, including with triggers. Yes, you should still be cautious and aware of how you are using triggers, including the possibility of introducing unintended blocking or hidden data processing that are hard to track down. However, don't be afraid of using them appropriately.

But why am I talking about functions when describing triggers?

In PostgreSQL, a trigger is just an instruction to execute a designated function in response to a specific DML action. The function itself isn't tied to any table or trigger type (INSERT, UPDATE, DELETE, etc.). Therefore, one trigger function can be referenced and used by many tables and DML commands. At first, this may seem like a management headache if you're used to developing individual trigger scripts for each table and DML action in SQL Server.

This provides a lot of flexibility in how trigger functions are developed. You could have one function per table and internally check to see which operation is calling the trigger to consolidate code. Or you can create one function to perform the same task on multiple tables, where it makes sense. This simplifies the management of code and reduces the overall number of trigger functions that need to be maintained.

Additionally, PostgreSQL triggers can apply a filter against the incoming data modification and only execute when certain conditions are met. And, triggers can be executed per row, not just per batch like SQL Server, often simplifying the programming necessary within the trigger to perform the appropriate action.

To creat triggers, a role must have the USAGE and CREATE privileges on the schema.

Types

Types in PostgreSQL allow you to create an entirely new datatype that can be used in the current database using one of five different forms; composite, enumerated, range, base, and array. For most users, the composite and enumerated types are useful for both data integrity and programmatic simplification. Both range and base types require additional function development and maintenance overhead.

Take, for example, the movie rating of a film in our sample database. While it is possible to add a constraint on the column to ensure the values come from a specified list of enumerated values, it lacks context or transparency to do so. Creating a new enumerated type, called `mpaa_rating`, highlights the intent of the column along with an easy reference for finding and maintaining acceptable values. In addition, the enumerated type can also provide custom sorting based on what the ratings values mean, rather than just sorting them alphanumerically.

To create a type, a role must have the CREATE privilege in the database.

Domains

Domains in PostgreSQL are a user-defined datatype with optional constraints that are defined in the current database. The underlying datatype used by the domain must already exist (i.e., TEXT, INT, etc.).

Domains are useful when a datatype is used in multiple places and must honor the same constraints. An email address or postal code, where check constraints could validate the format of the input, are examples of when a domain may be useful.

To create a domain, a role must have the USAGE privilege on the underlying type.

Conclusion

PostgreSQL, like all modern relational databases, has a myriad of core objects that help define datatypes, schema structure, programmatic functions, and more. The core development team has a long history of using the ANSI SQL standards to guide functionality and object support. The result is a long list of supported database objects that remain stable and often sets the foundation for unique ways of extending that functionality. PostgreSQL is a very versatile database, and the breadth of objects and extensibility help make that possible.

10
Introducing PL/pgSQL

An inherent need within any database management system is a language to create functions and other constructs including IF/THEN statements and other procedural controls as well as variables, transaction management, error handling and more. This chapter will cover PL/pgSQL, the primary procedural language used within PostgreSQL. We'll cover the following:

- The purpose and definition of procedural languages within PostgreSQL

- Basic behaviors of the PL/pgSQL language

- Using PL/pgSQL to create functions and other objects

- Flow control and error handling within PL/pgSQL

You'll notice that within the book, there isn't a chapter just on SQL. This is because with PostgreSQL's fairly strict adherence to the SQL standard, almost any resource will get you the basics to perform fundamental SELECT/INSERT/UPDATE/DELETE statements. Instead, we'll show you some of what is possible using PL/pgSQL to consume and control SQL. To get started, let's detail a little more what a procedural language is within Postgres.

Purpose of a Procedural Language

A standard installation of PostgreSQL comes with four different procedural languages enabled:

- PL/pgSQL

- PL/Python

- PL/Tcl

- PL/Perl

Each of these languages allows you to create functions and procedures, control flow, define variables and more. Each one does this in the unique language that defines it. Within all of them though, it's SQL that does the interaction with the underlying database objects.

The ANSI SQL standard doesn't define a lot of language constructs such as IF/THEN statements or variables. Yet, it's very common to need these types of flow control within the code running on a database system. Additional work such as error handling and transaction management are separated from ANSI SQL within PostgreSQL. All this leads to the need for a procedural language. Finally, storing code for reuse within the database in the form of functions or procedures is a very good practice and you'll need a procedural language to make that happen.

While most objects can be created and controlled with any of the procedural languages, most people are more comfortable working within a database using SQL style syntax. This is why we'll focus on PL/pgSQL here in this chapter and use it in the rest of the book.

Basic PL/pgSQL Syntax

The core syntax for PL/pgSQL consists of blocks, variables and error handling. There are a lot of additional behaviors, and we'll go through a number of them in this chapter, but it all starts with the block construct.

Blocks

The core of PL/pgSQL is what is called a block. A block consists of a series of statements starting with DECLARE and continuing with BEGIN and END. So, the core syntax would look something like Listing 10-1:

Listing 10-1. *Showing a block of PL/pgSQL code*

```
DO $$
<<block_example>>
DECLARE
      neededname varchar(2000);
BEGIN

SELECT
      full_name
INTO
      neededname
FROM
      customer
WHERE
      customer_id = 4299;
END;
$$
```

The block is defined by the label, in this case <<block_example>>, and then the statements defined between the BEGIN and END statements. The label itself is optional and doesn't have to be included. The block is actually just considered text, and it gets interpreted into the correct statements within PostgreSQL.

NOTE: Individual statements within a block, excluding DECLARE, BEGIN, and the final END, generally should terminate with a semi-colon.

In addition, we've defined escape characters, $$. Known as "dollar quoting", this is to allow the block, which is just text, to be able to use single quotes as they are within SQL. Otherwise, if you referred to text like this, 'some value', you would instead have to do it like this ''some value'', using two single quotes instead of one.

Within the block, the DECLARE statement is where we can define variables (more on that in the next section). Then, there is a BEGIN and END that defines this block. You can, within a block have other blocks of code, also grouped by the BEGIN and END statements. Each of the statements is terminated with a semi-colon, but, not the escape characters, $$.

Variables

In the previous section, we saw an example of a variable in use in Listing 10-1. We defined neededname as a varchar(2000) value and then used it in the query replicated in part here in Listing 10-2:

Listing 10-2. A subset of the earlier query showing variable use

```
SELECT
        full_name
INTO
        neededname
FROM
        customer
WHERE
        customer_id = 4299;
```

Listing 10-2 shows how the value from the column, full_name, is used to load the variable, neededname.

The core syntax for variables is to define a name and a data type, similar to this pseudocode in Listing 10-3:

Listing 10-3. Pseudocode showing variable declarations

```
...
DECLARE
        somename text;
        somevalue integer;
        somedate date;
BEGIN
...
```

You can also assign values when you define the variables like this in Listing 10-4:

Listing 10-4. Adding values to the variable declarations

```
...
DECLARE
      somename varchar(50) := 'Victor von Frankenstein';
      somevalue integer := 42;
      somedate date = '1/11/2024';
BEGIN
...
```

And you'll note that we used both "=" and ":=" because either will work, however we strongly recommend sticking with := for assignment, to reduce possible confusion for future readers of your code. Using just = for assignment, while it works, is very much considered bad practice.

As you get into blocks and sub-blocks, you can declare more variables within the sub-blocks. Those variables will only be available within the sub-block (you can think of them as locally scoped). You can refer to variables in the outer blocks, but if the same name as the sub-block variable, you'll need to include the outer block name in order to differentiate between the two.

Variables are like parameters, but parameters are defined with the function or procedure and not within the code block. A function or procedure can have both parameters and variables. We'll cover parameters in more detail in the section called Creating Functional Objects

Error Handling

You can add error handling through the raise statement. Then, there are various different levels that you can raise. These result in information being returned to the client in the case of:

- info
- warning
- notice
- exception

Or they'll be system only in the case of:

- debug

- log

The default level, if you don't supply one, is exception. Listing 10-5 shows the minimum to raise an exception:

Listing 10-5. Minimum code block to raise an exception

```
DO $$
BEGIN
RAISE 'my error message';
END $$;
```

The output from this error would look like Figure 10-1:

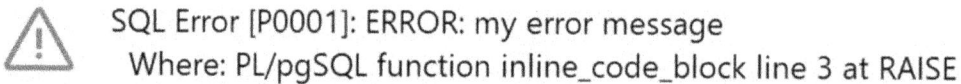

⚠️ SQL Error [P0001]: ERROR: my error message
   Where: PL/pgSQL function inline_code_block line 3 at RAISE

Figure 10-1. DBeaver shows the default error output

You can get much more sophisticated. Also, since raise supports different levels, we would suggest defining which level you're using at all times. In addition to the simple error message as shown in Listing 10-5, you can pass on additional information through the use of using and either:

- hint: additional information to assist in troubleshooting

- detail: information about the error

- errcode: the defined error code name or error code number that you intend to raise

Listing 10-6 shows using in action:

Listing 10-6. Raise exception with the addition of an errcode value

```
DO $$
BEGIN
        RAISE EXCEPTION 'An error message relating to dates'
            USING errcode = 22007;
END $$;
```

The output within DBeaver will now show the errcode value (which is for invalid_datetime_format):

> ⚠ SQL Error [22007]: ERROR: An error message relating to dates
>   Where: PL/pgSQL function inline_code_block line 3 at RAISE

Figure 10-2. The error now shows 22007 as defined by the code

Most of the time, you won't simply have an error raised like this. Instead, you'll be evaluating behaviors and using procedure language controls such as IF/THEN or CASE to decide to raise an error. We'll explore that procedural language now.

Procedural Language

A lot of the code that we write will be extremely straight forward CRUD style statements:

- CREATE
- READ
- UPDATE
- DELETE

Many of these will just work. There won't be a need for any kind of flow control. However, some of our code will benefit from the ability to decide if different paths through the code are superior. This is especially true of error handling in cases where it's very likely we would only want to raise an exception if a certain value is found. That's where something like the IF/THEN and other procedure language constructs are used.

IF/THEN

The IF/THEN construct within PL/pgSQL is fairly straight forward. You start with IF and then define a Boolean expression to evaluate. If that expression is true, THEN it continues into the block. You then close off the conditional with an END IF. In a nutshell, that's how it works. Listing 10-7 shows it in action:

Listing 10-7. Error handling using an IF statement

```
DO $$
DECLARE
      desiredtitle text;
BEGIN
      SELECT
            title
      INTO
            desiredtitle
      FROM
            film
      WHERE
            film_id = 18;

      IF desiredtitle <> 'On Golden Pond' THEN
            RAISE warning 'Incorrect Title. Title returned was: %',
desiredtitle;
      END IF;
END $$;
```

The query is pulling the title column from the film table and loading it into the desired title variable. From there, the IF statement determines if the value does not equal 'On Golden Pond'. If it does not, the THEN branch will be followed and run the raise warning command. The output from running the code is in Figure 10-3:

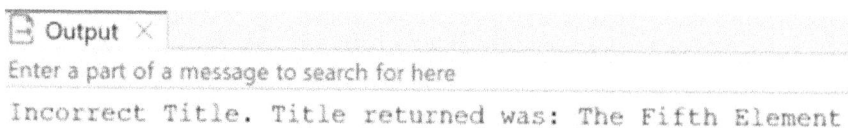

Output ×

Enter a part of a message to search for here

Incorrect Title. Title returned was: The Fifth Element

Figure 10-3. Output from the IF/THEN statement

Since the film for film_id 18 is 'The Fifth Element', our check for 'On Golden Pond' raises the warning message.

You can add additional checks using ELSEIF which will function in the same way. Finally, you can wrap it all up with an ELSE as a final possible command.

CASE

Another way to control the flow of code is through a CASE statement. While an IF/THEN statement works off the concept of evaluating any kind of condition, the CASE statement allows for evaluating a single condition at a time and then working off the values of that condition. Otherwise, in many respects, they are similar. You can have multiple WHEN evaluations, each on a single condition.

Listing 10-8 shows the basic syntax in action:

Listing 10-8. Evaluating the CASE of a count of film genres

```
DO $$
DECLARE
      genres int;
      filmdef varchar(50);
BEGIN
      SELECT
            count(fg."name") INTO genres
      FROM film f
        JOIN film_genre fg
          ON  fg.genre_id = ANY(f.genre_ids)
      WHERE film_id = 18
      GROUP BY f.title;

      CASE WHEN genres = 1 THEN filmdef := 'Narrow';
      WHEN genres BETWEEN 1 AND 3 THEN filmdef := 'Medium';
      ELSE filmdef := 'Wide';
      END CASE;

      RAISE NOTICE 'Film definition is % with % genres', filmdef,genres;
END $$
```

The CASE is made against the count of genres for the film in question. In this case, there are five genres for the film. The evaluation will check each of the first two conditions, but since they will not be reached, the ELSE condition will act as a final place to determine what to do within the code.

NOTE: There is also a CASE statement within the SQL standard, but that is distinct from this CASE statement that is a part of PL/pgSQL. Don't confuse the two.

Loops

There are three basic types of looping within PL/pgSQL:

- Loop: runs a loop until an exit or return statement occurs

- For Loop: runs until a specified range has been exhausted

- While Loop: runs until a condition is no longer true

Each of these satisfies different logical constructs within code, even though they are very similar in nature. Let's explore how each one works.

LOOP

To see LOOP in action, we'll take the most basic approach as shown in Listing 10-9:

Listing 10-9. *Using a counter value within a LOOP*

```
DO $$
DECLARE
      counter int := 1;
BEGIN
      LOOP
            RAISE NOTICE 'counter = %', counter;
            IF counter > 5 THEN
                  EXIT;
            END IF;
            counter := counter + 1;
      END LOOP;
END $$
```

Basically, if we didn't increment the value of counter, the loop would run forever. But because we keep increasing the counter, you'll only get the five executions. We're using RAISE NOTICE to show how the loop is behaving as you can see the values incrementing. However, this example, while a classic description of a LOOP function, is more like a FOR LOOP.

Listing 10-10 shows a different kind of example:

Listing 10-10. Using LOOP to walk through records

```
DO $$
DECLARE
     rec record;
BEGIN
     LOOP
          SELECT
                s.road_ref,
                s.street_name,
                s.store_id
          INTO
                rec
          FROM
                store s
          WHERE
                s.road_ref IS NOT NULL LIMIT 1;

          IF rec.street_name = 'Broadway' THEN
                EXIT;
          ELSE
                UPDATE store
                SET road_ref = NULL
                WHERE store_id = rec.store_id;
          END IF;

     END LOOP;
END $$
```

In this example, rows are retrieved, one at a time from the store table within the loop. Then, the value of street_name is checked to see if it equals 'Broadway'. When that happens, the loop will exit. Otherwise, the store is updated, and the queries continue.

FOR LOOP

The FOR LOOP lets us define a limit on the number of loops that will occur. Listing 10-11 shows a simple example:

Listing 10-11. Using the FOR LOOP

```
DO $$
BEGIN
    FOR counter IN 1..3 LOOP
        RAISE NOTICE 'Counter: %', counter;
    END LOOP;

END $$
```

Unlike the LOOP operation, we don't have to use EXIT or RETURN to leave the loop. This will only run three times, no matter what with results shown in Figure 10-4:

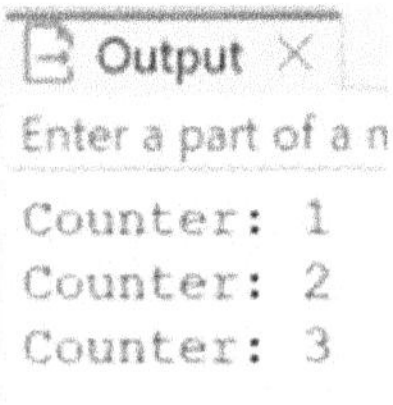

```
Output ✕
Enter a part of a n
Counter: 1
Counter: 2
Counter: 3
```

Figure 10-4. Three executions in the loop

You can use EXIT in a FOR LOOP as well. Plus, we can use the loop on result sets from queries as shown in Listing 10-12:

Listing 10-12. *Using LOOP with a result set*

```
DO $$
DECLARE
        counter int := 1;
        soundrec record;
BEGIN
        FOR soundrec IN
          SELECT
                fc.job
          FROM
                film_crew fc
          WHERE
                fc.department = 'Sound'
          GROUP BY
                fc.job
          ORDER BY
                fc.job DESC

        LOOP
                RAISE NOTICE '% ',soundrec.job;
                IF counter < 10 THEN
                        counter := counter + 1;
                ELSE
                        EXIT;
                END IF;

        END LOOP;

END $$
```

You could limit the results using LIMIT as we did earlier. However, for illustration purposes, we used the counter to limit the number of rows processed.

WHILE LOOP

The WHILE LOOP uses a check condition to determine whether to continue the loop. Listing 10-13 shows a simple example:

Listing 10-13. Example of a WHILE LOOP

```
DO $$
DECLARE
      future time;
      checktime time;
BEGIN
      future := clock_timestamp() + INTERVAL '2 seconds';
      checktime := clock_timestamp();

      WHILE future > checktime LOOP
            RAISE NOTICE '% %',future,checktime;
            PERFORM pg_sleep(1);
            checktime := clock_timestamp();
      END LOOP;
END $$
```

The code sets two values, future and checktime, with future being 2 seconds ahead. So, the while loop will run until checktime catches up and passes future. We added the pg_sleep() command just to limit the number of loops for the demonstration.

There is additional functionality within loops, but these examples of the three different loops cover most of the basics.

Creating Procedural Objects

Throughout this chapter, we've been calling code that would have to be stored in a file, or typed by hand because it wouldn't persist within the database. However, it is possible to create procedural objects within PostgreSQL using PL/pgSQL. The three we'll go over are functions, procedures and cursors.

Functions

A function is a way to store code within the database that is capable of returning a result set. A function differs from a procedure mainly on this alone. Procedures, explained more in the next section, cannot return results. So, if you want to have a query that you can run repeatedly to return result sets, you use a function. Listing 10-14 shows a very simple example:

Listing 10-14. Retrieving a list of genres from the database

```
CREATE FUNCTION genre_list ()
RETURNS TABLE (genre_id int,
genre_name TEXT)
AS $$
BEGIN
        RETURN QUERY
SELECT
                fg.genre_id,
                fg.name
FROM
public.film_genre AS fg;
END
$$ LANGUAGE plpgsql;
```

The basics are pretty straight forward. You use the CREATE FUNCTION to define the name of the function, genre_list. Then, assuming your function returns anything, you have to define it. Here we defined a table with data types that match the SELECT list later. We then define the RETURN as a QUERY and put it in the actual SELECT statement. Finally, we do have to define the language that the function is running under. It could be SQL or any of the procedure languages, but in this case, it's plpgsql.

To see the function in action, we just use it in a query as shown in Listing 10-15:

Listing 10-15. Querying the new function

```
SELECT
      gl.genre_id,
      gl.genrename
FROM
      Genre_list() AS gl;
```

This will result in the information shown in Figure 10-5:

SELECT gl.genre_id, gl.genrename FROM genrelist()

	genre_id	genrename
1	28	Action
2	12	Adventure
3	16	Animation
4	35	Comedy
5	80	Crime
6	99	Documentary
7	18	Drama
8	10,751	Family
9	14	Fantasy
10	36	History
11	27	Horror
12	10,402	Music
13	9,648	Mystery
14	10,749	Romance
15	878	Science Fiction
16	10,770	TV Movie
17	53	Thriller
18	10,752	War
19	37	Western

Figure 10-5. *A list of genres from the database*

Because functions are called from a SELECT statement, you can treat them like tables and join them on appropriate columns.

Most functions that return data will probably include filtering through a WHERE clause. We can modify existing functions using ALTER FUNCTION. However, you can't change the name or parameters in that way, Since the Genre_list function does already do what it says, return a list, let's create a different function:

Listing 10-16. Using parameters with a function

```
CREATE OR REPLACE FUNCTION genre (searchid int)
RETURNS TABLE (genre_id int,
genrename TEXT)
AS $$
BEGIN
      RETURN QUERY
SELECT
            fg.genre_id,
            fg.name
FROM
            bluebox.film_genre AS fg
WHERE
      fg.genre_id = searchid;
END
$$ LANGUAGE plpgsql;
```

For this function, instead of just CREATE, we're using CREATE OR REPLACE. As long as you don't change the parameters or the RETURNS definition, you can edit the internals of the function while maintaining the object ID for the function. This means that other functions, procedures or whatever, that reference this function, won't have to be recompiled.

The parameter is defined within the parenthesis. You can define it by name and data type, or you can just put in data types, then use their ordinal position within the code like this: ...fg.genre_id = $1 .... Otherwise, defining a parameter is basically the same as defining variables. In fact, you can add a DECLARE before the BEGIN within the function and create variables, just like in the code blocks we did earlier in the chapter.

To see this in action, we can call it just the same as we did in Listing 10-15, but we have to provide a parameter value:

Listing 10-17. Retrieving data using a parameter

```
SELECT
      g.genrename
FROM
      genre(27) AS g;
```

There are all sorts of additional code you can put within functions. You can have them return individual values instead of tables or sets of data. Functions can be made to manipulate data as well. Exception handling can also be added. You can also have them include much larger sets of queries. They can, and do, frequently get much more complicated.

Procedures

As was already stated earlier in the chapter, in PostgreSQL, procedures are basically functions that don't return data. The exception to that is the use of INOUT parameters, which we'll cover in a little bit. Otherwise, defining a procedure is a lot like defining a function as shown in Listing 10-18:

Listing 10-18. A procedure for adding a new genre

```
CREATE OR REPLACE PROCEDURE new_genre (genrename TEXT)
AS $$
BEGIN
INSERT
      INTO bluebox.film_genre (name)
VALUES (genrename);
END
$$
LANGUAGE plpgsql;
```

Just like the function, you can use CREATE OR REPLACE with procedures. The same rules apply, you can't change the parameters or it becomes a new procedure. To change the parameters, you would need to DROP and then CREATE the procedure. Other than that though, the definition looks a lot the same as creating a function. The difference is in how a procedure is used:

Listing 10-19. Adding a new genre through the new procedure

```
CALL new_genre('Anime');
```

Instead of using the SELECT statement, you place a CALL to the procedure. Once done, in this case, we get a new row added to the genres table as shown in Figure 10-6:

SELECT gl.genre_id, gl.genrename FROM genrelist()

	123 genre_id	ABC genrename
1	28	Action
2	12	Adventure
3	16	Animation
4	35	Comedy
5	80	Crime
6	99	Documentary
7	18	Drama
8	10,751	Family
9	14	Fantasy
10	36	History
11	27	Horror
12	10,402	Music
13	9,648	Mystery
14	10,749	Romance
15	878	Science Fiction
16	10,770	TV Movie
17	53	Thriller
18	10,752	War
19	37	Western
20	1	Anime

Figure 10-6. genres table showing the new genre

To see the INOUT parameters in action, we'll create a new procedure:

Listing 10-20. Getting a count of films in a genre

```
CREATE OR REPLACE PROCEDURE
    genre_count(genreid int, INOUT genrecount int )
AS $$
BEGIN
        SELECT
        count(*)
INTO
        genrecount
FROM
        film AS f
WHERE
        genreid = ANY(f.genre_ids);
END
$$
LANGUAGE plpgsql;
```

The only substantial new thing is the addition of the INOUT to the parameter genrecount. That designates this a parameter that will have an output value. It can also have an input value, but the presumption is that the procedure is going to change the value of the parameter for the calling code. To call this, we'll use the code in Listing 10-21:

Listing 10-21. Consuming the INOUT parameter

```
DO $$
DECLARE genre_counts int;
BEGIN
        CALL genrecount(genreid => 27, genrecount => genrecounts);
        RAISE NOTICE 'Films in genre: %', genrecounts;
END $$
```

In this case, instead of using the ordinal position of the parameters, we're using their names to pass in values. You'll notice that for the INOUT parameter, there's nothing that needs to be done on this side of the code. The value will be changed by the procedure.

Cursors

The final functional object we'll cover here are cursors. Cursors within PostgreSQL serve a different function than in a lot of other relational database management systems. Yes, they can be used for row-by-row processing, although that is an inefficient use of cursors within PostgreSQL and should be avoided in favor of using SQL to perform set operations. However, in addition to row-by-row processing, cursors are a mechanism of memory management within PostgreSQL. When you have very large data sets, you can avoid memory bottlenecks by using a cursor to process smaller batches of rows. A very common way to use this is in combination with a function.

To start with, we'll define a very simple cursor and show row-by-row processing. A cursor can be declared simply as a cursor object in your code. Then, later you define how it's used later in the code. However, more frequently, a cursor will be bound to a query through the use of FOR in the DECLARE statement.

Listing 10-22 shows how a couple of rows can be processed from a cursor:

Listing 10-22. Processing individual rows in a cursor

```
DO $$
DECLARE
counter int;

filmcrew CURSOR FOR
  SELECT person_id, job
  FROM film_crew;

rec record;

BEGIN
      OPEN filmcrew;
      counter = 0;
```

```
    WHILE counter < 2 LOOP
            FETCH NEXT FROM filmcrew INTO rec;

            counter = counter + 1;

            RAISE NOTICE 'Job: %', rec.job;
        END LOOP;
END; $$
```

The cursor is declared with the name filmcrew and the query to pull data from the film_crew table. The cursor is then opened, using the OPEN statement. From there, we loop through the results of the cursor, one row at a time, until we meet the requirements of the WHILE loop.

In order to see a cursor working with a function, first we'll need a function. Listing 10-23 shows one that returns more than 347,000 rows in our sample database, bluebox:

Listing 10-23. A function to return film crew information

```
CREATE OR REPLACE FUNCTION film_crew_info()
RETURNS TABLE (personname TEXT, title TEXT,
               department TEXT, job TEXT)
AS $$
BEGIN
RETURN QUERY
    SELECT
        p.name AS personname,
        f.title,
        fc.department,
        fc.job
    FROM
        film_crew AS fc    JOIN person AS p ON
        fc.person_id = p.person_id
    JOIN film AS f ON
        fc.film_id = f.film_id;
END
$$ LANGUAGE plpgsql;
```

We can then choose how we want to bring data back from the function using FETCH:

Listing 10-24. Consuming batches of rows from a cursor

```
BEGIN;
DECLARE
    filmcrew CURSOR FOR
        SELECT * FROM film_crew_info();

FETCH 15
FROM
filmcrew;

COMMIT;
```

This will pull 15 rows in a batch out of the cursor looking like this:

	ᴬᴮᶜ personname	ᴬᴮᶜ title	ᴬᴮᶜ department	ᴬᴮᶜ job
1	Tom Cruise	Mission: Impossible - Dead Reckoning Part One	Production	Producer
2	Lalo Schifrin	Mission: Impossible - Dead Reckoning Part One	Sound	Main Title Theme Composer
3	James Mather	Mission: Impossible - Dead Reckoning Part One	Sound	Supervising Sound Editor
4	Glenn Freemantle	Mission: Impossible - Dead Reckoning Part One	Sound	Sound Designer
5	Erik Jendresen	Mission: Impossible - Dead Reckoning Part One	Writing	Writer
6	Jill Taylor	Mission: Impossible - Dead Reckoning Part One	Costume & Make-Up	Costume Design
7	Enos Desjardins	Mission: Impossible - Dead Reckoning Part One	Sound	Sound Effects Editor
8	Mark Taylor	Mission: Impossible - Dead Reckoning Part One	Sound	Sound Re-Recording Mixer
9	Rebecca Sheridan	Mission: Impossible - Dead Reckoning Part One	Directing	Script Supervisor
10	Amy Byrne	Mission: Impossible - Dead Reckoning Part One	Costume & Make-Up	Hair Designer
11	Raffaella Giovannetti	Mission: Impossible - Dead Reckoning Part One	Art	Set Decoration
12	Tom Kemplen	Mission: Impossible - Dead Reckoning Part One	Crew	Visual Effects Editor
13	Wade Eastwood	Mission: Impossible - Dead Reckoning Part One	Crew	Stunt Coordinator
14	Max Aruj	Mission: Impossible - Dead Reckoning Part One	Crew	Additional Music
15	Rowan Watson	Mission: Impossible - Dead Reckoning Part One	Sound	Sound Effects Editor

Figure 10-7. 15 rows from a cursor

With cursors, you're not just limited to moving forward through them. You can also move backwards. You can define save points. They can be passed to and from functions and procedures. Cursors within PostgreSQL and PL/pgSQL have some utility but are infrequently used.

Conclusion

PL/pgSQL, and all the other procedural languages, have a very broad set of functions and language constructs. This chapter just introduced some of the most commonly used. There is still more to learn with PL/pgSQL. However, this chapter took you through the starting point using blocks. We then covered variables which are extremely common. We introduced conditional flow statements like IF/THEN so you can control your code. Finally, we showed how functions and procedures can be used to help you manipulate data in a more repeatable fashion. While there is a lot to PL/pgSQL, the fundamentals are fairly straight forward.

11
Query Tuning and Indexes

If you've been using databases for a while, you know that query tuning is often an art more than a science. The principles that you've learned tuning queries in one database generally apply to the next. PostgreSQL is no exception.

The challenge, however, is knowing how to find problematic queries, generate a representative query plan, and then extract relevant information from that plan. This is where the nuanced art of tuning queries starts to come into play.

In this chapter, we're going to show you those basic building blocks and give you some initial pointers on where to start. Once you know how to start attaining the information, there are other books and resources that can take you deeper into the query tuning rabbit hole.

EXPLAIN

EXPLAIN is the PostgreSQL command that retrieves an estimated or actual query plan. The command sounds active, as if in our new world of AI everywhere, PostgreSQL EXPLAIN will walk you through each part of the query and help you understand where it could be improved. But of course, that's not what EXPLAIN does at all.

The statistics-based query planner works as quickly as possible to find the best plan in the shortest amount of time. EXPLAIN simply produces the textual representation of the chosen plan. That's right, the *textual* representation. There is no built-in graphical query plan viewer because there is no official IDE that nearly every PostgreSQL developer uses, like SQL Server has SSMS, with years of development to make it the standard plan viewer. We'll get back to that later.

Estimated Query Plans

Used by itself, EXPLAIN produces an estimated query plan without executing the query. A sample query and EXPLAIN output are shown in Listing 11-1.

Listing 11-1. Showing the estimated query plan

```
EXPLAIN
SELECT * FROM film
WHERE release_date > '2023-10-01'::date;

QUERY PLAN                                                        |
------------------------------------------------------------------+
-> Seq Scan on film  (cost=0.00..962.55 rows=15 width=778)|
   Filter: (release_date > '2023-10-01'::date)                    |
```

In the estimated query plan above, we learn two valuable pieces of information. First, the query is going to scan the entire film table (Seq Scan) and PostgreSQL estimates it will take 962.55 units of work and return 15 rows of data, the information inside of the first parenthesis of each node.

```
-> Seq Scan on film  (cost=0.00..962.55 rows=15 width=778)|
```

To see if PostgreSQL estimated correctly and get the actual values, we must use some of the options with EXPLAIN.

EXPLAIN Options

The EXPLAIN command has several options that you can add which will change the output to provide more detail. Some of these options would be analogous to setting I/O statistics or timing on when retrieving an execution plan in SQL Server.

By default, the COSTS and TIMING options for the EXPLAIN command are enabled and should generally be left that way. Because they default to true, the options themselves do not have to be added when running EXPLAIN. You'll see the cost and timing values in the example query plans that follow.

The other options include ANALYZE, VERBOSE, SETTINGS, GENERIC_PLAN, BUFFERS, WAL, SUMMARY, and FORMAT. We'll address some of these options as we go.

Adding run-time statistics

Adding the most common option, ANALYZE, to the EXPLAIN command (Listing 11-2) will produce the query plan with additional run time statistics for review. Recognize, however, that this does execute the query to completion. If a query requires heavy I/O or memory use to complete, or data modifications in the case of DML statements, those modifications will occur before the plan is returned.

Listing 11-2. Adding the ANALYZE option to EXPLAIN

```
EXPLAIN ANALYZE
SELECT * FROM film
WHERE release_date > '2023-10-01'::date;

QUERY PLAN                                                    |
--------------------------------------------------------------+
Seq Scan on film  (cost=0.00..962.55 rows=15 width=778)|
(actual time=13.870..27.588 rows=63 loops=1)          |
  Filter: (release_date > '2023-10-01'::date)          |
  Rows Removed by Filter: 7939                          |
                                                        |
Planning Time: 0.206 ms                                 |
Execution Time: 27.649 ms                               |
```

Adding the ANALYZE command provides us with some added details. First, we can see that the second set of parenthesis contains actual values for time, rows, and loops from this node.

```
-> Seq Scan on film (cost=0.00..962.55 rows=15 width=778)|
        (actual time=13.870..27.588 rows=63 loops=1) |
```

This tells us the query took 27ms to scan the film table and return 63 rows, about 4x more than the estimated 15.

Second, to return those 63 rows, PostgreSQL scanned the entire table row by row and filtered out 7939 rows that had a `release_date` value less than '2023-10-01'.

And finally, generating this execution plan took 0.206ms and another 27.649ms to run to completion.

Execution plans certainly get longer and more complicated as query complexity increases but working your way through plans to find areas for optimization starts by looking at these same values, node by node.

Note: In an unfortunate name collision, the ANALYZE option of the EXPLAIN command is not the same as the SQL command ANALYZE.

We'll discuss the ANALYZE command later in this chapter.

BUFFERS

The second most useful EXPLAIN option is BUFFERS. It's so helpful, in fact, that there have been years of discussions about whether to make it the default option when generating an actual query plan.

Buffers are the 8Kb pages on disk that store the data for your database. These pages can reside in the shared buffers memory (fastest), the disk cache (fast), or on the physical to disk (slowest).

The general principle, however, is straightforward. The more pages a node reads to access the required data, the more work it needs to do and the slower it will make the query. Remember, it's a principle, not a rule.

Yes, a higher value for actual time will often relate proportionally to a higher amount of buffer usage, but being able to measure the total amount of data that is needed can make it much easier to pinpoint problematic nodes. (e.g. does this query take megabytes, gigabytes, or terabytes of processed pages to retrieve the data and return a result?)

Let's return to our simple query from the film table, but this time add the BUFFERS option (Listing 11-3).

Listing 11-3. Add additional BUFFER information to EXPLAIN output

```
EXPLAIN (ANALYZE, BUFFERS)
SELECT * FROM film
WHERE release_date > '2023-10-01'::date;

QUERY PLAN                                                        |
------------------------------------------------------------------+
Seq Scan on film  (cost=0.00..962.55 rows=15 width=778)           |
(actual time=1.001..3.719 rows=63 loops=1)                        |
  Filter: (release_date > '2023-10-01'::date)                     |
  Rows Removed by Filter: 7939                                     |
  Buffers: shared hit=862                                          |
Planning Time: 0.295 ms                                           |
Execution Time: 3.801 ms                                          |
```

In this updated query plan, we can now see that producing the result for this query required 862 pages to be accessed, or approximately 7MB of data (862 page * 8Kb = 7.136 MB).

Note: You probably noticed that adding BUFFERS as a second option for EXPLAIN required us to use parenthesis around both options but using just ANALYZE by itself didn't. This is primarily for backwards compatibility to when EXPLAIN had fewer options.

Using the ANALYZE or VERBOSE options without any others does not require parenthesis. However, adding more options to EXPLAIN ANALYZE requires that all options be contained in parentheses.

When you read the values for buffers, you may have noticed that EXPLAIN generally prints out four different types of buffer usage dealing with shared buffers: hit, read, written, and dirtied. In most cases, we're primarily concerned with hit (the pages were already in shared buffers) and read (the pages were not in the shared buffers). If all, or most of the pages necessary to satisfy a query can come from shared buffers (shared hit), the operations will be faster. The more pages that must first be read into shared buffers to satisfy the query, the slower those operations will typically be.

Having this information available as you begin to look at more complex query plans can quickly highlight where the bottleneck is and focus your attention.

Buffer Values Are Cumulative

Up to this point we've left out one important piece of information when talking about query plans, mostly because our example plan only has one Seq scan node. However, as more operations are needed to process the data and return the desired result, additional nodes will be added. Some of the query metrics associated with each node, like buffer values, are the cumulative sum of all metrics from nodes that were executed earlier in the query.

To demonstrate this, we need to change our query just a bit, adding joins with two additional tables. (Listing 11-4)

Listing 11-4. Adding buffer counts is cumulative for all earlier nodes

```
EXPLAIN (ANALYZE,BUFFERS)
SELECT * FROM film f
      JOIN film_cast fc USING (film_id)
      JOIN person p USING (person_id)
WHERE release_date > '2023-10-01'::date;


QUERY PLAN                                                      |
----------------------------------------------------------------+
Nested Loop  (cost=0.84..2664.14 rows=445 width=926)            |
    (actual time=0.432..296.535 rows=2265 loops=1)              |
  Buffers: shared hit=8790 read=1445                            |
  -> Nested Loop  (cost=0.42..2425.16 rows=445 width=801) |
           (actual time=0.425..11.842 rows=2265 loops=1) |
      Buffers: shared hit=1127 read=48                          |
      -> Seq Scan on film f                                     |
           (cost=0.00..962.55 rows=15 width=778                 |
           (actual time=0.413..2.269 rows=63 loops=1) |
          Filter: (release_date > '2023-10-01'::date)           |
          Rows Removed by Filter: 7939                           |
          Buffers: shared hit=862                                |
      -> Index Scan using film_cast_pk on film_cast fc   |
           (cost=0.42..97.18 rows=33 width=31)                  |
           (actual time=0.117..0.142 rows=36 loops=63)|
          Index Cond: (film_id = f.film_id)                     |
          Buffers: shared hit=265 read=48                        |
  -> Index Scan using person_pkey on person p                   |
        (cost=0.42..0.54 rows=1 width=133)                      |
        (actual time=0.125..0.125 rows=1 loops=2265)            |
      Index Cond: (person_id = fc.person_id)                    |
      Buffers: shared hit=7663 read=1397                        |
Planning:                                                       |
  Buffers: shared hit=22                                        |
Planning Time: 0.282 ms                                         |
Execution Time: 296.802 ms                                      |
```

Using the buffer values as an example, we can see that the inner most nodes, the Seq Scan on film and the Index Scan on film_cast_pk, were executed first as two sides of a nested loop. Most of the data necessary for these two operations was available in shared buffers (shared hit: 862+265=1,127) and a small fraction of pages needed to be read into shared buffers (shared read=48). These totals match the cumulative values of the `Nested Loop` parent node shown in Listing 11-5.

Listing 11-5. *Total buffers for the nested loop join*

```
->  Nested Loop  (cost=0.42..2425.16 rows=445 width=801) |
          (actual time=0.425..11.842 rows=2265 loops=1) |
      Buffers: shared hit=1127 read=48                   |
```

The result of the Nested Loop operation is then joined to the person table using an `Index Scan` on `person_pkey`. The sum of these two nodes becomes the total amount of buffer "work" that the query performed as seen in the top-level Nested Loop node (Listing 11-6). The number of pages that were found in shared buffers (`shared hit`) during this query execution was 8,790 (1,127+7,663), while the total number of pages accessed from disk (`shared read`) was 1,445 (48+1,397).

Listing 11-6. *Total buffers needed for the entire query*

```
Nested Loop  (cost=0.84..2664.14 rows=445 width=926)   |
    (actual time=0.432..296.535 rows=2265 loops=1)     |
  Buffers: shared hit=8790 read=1445                   |
```

Query Cost and Actual Time

For each query node, cost is the estimated measure of arbitrary units that the query planner assigned to each node based on table statistics and other settings. This isn't a cost based on something tangible, like the amount of CPU, but should be proportionally relevant within an individual execution plan. Costs are used to determine the best query plan in the shortest amount of time possible. For instance, if a join could be accomplished by a hash join or a nested loop, the one that was estimated to cost less would typically be chosen unless there were other factors beyond the join operation.

Time, on the other hand, is the actual measure of time in milliseconds that a particular node takes to execute. The total actual time for the query is typically the sum of all node timings below (taking things like loops into account).

Finally, you may have noticed that query cost and actual time are each represented by two values: the cost/time to start the operation, and the total cost/time for that operation. Another way to think about the first value for each of these measurements is whether the operation had to delay work because of another operation (i.e. the output of a join). Anything other than zero means something else took time before this node could begin its work.

Primary Node Types

Now that we have a basic overview of how to read a query plan produced by EXPLAIN and what some of the key metrics are to measure the amount of work individual nodes and the overall query is doing, we need to talk about the basic node types in PostgreSQL.

At a high level, PostgreSQL query plan nodes can be broken down into three distinct categories: scan nodes, join nodes, and other nodes that perform special tasks like grouping or aggregating data.

Scan Nodes

Scan nodes handle reading data. Although there are many built-in scan nodes for things like scanning a CTE or Function result, there are only three node types that beginners need to focus on to gain the biggest bang for their query tuning effort.

Sequential Scan: Scan through all physical pages of a table, either because an index does not exist for the given predicate or because PostgreSQL has determined it's faster to just scan the table. In many cases this will be a slower operation than using an index, however, you will often see a sequential scan for smaller tables even if indexes exist. Based on the query planner calculations, scanning a smaller heap-based table can be more efficient than jumping around the disk to retrieve and scan individual pages, especially in cases where you need to read data from the table anyway.

Index Scan: Index scans use the specified index to locate pages (and often specific rows) of data to find and return. However, because the index didn't contain all the columns needed from the table, a second set of reads will occur to retrieve the actual data pages. This means that often PostgreSQL determines that a sequential scan is cheaper when a large enough percentage of a heap pages will need to be accessed even with the help of an index.

There are ways to influence this choice, but for now, it's good to realize that seeing a sequential scan of a table even when a matching index exists might not be a bad thing and PostgreSQL is helping the query execute faster… in theory.

Index-Only Scan: This is the most efficient scan node of the three. When you see this type of scan node, it indicates that all required columns are available within the index and no secondary heap data access is needed. This will occur if only the indexed columns are referenced, or when you create a covering index that includes other columns.

Join Nodes

There are three primary join nodes that can be used for gathering data across tables based on the join keys.

Nested Loop Join: A nested loop join does exactly what you would expect. For each row of the outer table, search all rows of the inner table. Typically, nested loop joins are the least efficient way to join a table to produce results, however, nested loop joins are always available to the planner when other methods are deemed more expensive or unusable. Nested loop joins efficiency can often be improved significantly by ensuring there is a matching index for the join key on the inner table.

Hash Join: Hash joins use a two-step process to perform the join operation. First, the inner table (typically the smaller one) is read, and a hash table is created in memory for the join keys. Once the hash table is created, it scans the outer table and probes for matching rows.

Merge Join: A merge join requires that the joining key values are sorted in the same order on both sides of the join before parallel processing of each table begins. When the join keys are already sorted appropriately, like when using indexes, this can often be the fastest join method. However, if data on one or both sides of the join must be sorted first, the process could be much slower.

Other Nodes

Merging data from different tables and selecting it in the most efficient way is almost always what matters most. However, like all other relational databases, PostgreSQL has many other node types that perform specific tasks when appropriate.

When reading execution plans, you'll be able to identify nodes that are used because of specific SQL query commands. A few common nodes include:

- **Aggregate:** Perform the specified aggregation method

- **Append:** Concatenate the results of sub-plans, typically something like a UNION ALL.

- **Sort:** Sort the output of the previous node based on the ORDER BY columns or GROUP BY column if a specific ORDER BY isn't defined.

- **Group:** Take input data from the previous node and produce the GROUP BY output. The data must be pre-sorted, which often results in a Sort node before the Group node.

- **Window Aggregate:** Performs aggregation of data from the previous node based on the specified window function.

- There are many other nodes, and more can be added to the query planner through extensions including new types of scans and join nodes to read unique data types as necessary.

Additional Areas to Troubleshoot

Now that we've talked about the basics of how to read a query plan and the kinds of nodes you will often see, let's talk about a few other things to be on the lookout for which might be impacting the performance of your query. Again, this isn't a complete list, just a few additional tips that can often make a positive impact once remediated.

First things first – work_mem

In Chapter 5 we discussed the importance of the work_mem setting in PostgreSQL. Set to 4MB by default, this is a hard limit for each node of a query plan that needs to gather, hash, or sort data along the way. If there is more data for a particular operation than this value, PostgreSQL will have to use external disk space to complete the operation.

Fortunately, this setting can be changed in two ways. First, at a global level in the postgresql.conf file, as we discussed in Chapter 5. Use caution, however, when setting this value globally. Setting it too high could create a server-wide resource issue during times of high load.

Second, work_mem can also be set in a session to accommodate specific, often resource hungry queries. Maybe you have a set of reports that run each night, and they take a significant amount of time to run. These queries probably have numerous aggregations, groupings, and sorting operations to get results for the report. If PostgreSQL must keep using external disk to perform these operations, the query is going to be slow and use a significant amount of I/O to perform the work.

So, how do you identify when a query is slow because it uses the external disk? We're glad you asked.

External Sort Disk

When an operation in a query plan sorts, aggregates, or creates hash tables, there's always a chance that there is more data to process than work_mem available. This causes the query processor to use the external disk for storage as the process does its work. As soon as any part of the plan moves from memory to disk, there is a chance that it will become slower, particularly as data grows.

Using the default value of 4MB for work_mem, the query in Listing 11-7 produces an external disk operation with our sample dataset. You'll notice that it also planned multiple worker processes.

Listing 11-7. Query to demonstrate an external disk operation

```
EXPLAIN (ANALYZE, BUFFERS)
select
    f.film_id,
    f.title,
    rental.store_id,
    sum(payment.amount) as "gross revenue"
from film f
inner join inventory on
    inventory.film_id = f.film_id
inner join rental on
    rental.inventory_id = inventory.inventory_id
inner join payment
    on payment.rental_id = rental.rental_id
where payment.amount is not NULL
    AND rental_period <@ tstzrange('2024-04-01', '2024-07-01')
group by f.title,
        f.film_id,
        rental.store_id
order by
    sum(payment.amount) desc
```

In the explain plan, we can see multiple references to "external merge disk", with each worker part of a larger parallel hash join (Listing 11-8).

Listing 11-8. *Multiple external disk operations*

```
QUERY PLAN
----------------------------------------------------------------+
Sort  (cost=567486.06..569599.99 rows=845574 width=62)
       (actual time=3835.880..3901.206 rows=71376 loops=1)
  Sort Key: (sum(payment.amount)) DESC
  Sort Method: external merge  Disk: 3552kB
...
     -> Sort  (cost=312776.33..313657.13 rows=352322 width=37) (actual
time=3245.047..3330.326 rows=299214 loops=3)
        Sort Key: f.film_id, rental.store_id
        Sort Method: external merge  Disk: 13896kB
       Buffers: shared hit=151144 read=37314,
           temp read=28699 written=28787
         Worker 0:  Sort Method: external merge  Disk: 15064kB
         Worker 1:  Sort Method: external merge  Disk: 13984kB
...
Planning:
  Buffers: shared hit=20 read=26
Planning Time: 0.904 ms
Execution Time: 3908.013 ms
```

When PostgresSQL needs to use external disk, it tells us how much disk space was needed above and beyond the memory it had available. In the explain plan above, we see that multiple workers all had to use external disk to complete their branch of the execution, ranging anywhere from ~4MB to ~15MB. To do this work in memory, we can set work_mem to a different value for this session.

Setting the value to something slightly more than work_mem + external disk value (Listing 11-9), should allow the plan to do those operations in memory. In this case, with some experimentation, setting work_mem to at least 28MB provided the resources necessary to short in memory and reduce the execution time by 40%. The exact work_mem value that you need to use may differ slightly and is very dependent on how much data you have in the table, etc.

Listing 11-9. Setting work_mem for a session to reduce external disk operations

```
SET work_mem = '28MB';
...
->  Sort  (cost=278708.83..279589.63 rows=352322 width=37)
       Sort Key: f.film_id, rental.store_id
       Sort Method: quicksort  Memory: 27108kB
       Buffers: shared hit=150587 read=37929
       Worker 0:  Sort Method: quicksort  Memory: 26743kB
       Worker 1:  Sort Method: quicksort  Memory: 27093kB
...

Planning:
  Buffers: shared hit=17 read=29
Planning Time: 1.966 ms
Execution Time: 2456.494 ms
```

The one challenge with finding these problematic queries is that there is no PostgreSQL statistic view or metric that identifies each query that spills to disk. To find and track these queries over time, you must use a tool like "auto explain" to log slow queries and parse the plans separately. We'll discuss this in more detail at the end of the chapter.

Indexes

Indexes in relational databases like PostgreSQL are one of the most essential components to ensuring that the database is fast and efficient at querying data. When managed appropriately, indexes will often improve query performance more quickly than other methods. Again… when managed appropriately.

The same things you know about indexes in other database systems also hold true for PostgreSQL. Don't create an index for every column. Be diligent to root out duplicate indexes. Cull indexes that are never used. And a handful of other time-tested, sage advice.

Still, it's good to review the standard, and unique, features of PostgreSQL indexes to ensure your application is performing at the highest level.

Sequential Scans

In Chapter 9 we highlighted the six different index types that ship with PostgreSQL core. Adding indexes to tables is primarily to reduce the amount of effort the query planner and executor must expend to retrieve the requested data efficiently. Hopefully, that's a foundational understanding of why indexes are important.

When it comes to PostgreSQL this generally means trying to avoid sequential scans by using indexes where it makes sense. But remember from earlier in the chapter, even when a matching index exists, the PostgreSQL query planner is still more likely to choose a sequential scan once the estimated number of matching rows for a table reaches a calculated threshold of "work".

This doesn't specifically mean that every time a table is estimated to return more than 10% of the rows, for example, that the planner will always choose a sequential scan. PostgreSQL uses a cost-based planner, and the table storage is heap-based. Therefore, the query planner is more likely to choose a sequential scan when a lot of rows are going to be returned because the added effort of looking up the data pages in the index still requires the matching data pages to be retrieved. It's essentially twice the effort when scanning the pages in and filtering them ends up being more efficient from a cost perspective.

You'll also see this a lot on relatively small tables of data, even in the thousands of rows. Any time most of that small table is going to be needed to satisfy a query, the index scan will be skipped because reading in a few hundred pages of data is faster than picking and choosing through the index.

Regardless, utilizing indexes and the features that matter can have a big impact on performance, index maintenance, and index size.

B-Tree Deduplication

B-Tree indexes typically have a 1:1 ratio with the number of rows in the table. Even when many rows use the same indexed value, there is still a row in the index to point to each specific location of the matching data.

Starting in PostgreSQL 13, B-Tree indexes can be deduplicated so that one index entry can refer to multiple locations of data for the same value. This has two benefits. First, indexes are smaller because there are fewer rows in the index while still maintaining a pointer to every piece of data in the matching table. Second, because the indexes are smaller, fewer pages of data need to be read for an index scan operation which essentially means less overall effort.

The one gotcha is that existing indexes are not deduplicated when upgrading from a PostgreSQL 12 or below. Newer entries will be deduplicated, but if you want to ensure that older B-Tree indexes are fully deduplicated, you must reindex each of them after upgrading to PostgreSQL 13 or above.

Listing 11-10 demonstrates the impact of B-Tree deduplication on the total size of the index.

Listing 11-10. B-Tree indexes with and without deduplication

```
-- Automatic deduplication
CREATE INDEX rental_inventory_id_idx ON bluebox.rental USING btree
(inventory_id);

-- No deduplication
CREATE INDEX rental_inventory_id_idx_nondedup ON bluebox.rental USING
btree (inventory_id) WITH (deduplicate_items=OFF);

-- Query the size of the indexes
SELECT indexname, pg_size_pretty(pg_relation_size(pg.oid)) index_size
       FROM pg_indexes pi
JOIN pg_class pg ON pi.indexname = pg.relname
WHERE pi.tablename = 'rental'
AND indexname~*'inventory_id';
```

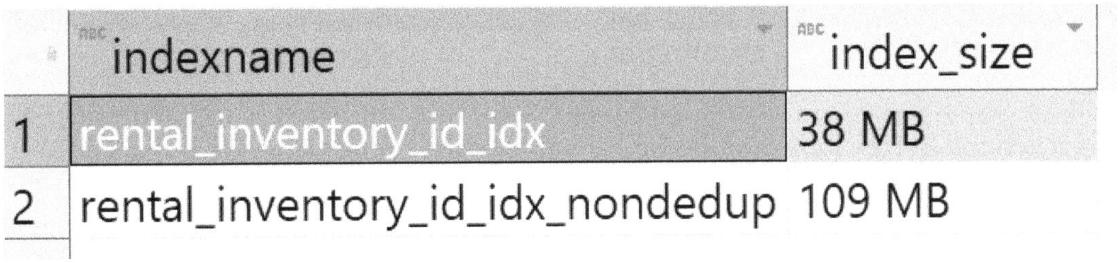

	indexname	index_size
1	rental_inventory_id_idx	38 MB
2	rental_inventory_id_idx_nondedup	109 MB

Figure 11-1. Index size differences with deduplication

As you can see, this one column index is nearly three times smaller with deduplication. That's a huge win as the index grows.

Functional Indexes

There are other times where the form of a predicate would preclude PostgreSQL from using the index. If you always search for rows with a lowercase string or a specific part of a range value, a generalized B-Tree index won't be used. In these cases, a functional index is needed.

For example, we often need to query the list of rentals that are outstanding. This is shown in the `rental_period` range type when the upper value is NULL. To demonstrate the impact of adding appropriate indexes, we'll use the query shown in Listing 11-11 and focus on the buffers read, the scan method, and the total time of execution without an index and then with a functional index.

Listing 11-11. Query for all rentals that are currently on loan

```
EXPLAIN (ANALYZE,buffers)
SELECT count(*) FROM bluebox.rental
WHERE upper(rental_period) IS NULL;
```

Without an index, PostgreSQL must do a sequential scan. If there is a lot of data and there are workers available, it will likely try to do a parallel scan to speed up the data retrieval. Regardless, it will have to read all pages of data for this table and then filter out rows that don't match.

Buffers	Method	Execution
52,000 (~415MB)	Parallel Scan	990ms

Adding a general B-Tree index on the upper value of the rental period (Listing 11-12) does have a dramatic impact on the query execution, at the expense of a larger index.

Listing 11-12. Create a functional index on the upper range value

```
CREATE INDEX rental_rental_period_upper ON bluebox.rental
USING btree (upper(rental_period))
```

Index Name	Index Size	Total Buffers	Scan Method	Total Execution Time
rental_rental_period_upper	86MB	13 pages (~100kB)	Bitmap Index Scan	1.2ms

The number of buffers read, and the query execution time is dramatically reduced! The index size is still large, which leaves us with an opportunity for more improvement with a partial index where it makes sense to use them.

Partial Indexes

Because PostgreSQL has a heavy tendency towards sequential scans when many rows match a filter rather than using the index, partial indexes can reduce the size of the index further and the overhead of maintaining that index.

If we add an index that only tracks outstanding rentals where the upper value of the rental period is NULL (Listing 11-13), we retain the value of the functional index but with significant savings in disk space used.

Listing 11-13. Create a filtered index

```
CREATE INDEX rental_rental_period_upper_null ON bluebox.rental
   USING btree (upper(rental_period))
WHERE upper(rental_period) IS NULL;
```

Index Name	Index Size	Total Buffers	Scan Method	Total Execution Time
rental_rental_period_upper_null	88kB	11 (~100KB)	Index Only Scan	1.3ms

As with any use of a feature like functional or partial indexes, your milage may vary. You must understand the query patterns of your application and if the index will be usable in the variety of cases that you need.

Composite Indexes

Earlier we talked about the problem of an index scan still requiring a second trip to the heap to get the matching pages of data. If some queries always filter on multiple columns of data, it can be beneficial to use a composite index.

Let's consider, for instance, that our customers always search for available inventory at a specific rental location (`store_id`). To determine which films are currently available, we need to filter inventory that is currently out on rental (WHERE `upper(rental_period)` IS NULL). An example query to get the information is shown in Listing 11-14.

Listing 11-14. Searching a specific store for rental inventory out on loan

```
EXPLAIN (ANALYZE,buffers)
SELECT DISTINCT film_id, title, popularity, rating, release_date
FROM film f
     JOIN inventory i USING (film_id)
WHERE i.store_id = 112
     AND f.title ~* '^s'
     AND inventory_id NOT IN (
   SELECT inventory_id FROM rental WHERE store_id=112
   AND upper(rental_period) IS NULL)
ORDER BY title, release_date, popularity DESC;
```

With the partial index in place from the previous section, this query performs an index scan on store_id and upper(rental_period).

```
...
  ->   BitmapAnd  (cost=753.95..753.95 rows=156 width=0)        |
            (actual time=4.098..4.115 rows=0 loops=1)           |
        Buffers: shared hit=34 read=11                          |
    ->  Bitmap Index Scan on rental_store_id_idx               |
            (cost=0.00..341.86 rows=31123 width=0)             |
            (actual time=3.091..3.092 rows=36823 loops=1)      |
          Index Cond: (store_id = 112)                         |
          Buffers: shared hit=34                               |
    ->  Bitmap Index Scan on rental_rental_period_upper_null|
            (cost=0.00..411.76 rows=25511 width=0)             |
            (actual time=0.252..0.268 rows=9875 loops=1)       |
          Index Cond: (upper(rental_period) IS NULL)           |
          Buffers: shared read=11                              |
...                                                             |
Planning:                                                      |
  Buffers: shared hit=30 read=2                                |
Planning Time: 1.099 ms                                        |
Execution Time: 7.832 ms                                       |
```

While the ability to make use of two different indexes like this is pretty cool, if it turns out that the application only ever searches for available (or rented) films by store, rather than maintain two separate indexes, we could create a single multi-column index (Listing 11-15) to reduce overhead for these very focused queries.

Listing 11-15. *Create a composite index by store and outstanding rentals*

```
CREATE INDEX rental_store_id_upper_rental_null_idx
ON bluebox.rental USING btree (store_id, upper(rental_period))
WHERE upper(rental_period) IS NULL;
```

On this sample database with around 5 million rental records, the created index is less than 100kB in size. The same query, however, executes 50% faster!

```
...
SubPlan 1
  ->  Bitmap Heap Scan on rental
        (cost=5.49..606.35 rows=156 width=4)
        (actual time=0.013..0.069 rows=69 loops=1)
        Recheck Cond: ((store_id = 112)
                      AND (upper(rental_period) IS NULL))
        Heap Blocks: exact=54
        Buffers: shared hit=56
        ->  Bitmap Index Scan on
            rental_store_id_upper_rental_null_idx
              (cost=0.00..5.46 rows=156 width=0)
              (actual time=0.007..0.007 rows=69 loops=1)
            Index Cond: (store_id = 112)
            Buffers: shared hit=2


...
Planning:
  Buffers: shared hit=13
Planning Time: 0.414 ms
Execution Time: 3.096 ms
```

Granted, this is a sample database with a relatively small set of data. While your mileage may vary, it's worth remembering that in some situations, composite indexes are a great tool to have at your disposal.

One drawback to consider is that the more columns you add as part of the index key, the greater potential to have more frequent page splits at the index level as time goes on. Like other in database management systems, indexes are stored in sort order on each index page. At some point, if PostgreSQL needs to insert an index reference to a page but there's no more space, the page is split in half to create room while keeping the index in order.

The full process is a bit more complex than that, but the principle holds true. Don't simply create multi-column indexes to satisfy every query that filters on two or more columns, after all, Postgres can always make use of bitmap joins if it needs to. That said, when it will help in a specific way and you understand the overhead you may incur, go for it. Just be aware that you may be creating more maintenance overhead on the indexes, and we want PostgreSQL to avoid unnecessary work whenever we can.

Covering Indexes

Composite indexes shouldn't be confused with covering indexes, even though they can often serve a similar purpose.

Remember that even when there is an index scan in PostgreSQL, the plan executor must retrieve the data pages separately, which can cause a lot of extra I/O on disk. Sometimes, there are queries that are filtered on the same column, and always request the same subset of columns from a table. In these cases, it may be helpful to include columns with the indexed value to save an extra request for the data pages.

Looking at our sample query from before, we can see that we return the title of the film and a few key metrics to display to a customer that is searching for films. We still only need to filter on the film_id column, but if we can eliminate a second trip to retrieve more data pages by creating a covering index (Listing 11-16), the query may be more efficient.

Listing 11-16. *Create a covering index for film properties*

```
CREATE INDEX film_film_id_incl ON bluebox.film
USING btree (film_id)
INCLUDE (title, popularity, rating, release_date);
```

With that index in place, the query time is reduced another 40% because PostgreSQL can retrieve all data from the index alone; an Index Only Scan.

```
...
 ->  Index Only Scan using film_film_id_incl on film f
        (cost=0.28..0.75 rows=1 width=38)
        (actual time=0.001..0.001 rows=0 loops=291)
                Index Cond: (film_id = i.film_id)
                  Filter: (title ~* '^s'::text)
                Rows Removed by Filter: 1
                        Heap Fetches: 0
                        Buffers: shared hit=583
Planning:
  Buffers: shared hit=13
Planning Time: 0.323 ms
Execution Time: 1.937 ms
```

Covering indexes, like composite indexes, can be tricky business. As with many things in technology, new tools become our hammers, and every performance tuning problem looks like a nail. Obviously, this will increase the size of your index, which comes at some cost, but if it effectively reduces the amount of work needed to satisfy the query, consider using one.

Logging Query Plans

We've talked about a lot in this chapter. Learning how to read an explain plan, thinking about some common indexing patterns, and knowing a few parameters that can be adjusted to help queries perform better is just the tip of the iceberg. If you are writing complex queries or triaging a query that is causing performance problems, these first steps will get you started on your query tuning journey.

But how do you find queries that may be causing performance issues over time? `pg_stat_statements` and `auto_explain`.

For the rest of this chapter, we'll just be talking about auto explain. Using various monitoring views in PostgreSQL will be covered in Chapter 15, including the use of pg_stat_statements to identify query performance over time.

Auto Explain

PostgreSQL doesn't include a "fancy", built-in mechanism like SQL Server Query Store for recording individual query plans, coupled with individual statistics, over time. All the data and metrics are available, they just need to be stitched together using external programs or specific extensions.

Instead, the auto_explain extension ships with PostgreSQL as a core module which can be used to log an execution plan for queries that meet specified criteria. The purpose of auto_explain is not to log every execution plan. Doing so will fill the log quickly and you will incur (some) overhead on every query execution for almost no return.

To enable auto_explain, it must first be enabled in the configuration to be loaded when the PostgreSQL cluster starts. This is accomplished by adding it to the shared preload libraries setting in configuration.

postgresql.conf

```
shared_preload_libraries='auto_explain'
```

Once the library is loaded, you need to configure the thresholds so that PostgreSQL knows when it should consider running EXPLAIN on the query to log it for later inspection. These configuration settings are also added to the postgresql.conf file, or through a UI console from your chosen provider.

If you use a tool like Redgate Monitor to log queries and execution plans, the vendor will often provide recommended settings to ensure you get the most value out of logging plans. The main settings you need to think about and change fall into two categories: what criteria must be met to log an execution plan, and if it will be logged, what query plan metrics are added to the plan itself.

Criteria to trigger plan logging

auto_explain.log_min_duration (default: -1):
Queries that take longer to execute than this value are candidates to be logged, after considering additional settings. Setting this to a zero or a low value (100ms or less), is not recommended, otherwise there will be significant overhead simply trying log nearly every query.

Instead, take time to consider how to define what a "slow" query is for your application or organization. If you expect most queries to execute in under 200ms (even "complex" queries), then make that your threshold to log queries that take longer. Because of the overhead that's incurred, your organization may only want to log queries that are clearly slow, maybe setting the value to a few seconds.

auto_explain.sample_rate (default: 1):
Once a query has exceeded the execution time threshold, sample some fraction of the queries that could be logged. This is a fractional value between 0 and 1. By default, auto_explain will sample all queries that exceed the minimum time. Setting this value correctly can take some time and is very dependent on your application, the load on your database server, and how often you expect queries to exceed the timing threshold.

Generally, the lower your logging threshold, the smaller fraction of plans you should sample. The higher the execution time threshold is set, the more queries you should log.

The only drawback to a lower sampling frequency is that you can miss logging some execution plans if a query is long but runs infrequently. Even though it is eligible, it might not be sampled and there's no way to go back and retrieve the query plan later. We recommend doing some back of the napkin calculations based on your typical transactions per second and start with some fraction of that number. If you continue to miss logged execution plans for queries of interest, consider raising the minimum execution time parameter along with the sampling rate so that more query plans are logged, but only for queries that are truly slow and of interest.

auto_explain.log_format (default: text):
The format of the execution plan that is logged. Most tools that can read PostgreSQL logs and help you dig into execution plans will have a preferred format like JSON. If you're not using a tool to help you automate the collection of execution plans (you should be!), use something like 'text' to start so that the plans are readable like normal execution plans.

auto_explain.log_analyze (default: off):
This setting determines if auto_explain logs an estimated query plan or **executes** EXPLAIN ANALYZE to acquire actual runtime metrics. Estimated plans are cheaper to create and have significantly lower impact on the execution and logging process, however, there is less actionable data to help identify the nodes of the plan which need attention.

You will get the most valuable information by turning this on, however, you will incur more overhead on each query.

auto_explain.log_(buffers | wal | timing | triggers | etc.):
The other settings help you further configure what kind of information is logged along with the execution plan. Some of these, like log_timing, will incur more overhead, so be thoughtful about when to enable it. One way to manage this trade-off is to try to log the queries with minimal information via auto_explain, and then once you know

which queries to dial in on, make use of the SQL level EXPLAIN command to get those additional details.

Reading Execution Plans from the Log

Accessing execution plans from the logs depends on your permissions and hosting environment. The most convenient way is to use an extension like `file_fdw` or a vendor specific extension like `log_fdw`. This provides a mechanism to query logs like a regular table to extract the information, like execution plans, that you need. See the documentation from your PostgreSQL provider to better understand what options they provide for reading PostgreSQL logs.

More Resources

This chapter is just the beginning on using EXPLAIN, indexes, and auto_explain. However, regardless of how you obtain an execution plan, it can be helpful to have a tool that reads the plan and provides insights on areas for improvement. At the time of this writing, a few options you can explore include:

explain.depesz.com:

A free, online query plan analyzer that is popular within the community. It is not a visual query plan viewer but focuses instead on offering a clear view of where time and effort are being spent to help you focus your work.

explain.dalibo.com

This is an open-source plan visualization tool. It shows node relationships and highlights areas for improvement, similar to explaining.depesz.com.

pgMustard.com

pgMustard is a subscription product that provides insights into query plans using machine learning and unique ways of identifying areas for improvement.

Redgate Monitor

Redgate Monitor provides query plan visualization for all queries logged by auto_explain, above and beyond the plethora of metrics it tracks and alerts on.

12
Backup and Restore

The backup process is a vital first step for the even more important process, a restore. A friend, Kimberley Tripp, once said, "You're only as good as your last restore." The issue is, the information under management within your PostgreSQL databases must be protected. One of the most fundamental protections is the ability to restore the data should something horrible occur. This chapter will introduce the concept of backing up a database and the process to restore databases as well. Topics will include:

- Defining a restore strategy

- Backing up an entire database

- Backing up the Write Ahead Log

- Restoring a whole database

- Restoring to a point in time

The single most important part of managing a PostgreSQL data store is the ability to recover in the event of a disaster. Backups are the first building block in your disaster recovery process.

Restore Strategy

Figuring out what backups you need to run, how you need to run them, and how often, means that you need to reverse your thinking. Instead of worrying about the backups, you need to focus first on your restores. In order to decide on a restore strategy, you need to understand two concepts first: Recovery Point Objectives (RPO) and Recovery Time Objectives (RTO).

Your Recovery Point Objective (RPO) is best described as the question: "How much data is your organization prepared to lose?". Yes, the answer is always zero initially, but then the costs of ensuring as close to zero data loss as possible are explained and suddenly, yes, the organization can afford to lose 5 minutes, 2 hours, a day, or even a week of data. This is primarily a business discussion, not a technical one. You have to understand the business in order to understand what amount of data loss is acceptable. However, with that amount in mind, you can then determine what type of backup, and its frequency, is most appropriate. For example, if a business says that a day of losses, while not ideal, wouldn't cause inordinate pain for the organization. Maybe they run off a data load that's easily repeatable, so having a daily backup is adequate. In this case, you simply need to schedule once-daily complete database backups and you're good to go. Another example would be that more than 10 minutes of lost data would be a problem. In this case, in addition to complete backups, you will need to capture the Write Ahead Log (WAL) at least every 10 minutes in order to provide the ability to restore your database to a point in time. And by "a point in time" we literally mean, selecting a date and time to restore your databases to. Regardless of the situation, you need to determine your RPO with your business providing input.

Next, you have to look at the Recovery Time Objective (RTO). This would be the amount of time it takes to restore a database, based on the RPO. This time is less business-oriented and more technical, although the business is going to want to weigh in. For example, if the RPO states that a daily database backup is adequate, then the RTO will simply be, how long does that restore process take, with larger databases expected to take longer. On the other hand, the RPO of 10 minutes means you'll first have to restore the database, and then replay the WAL files to a point in time. The combined time these take will be your RTO. You may find that the WAL replay time is too long, in which case, you need to get the complete backup more frequently so that you have fewer WAL files to replay. There are, of course, implications to all of this, but the basic concepts are simple.

With the RPO and RTO in hand, you can then decide what kind of backups you need to run, and how frequently you need to run them - all to ensure the ability to restore the information needed by the organization.

Database Backups

There are three mechanisms for getting a database backup. The first is to create what is called a dump. The second is to do a file system backup. And third is a more comprehensive mechanism for backing up the file system called a base backup. A dump file is basically an export of the database, each object definition, the tables, functions, etc., and all the data, database by database. The dump is internally consistent, meaning it will successfully restore all the data at the point you created the dump. The file system backup is simply a copy of the file system where the database is stored. However, in order for the file system backup to be internally consistent, your server must first be taken offline, which may be an issue for some organizations. The base backup is a way to basically do a file-based copy of the whole server (note, not individual databases) that includes the WAL, or Write Ahead Log, in order to completely recover the backup. The base backup is the foundation for a point in time recovery, covered in a later section of the book.

Let's get an overview of each of the two mechanisms, then we'll do a short comparison between them.

NOTE: It's worth mentioning that there are multiple third-party extensions that provide several additional mechanisms for backup and restore. You may want to research those in addition to understanding the native means of backup and restore, depending on your organization and its requirements. Additionally, some hardware configurations allow for different mechanisms of backup and restore, independent of PostgreSQL behaviors. These are also outside the scope of the book and require external research.

SQL Dump

A dump from PostgreSQL is quite literally a collection of the necessary SQL commands to recreate the database, including inserting all the data. That's it - it really is that simple. Creating a dump is also quite simple. A utility is built into PostgreSQL that performs the dump, pg_dump. You can run this remotely, providing the appropriate host and login, or you can run it locally on the server hosting PostgreSQL. Listing 12-1 shows the simplest pg_dump command, running locally:

Listing 12-1. Creating a dump of bluebox

```
pg_dump bluebox > bluebox.dmp
```

In order for this to run as is, the login that you're connected to in bash (or however you're running commands against your server) must have permissions to the PostgreSQL server, the database in question, and the file system. For example, we changed the login within the bash command to the postgres user using Listing 12-2 before running the command:

Listing 12-2. Changing the user in bash

```
su postgres
```

To be able to run the command, we also switched directories to the bu directory where the postgres login had permissions on this system. This isn't a requirement, merely the security setup locally, and yours may vary. A partial listing of the output is shown in Figure 12-1:

```
CREATE SEQUENCE public.country_country_id_seq
    START WITH 1
    INCREMENT BY 1
    NO MINVALUE
    NO MAXVALUE
    CACHE 1;


ALTER SEQUENCE public.country_country_id_seq OWNER TO postgres;

--
-- Name: customer; Type: TABLE; Schema: public; Owner: postgres
--

CREATE TABLE public.customer (
    customer_id bigint NOT NULL,
    store_id integer NOT NULL,
    full_name text NOT NULL,
    email text,
    phone text,
    zip_code integer,
    activebool boolean DEFAULT true NOT NULL,
    create_date date DEFAULT CURRENT_DATE NOT NULL,
    geog public.geography(Point,4326),
    last_update timestamp with time zone DEFAULT now()
);


ALTER TABLE public.customer OWNER TO postgres;
```

Figure 12-1. Some of the SQL output from a dump

You can see the basic commands for creating a sequence, a table, and altering ownership to show how a restore operation would work.

NOTE: While we used the somewhat standard *.dmp for the dump file output extension, others are possible. Robert Treat (our technical editor) recommends using *.sql if the dump doesn't require `pg_restore`, *.pgr if it absolutely requires `pg_restore`, and *.pgdump to show people you used the dump command to create the backup.

We can also run `pg_dump` remotely, away from the server, on a client machine, assuming security access. Listing 12-3:

Listing 12-3. *Dump data from a remote server*

```
pg_dump -U postgres -h db_server bluebox > bluebox.dmp
```

We have to provide the database user (in this case, postgres), the server We're connecting to, a server called db_server for the example, and then provide the database and the output file as well.

Not only do you control the name of the output file but, within your permissions of course, you control the path to the location of the output file:

Listing 12-4. *Controlling where the dump file goes*

```
pg_dump -U postgres -h db_server bluebox > \bu\bluebox.dmp
```

This is the same command as Listing 12-3, but now we have chosen to put the backup into the \bu folder.

That covers the basics of how to use `pg_dump`. From there you have a number of different options that you could add to change behaviors. A few of them include:

- -F: Determines the format for the dump file, which can include a compressed tar format as well as others. This is very commonly used to save space.

- -c: Adds `DROP` commands to the dump in order to clear the existing database during a restore operation

- -N: Allows you to filter the database objects being exported by the dump operation to exclude some objects based on namespace, or schema.

- -a: Dump only the data from the database.

- -s: Dump only the schema from the database.

- -C: adds a create database command to the dump (this will be covered in more detail in the Database Restores section.

For a complete listing of all that you can do with `pg_dump`, read the PostgreSQL documentation (https://tinyurl.com/mf8xvws5).

One additional way to use pg_dump is take advantage of a wrapper around pg_dump called pg_dumpall. This will back up all databases on a server. Further, since pg_dump doesn't include global objects such as roles, if you want to include those for your restore operation, you'll need to use pg_dumpall. You can even output it all to a single file, making it possible to transfer a whole server around. It does have limitations though, such as no compressed formatting on the file. It will limit the full extent of the functionality of pg_restore (more on that in the section on Database Restores).

File System Backup

There are actually two ways you can run the file system backup. I'll refer to the basic operation here but for point in time recovery, working with the Write Ahead Log (WAL), there's a second mechanism. We'll cover that in the Point in Time Recovery section.

The basic idea behind the file system backup is that you can use just about any command you want to copy and store the files that make up the database. You're simply dealing with files because - and this is the key - PostgreSQL itself has been shut down.

For most users, shutting down the database to take a backup is not practical, so this is not a commonly used approach to getting backups for PostgreSQL. That said, there are multiple third-party tools and advanced file system techniques that can be used to overcome these limitations, so we wanted to include it as part of the introduction to the concept. For many users however, instead of attempting to use this mechanism, it is advised to use pg_basebackup as described in the next section.

Base Backups

Base backups use another utility to perform the system level file copy but, unlike attempting to copy the file system yourself, the base backup can be run against a functioning PostgreSQL server. The mechanism uses a different utility, pg_basebackup. Basically, the process temporarily puts the server into a backup mode and then back to normal. For this to work, a checkpoint marker in the WAL files will be issued to the databases. Then, when the files are copied, the necessary WAL files are also copied (although a more advanced way involves streaming the WAL files as you go). Backups done through `pg_basebackup` are for the entire cluster, not individual databases or parts of databases. If you need that kind of behavior, `pg_dump` is still the go-to.

While base backups can be used just as backups for the databases on the cluster, they are generally used for more. Base backups are the foundation for a point in time recovery operation, and they are also used as the foundation for replication within PostgreSQL.

The most basic operation of `pg_basebackup` is shown in Listing 12-5:

Listing 12-5. *Running pg_basebackup*

```
pg_basebackup -D /bu/mybase
```

The directory that you send the output to must be empty. That means for repeated backups you either have to clear out the directory first, or go to a new directory. If the directory doesn't exist, `pg_basebackup` will create it. The output is visible in Figure 12-2:

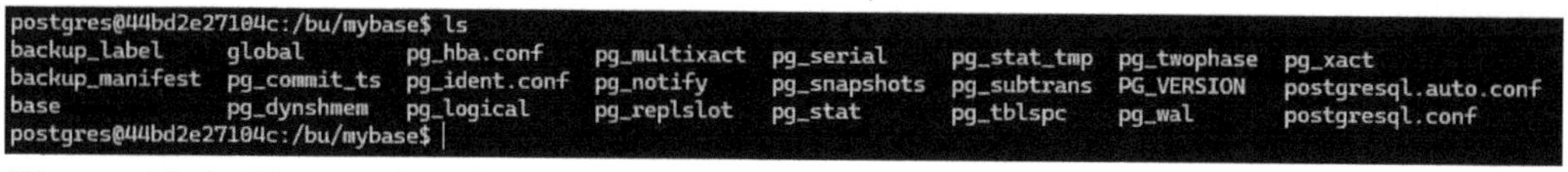

Figure 12-2. *The results of running pg_basebackup*

The output is a copy of all the file structures needed to restore the cluster.

The command is run using the replication protocol, so whatever user is used to run `pg_basebackup` must have `REPLICATION` permissions.

Otherwise, running `pg_basebackup` is somewhat similar to running `pg_dump`. There are a number of possible options that can affect how the backup runs as well. Here are just a few:

- -F: Similar to `pg_dump`, this lets you decide if you want plain text, the default, or compression to a tar file

- -X: This determines how to deal with the WAL files, -Xn for none, -Xf for "fetch" which retrieves the WAL files at the end, or -Xs for stream, copying the WAL files in line as the backup is created, the default.

- -Z: Gives you the ability to control how compression is run which can help you tune the load on the server.

- -P: Shows the progress of the backup process as it runs.

Comparing Backup Mechanisms

Now that you know the basic means of backing up the database within PostgreSQL, the question is simple: which one to use? In general, as was already stated, we would shy away from using file system backup because it requires you to completely shut down your cluster, so it comes down to either pg_dump or pg_basebackup.

The strengths of pg_dump are:

- You can back up individual databases.

- Individual parts of a database can be backed up.

- Backups themselves will generally be smaller.

- You can restore across versions of PostgreSQL. (It is recommended to always use newer pg_dump against older servers, but an older sql dump file, for example, will likely restore on a newer server. As always, testing is required to confirm it).

- The backup is complete, no WAL files needed.

The weaknesses for pg_dump are:

- It doesn't allow for a point in time recovery, which may be the biggest point against it.

- Generally longer time for backup and longer time for restore.

By contrast, there are strengths and weaknesses to pg_basebackup. The strengths include:

- The ability to perform a point in time recovery

- Foundation for a standby server and replication

- A faster backup process

And the weaknesses include:

- A larger amount of backup space needed.

- You must include WAL files (or stream them during the backup).

- You're always backing up the whole cluster.

- You can only restore to the same version the backup was taken from

With all that in mind, what is the answer? Well, it comes back to your recovery strategy. If your RPO suggests that a nightly backup is sufficient, you can probably just use pg_dump. As soon as the RPO suggests that a narrower window will be better, you're almost certainly going to be using pg_basebackup in order to be able to restore to a point in time. But, none of that precludes mixing and matching as needed. For example, while your standard backups may all be done through pg_basebackup, when it comes time to migrate to a new version of PostgreSQL, you may use pg_dump to get a backup that will move successfully. In other words, both tools have their purposes, so use them where it's appropriate and don't feel as if you need to show loyalty to one over the other.

Restoring a Database

If you're using pg_dump to create your database backups, you can restore a single database. Otherwise, if you're using pg_basebackup, you restore the whole file system of the server, meaning all of the databases in the cluster instead of just one. We'll cover how to restore backups from pg_basebackup in the next section on Point In Time recovery.

To get started with a restore of a database, you first need an empty database in which to run your restore command. That is, unless you run pg_dump with both -c to add DROP commands, and -C to add a CREATE DATABASE command. In which case, you'll just get a DROP DATABASE command before the CREATE DATABASE command.

For our purposes, let's assume that we ran the pg_dump command in Listing 12-1. If we want to restore that to the server, we first need to have an empty database. Let's run the commands here in Listing 12-6:

Listing 12-6. Preparing a database for a restore

```
DROP DATABASE bluebox;
CREATE DATABASE bluebox WITH TEMPLATE template0;
```

You will need to ensure that no one is connected to the database in order to drop it. Then, when you create a blank database, use template0. This is because it is somewhat common to put objects into template1 so that they are created with each new database.

Those objects will be backed up by the PostgreSQL backup process. So, in order to ensure a successful restore, they shouldn't be in the database. This is why it's good practice to always reference template0 when running a restore.

Since the backup from pg_dump is simply a set of SQL scripts that recreates the database, including all the data stored as plain text, you could just run that SQL script. Listing 12-7 shows how to use psql to do just that:

Listing 12-7. Using psql to run the backup scripts

```
psql -U postgres -d bluebox -f bluebox.dmp
```

That will only work if you created the backup as plain text. Since compression is very commonly used, it would take additional steps to get at the script. Instead, another utility is included with PostgreSQL, pg_restore. You will need to drop the database as before, but you don't have to create a new one. Listing 12-8 shows how to run pg_restore:

Listing 12-8. Running pg_restore as simply as possible

```
pg_restore -C -d postgres bluebox.tar
```

Several options are at work. The -d sets a database from which to run the necessary CREATE DATABASE statement, because pg_restore will handle that for you. You can also use -d to change the database you're restoring to. We also used -C which will create the database defined within the dump file. Finally, of course, you provide a path and file name for pg_restore to run against.

As with the other utilities, you can run pg_restore remotely from a client machine as well as from the machine hosting your cluster. In that case you just have to provide the host, a login and password.

You also get a lot of options on how you run pg_restore, similar to the other utilities. For example, Listing 12-9 doesn't actually restore a database. Instead, it lists the objects included in the dump:

Listing 12-9. Listing objects within the dump file

```
pg_restore -l bluebox.tar
```

The output will look something like Figure 12-3:

```
postgres@444bd2e27104c:/bu$ pg_restore -l bluebox.tar
;
; Archive created at 2024-07-10 14:47:03 UTC
;     dbname: bluebox
;     TOC Entries: 172
;     Compression: gzip
;     Dump Version: 1.15-0
;     Format: CUSTOM
;     Integer: 4 bytes
;     Offset: 8 bytes
;     Dumped from database version: 16.3 (Debian 16.3-1.pgdg110+1)
;     Dumped by pg_dump version: 16.3 (Debian 16.3-1.pgdg110+1)
;
;
; Selected TOC Entries:
;
7; 2615 33663 SCHEMA - geofaker postgres
8; 2615 2200 SCHEMA - public postgres
9; 2615 33664 SCHEMA - staging postgres
2; 3079 33665 EXTENSION - pg_stat_statements
4548; 0 0 COMMENT - EXTENSION pg_stat_statements
3; 3079 33696 EXTENSION - postgis
4549; 0 0 COMMENT - EXTENSION postgis
1719; 1247 34775 DOMAIN public bigint postgres
1722; 1247 34777 TYPE public mpaa_rating postgres
1725; 1247 34790 DOMAIN public year postgres
322; 1255 34792 FUNCTION geofaker n_points_in_polygon(public.geometry, integer) postgres
```

Figure 12-3. A listing of the objects within the dump file

This is just `pg_restore` reaching into the dump file and pulling out the information (no actual restore is run), but this helps the next piece of functionality within `pg_restore`: you can restore individual objects.

There are a number of parameters that you can supply `pg_restore` that lets you name individual objects. Let's say, someone accidentally dropped a function. You could use `pg_restore` to just restore_ that one function (created in a previous chapter) to the database using Listing 12-10:

Listing 12-10. Using pg_restore to restore a single object

```
pg_restore -d bluebox -P 'film_crew_info()' bluebox.tar
```

The key here is to ensure that the function name and all parameters are listed exactly as they are in the dump file. This is where the ability to list the objects in a dump from Listing 12-9 comes into play.

You can restore individual tables, indexes or even simply provide a list of objects, using -L and a file, to restore a subset of the dump file. If any of the objects already exist, you will generate an error.

There are a number of other mechanisms within pg_restore, including:

- -a: You can restore just the data and not the schema.

- -c: Issues DROP statements for all objects before restoring. This is used for restoring to an existing database instead of dropping and recreating it.

- -J: Defining a number of jobs, to run the restore in parallel on machines with multiple processors in order to speed up a restore.

- -n: Restore only the specified schema

- -s: A schema-only restore of the database (no data)

There are a number of additional options. For more information on pg_restore, please refer to the PostgreSQL documentation (https://tinyurl.com/mvxr62my).

Restoring to a Point in Time

While using pg_dump and pg_restore solves a whole lot of issues when it comes to recovery, the one thing they don't deal with is recovery to a point in time. That requires two things: archiving of the Write Ahead Logs (WAL) and using the results of pg_basebackup as the start point for the restore.

Let's be clear on the concept. With a backup from pg_dump, that dump file represents the only point in time to which you can restore. Being able to take advantage of the file level backups from pg_basebackup combined with the WAL, you can literally pick a moment - provided that you have the backup and the correct set of WAL files - that you wish to restore to. That moment can be in the middle of one of the WAL files, as long as it includes the time the pg_basebackup was taken, and the complete chain of WAL files from that moment until the one you're interested in.

In order to restore to a point in time, you must first have WAL Archiving enabled. The Write Ahead Logs are a series of rolling files, each 16MB by default. As each one fills, a new file with a new name is created. In these files are the logs of what happened on the database, from inserts to deletes and object creation. In order to use the WAL to effectively play back the transactions on your restore, you must first create an archive of WAL files.

WAL Archiving

To make this work, you have to have a location where you can write the WAL files. This can be anything from attached storage to cloud-based file shares or any other place where you can copy the files after they are filled. Next, you need to be able to create a batch command that can move the file to the appropriate storage location.

Once we have our storage in place, we have to make some configuration changes to our database. First, we have to change the wal_level within our PostgreSQL database. There are three options; minimal, replica, or logical. Each one adds additional information to the WAL. Minimal maintains as little information within the log as possible. Enough to support recovery from an unplanned outage, but not enough for a point in time recovery. You must use either replica or logical in order to enable WAL archiving. The default is replica, so unless you've explicitly changed your wal_level, this should be ready.

Next, we have to change the configuration setting archive_mode. The setting has three values: off (default), on and always.
'On' is self-explanatory, while 'always' is a setting for working with replication and goes far beyond our introduction to the concepts here. Editing the postgresql.conf file can be done through nano, vim, or whatever your OS allows. To find your configuration file, you can use the SQL command in Listing 12-11:

Listing 12-11. Locating the config file in PostgreSQL

```
SHOW config_file;
```

When you have the file open, you should see the `archive_mode` setting in the file. If not, you can add it. Set it so that it looks like this:

```
archive_mode = on
```

Next, you have to add, or change, the configuration setting for the `archive_command`. This is what will move the finished WAL files to your archive location. We have created a local directory, just for testing purposes, and we're copying the files to there through the command in Listing 12-12:

Listing 12-12. Archive command definition in postgresql.conf

```
archive_command = 'test ! -f /walarchive/%f $$ cp %p /walarchive/%f'
```

This is just a simple copy command to illustrate the process but, in production, you can and should absolutely make this more sophisticated. Better yet, you can look into some of the third-party scripts that manage this process for you. It verifies that the file doesn't exist through the test command, then it copies the file over. The %f is a placeholder for the file name. %p is a placeholder for the finished WAL file that is getting archived.

After you've made the changes to the configuration file, you will have to restart the cluster.

Recovery To a Point In Time

In addition to setting up WAL Archiving, the assumption is that you are running pg_basebackup on a regular basis. Both are necessary to arrive at a point in time restore. This process isn't simple. We would strongly recommend you practice this a bunch. Also, prep the restore scripts ahead of time so you're not scrambling to piece it all together in an emergency.

1. Assuming you can access the server, run the SQL function pg_switch_wal. This will close out the current WAL file allowing it to get archived, making it available for your restore later.
2. Stop the server (if it's online).
3. Remove all files and subdirectories in your data directory, or better still, in a new directory if you're on the same server.
4. Restore the Base Backup files from wherever they are stored.
5. Remove all files from pg_wal/, they're old since we have archiving.
6. Change settings in postgresql.conf to start the recovery process.
7. Create a file called recovery.signal in the cluster data directory.
8. Start the service.

We will need to address a few of these steps in more detail to understand how a restore to a point in time works.

Running pg_switch_wal requires a connection so you can run a query: SELECT pg_switch_wal(). That will cause the WAL to close the current file and because you have archiving set up, it'll get added to the archive location. If you can't connect, you can try to copy the file from the pg_wal directory to a safe location.

You can stop the server using the utility pg_ctl. Issue it a 'stop' command to stop the service. When it's time to start the service again, you can call, pg_ctl start.

Since the base backup copies all the files, to restore them you first need to remove them from the system. The process will be expecting to move files into those directories, and if files are there, it will cause errors instead of a successful recovery. The exception is the pg_wal directory. If you want to restore just the backups from pg_basebackup, that's fine. Leave pg_wal in place. However, since we're going to a point in time based on the archive of the WAL files, it's best to clean out this one folder after you restore the rest. How you remove the directory depends on the OS. Same thing with the copy from backup. If you do drop and recreate the directory, make sure you set the postgresql user as the owner with appropriate security:

Listing 12-13. Setting appropriate security in new folders

```
sudo chown postgres:postgres /var/lib/postgresql/16/data
sudo chmod 700 /var/lib/postgresql/16/data
```

There isn't a utility to launch recovery. Instead, you edit the postgresql.conf file. There should be a setting called restore_command within the configuration file. It's likely commented out. Remove the comment and edit the path. The default will be:

```
/path/to/database_archive/
```

In this case, we're going to change it to:

```
/walarchive
```

The full command would then be Listing 12-14:

Listing 12-14. Changes to the postgresql.conf file for a point in time restore

```
restore_command = 'cp /walarchive/$f %p'
```

Finally, because we want to restore to a point in time, we have to specify the stopping point. It can be a time, a log sequence number, a transaction id or, if we've created restore points (beyond the scope of the book), a restore point. Assuming time, I'll add this below the restore_command:

```
recovery_target_time = '2024-07-10 15:24:00 EDT'
```

As for the recovery.conf file, it's simply meant to be a safety switch. You'll create an empty file with that name. When the service is started again, recovery.conf will be renamed to recovery.done. This prevents the system from going into recovery every time it gets restarted.

With all that in play, your entire cluster will be restored. The files will be copied from their storage within the structures created by `pg_basebackup`. Then the entries in the necessary WAL files will be replayed until the point in time specified as recovery_target_time is met.

Conclusion

It bears repeating, your most important goal is to have a restore strategy, not a backup strategy. Define your RPO and RTO with the help of the business, and then use those definitions to build your backup mechanisms. Use a scheduling utility, such as cron, and backup your databases and WAL using the mechanisms that are best for your restore strategy. A very good practice is to run restores regularly, to be sure you know how to do so when you're in an emergency.

13
MVCC, VACUUM, and ANALYZE

In computer programming, there's a long-standing joke that there are three hard problems to get right: variable names, cache invalidation, and "off by one" errors. In database systems, one of the hardest problems to solve is how to effectively deal with concurrent operations and data access.

Over the years, database management systems have used various mechanisms for allowing concurrent access to data while trying to reduce conflicts between sessions. The most traditional approach was to use a locking method to prevent current access in a way that would violate the read-committed transaction isolation level. If a query needed to read a lot of rows or update a subset of data, the database system might lock a range of rows, access to the physical data pages, or the entire table of data. While this ensured that only one session could modify data at a time and all other sessions read the most up-to-date value, users and developers often had to contend with higher rates of blocking or deadlocks. I mean, SQL Server developers proliferated the NOLOCK keyword for a (misunderstood) reason, right?

However, modern applications of the last few decades require high levels of concurrency with minimum impact on the ability of other sessions to read and write data. Therefore, an approach that reduces or nearly eliminates the use of locking to accomplish this was needed. To that end, Multi-version Concurrency Control (MVCC) has been the method chosen by many relational databases for the last 20+ years to handle demanding workloads that increase year after year. While the implementations differ, the basic goal is the same:

Readers should not block writers, and writers should not block readers.

At a technical level, this is accomplished through row versioning, where each transaction retains their own snapshot of the database to ensure consistency with the chosen isolation level. Understanding how the row versions are managed in PostgreSQL is essential to maintaining a properly functioning database.

MVCC in PostgreSQL

PostgreSQL is unique in the way it manages concurrency and row versioning in at least two ways.

First, all information about a specific row version is maintained within the row itself using a few special columns that are never returned with the row data unless you specifically ask for them (and it's rarely helpful to do so, anyway). There is no extra versioning table or temporary table involved as databases like SQL Server use to manage row versions in snapshot isolation.

Second, every insert or update statement creates a new row version in the table, while every delete statement only marks the row for deletion later and does not immediately remove the data from the table. Transactions can only see row versions that they have access to (discussed more later), but every row version takes space on disk until that version is no longer needed by other transactions. These old rows, called *dead tuples*, are eventually cleaned up by the vacuum process and the space is returned to the table for new row data.

On the surface, managing row versions using data available in each row is a very straightforward way of implementing MVCC. However, as modern applications and their heavy workloads have required more concurrency, other flags and processes have been added to help keep tables and row versions well managed. Over time, these changes have allowed PostgreSQL to work well in very large and active environments, but it has complicated the process of supporting healthy table data and being able to understand its state.

Row Versions

Every row, in every table, stores additional information about the state of each row version to help determine which row versions are visible to any specific transaction. The hidden columns that pertain to our discussion of MVCC in PostgreSQL are *xmin* and *xmax*.

When a row is created, the transaction ID (XID) that created the row is stored in *xmin*, while the xmax column is initially left blank. When the row is eventually updated or deleted, the XID that changed the row version will be stored in the *xmax* column. The information in these two columns, along with a few other external bits about transaction state we won't discuss here, is then used to determine the visibility of a row version for any given transaction. Don't miss that one important nuance about updating rows.

Note: Every update to row data creates a new row version, even if no column values change.

In update heavy tables, this can mean that multiple row versions exist at one time until the vacuum process can clean them up.

Transaction IDs for row inserts or modifications are assigned when the first statement is executed within a transaction, not when the BEGIN command is issued (explicitly or automatically). For every transaction, PostgreSQL tracks the XIDs of any other transactions that are in progress (not yet committed/rolled back) when the current transaction began. From that point forward, a command within a transaction will only *see* rows that were committed before it started (i.e. a XID older than the current XID). All other rows that have a newer XID or that belong to a transaction that is still in progress, will not be available to the current transaction. The only exception is when there is a multi-statement transaction. The rows committed along the way within a transaction are available to later statements before the parent transaction.

To help you visualize what happens at the row level within a PostgreSQL table, let's demonstrate how MVCC works with a few simple illustrations.

Row Versions in Practice

Let's start our illustration with the simplest row version; a newly inserted row of data that has been committed, shown in Figure 13-1. The XID of the statement that inserted this row (xid=30) is saved in the *xmin* column. Because the *xmax* column is set to zero, this row has been committed and is available to any transactions with an XID > 30.

```
INSERT INTO mvcc_example (user_data) VALUES ('Hello!');
```

xmin	xmax	id	user_data
30	0	1	Hello!

Figure 13-1. Transaction ID values for a newly inserted row

When a row is deleted as shown in Figure 13-2, the *xmax* column is set to the XID that deleted it. This is known as a *dead tuple* because the row still exists within the table until it is vacuumed, but new transactions will not see this row version.

```
DELETE FROM mvcc_example WHERE id=1;
```

xmin	xmax	id	user_data
30	75	1	Hello!

Figure 13-2. Because both xmin and xmax are populated, this is considered a dead tuple

And finally, whenever a row is updated, the previous row version visible to the current transaction is deleted (*xmax* set to the current XID), and a new row version is created with *xmin* set to the current XID, shown in Figure 13-3.

```
UPDATE mvcc_example SET user_data = 'Hello World!';
```

Xmin	xmax	id	user_data
30	75	1	Hello!
75	0	1	Hello World!

Figure 13-3. Updating a row version creates a new row and marks the old previous one as a dead tuple

The same holds true even if no data changes within the row version itself, like when a value gets updated to itself. PostgreSQL does not check to see if any column values changed within a row. It simply creates a new row version just like any other update process, shown in Figure 13-4.

```
UPDATE mvcc_example SET user_data = user_data;
```

xmin	xmax	user_data
30	75	Hello!
75	0	Hello!

Figure 13-4. Updating to the same values still creates a new row version

Row Visibility

Having this basic understanding of how row versions are tracked, we next need to talk about how any given transaction knows which rows should be visible to the current transaction. To be visible to the current transaction, other row versions must meet the criteria shown in Figure 13-5.

xmin	xmax
• **Less than current XID** • **Is a committed transaction** • **Was not in process when the current transaction began**	• Is either: • zero • greater than XID of the current transaction

Figure 13-5: Row visibility criteria

This helps us see how a "snapshot" of the data is used for each transaction. You may have noticed, however, that XIDs are integers. At some point, PostgreSQL would theoretically run out of integer values to use. Granted, in real life this is less likely if XIDs were tracked with a signed 64-bit integer (it could track more than 18 quintillion transactions after all), but what happens if XIDs are smaller, and the system can't generate new XIDs "in the future?"

Transaction ID Space

It turns out that PostgreSQL XIDs are signed 32-bit integers held in a circular space, not a linear one. This means that for any given XID, there are ~2.1 billion XIDs that are "in the past" (visible) and ~2.1 billion XIDs that are "in the future" (invisible) as shown in Figure 13-6.

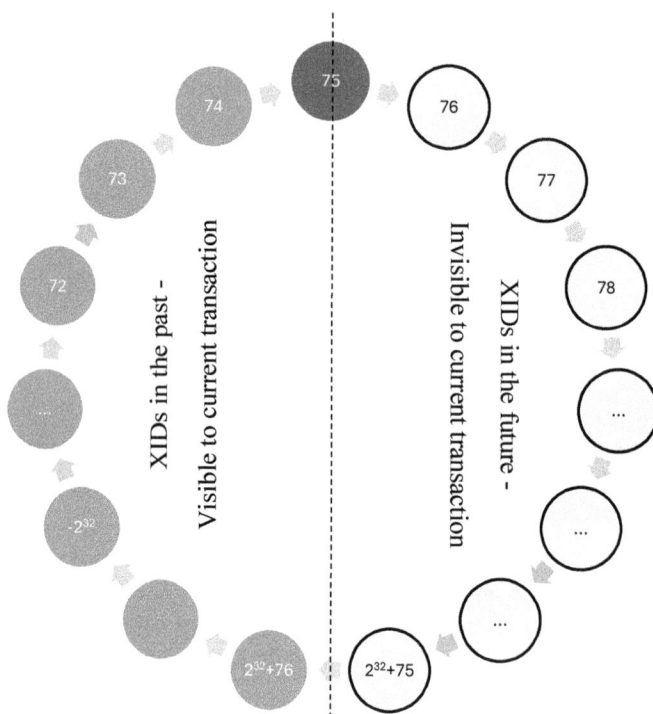

Figure 13-6. Transaction IDs are circular and will eventually need to be reused

Even though there are technically ~4.2 billion available XIDs, from the perspective of any given transaction, there are only ~2.1 billion XIDs in the past that are currently visible. At some point, when XIDs start to be reused, committed transactions from a long time ago will start to look like they are in the future and data will suddenly appear to be lost.

Obviously, this isn't good for data integrity. The rows of data still exist, but the transaction with a reused XID thinks those old rows are for future XIDs, even though they may have been committed months or years ago. PostgreSQL needs to do something to ensure that old rows stay visible while also allowing XIDs to be reused. This is one of the jobs of the vacuum process.

The Vacuum Process

While the MVCC implementation for PostgreSQL works very well to accomplish high levels of concurrency, there are two main challenges that must be dealt with over time because of it. Dead tuples and XID maintenance. Tackling these two challenges is the primary focus of the vacuum process.

VACUUM and autovacuum

The VACUUM command in PostgreSQL can be run at any time. Listing 13-1 shows how to manually start the vacuum on a table, or the entire database. That said, manually starting the vacuuming process should not be necessary most of the time. If you are regularly vacuuming tables through SQL, other settings likely need to be tuned for autovacuum to run properly, which we'll discuss next.

Listing 13-1. Vacuuming an individual table or entire database

```
-- vacuum one table to remove dead tuples and freeze rows
VACUUM bluebox.rental;

-- on very rare occasions, you may choose to vacuum the entire database
VACUUM;
```

Note: Users new to PostgreSQL often see mention of the VACUUM FULL command. This command acts more like a "deep cleaner" of the table by removing dead tuples and then reorganizing live tuples onto pages with available space. It then removes pages with no data, which shrinks the overall footprint of the table on disk. However, VACUUM FULL will maintain an **access exclusive lock** on the table, blocking both reads and writes, while it works and is *rarely* what you really need.

Our advice, and that of the PostgreSQL community, is to not use VACUUM FULL unless it is absolutely necessary, and you understand the consequences on the runtime performance of your database.

Instead of manually vacuuming tables, however, PostgreSQL runs a database process called *autovacuum* to vacuum tables automatically. Every time the process starts, it looks for tables that have reached the configured threshold of modified rows. When it finds a table that is eligible for vacuuming, it begins scanning the data pages and removing dead tuples.

By default, the threshold (technically called the scale factor) is set to 20% + 100 modified rows before the table will be vacuumed. The larger a table gets, however, the longer it takes for the table to meet that threshold and vacuuming to take place. For instance, a table with 100,000 rows will be eligible for vacuuming once 20,100 rows have been modified. A table with 10 million rows, however, will wait until more than 2 million rows have been changed. That's a lot of dead tuple space potentially being wasted, not to mention the other maintenance that's not being completed when a table is vacuumed.

Fortunately, you can both configure the cluster wide settings for autovacuum *and* tune individual tables as necessary. This is typically needed the larger a table gets, especially tables that have heavy update or delete operations. Listing 13-2 shows how to change these settings for a table to encourage autovacuum to run more frequently.

Listing 13-2. Setting a table specific threshold for modified rows before vacuuming

```
-- set the autovacuum percentage threshold to 5% for this
-- large, update heavy table
ALTER TABLE rental SET (autovacuum_vacuum_scale_factor=0.05);
```

If your cluster has adequate memory for the autovacuum process to work efficiently, it's usually better to have the vacuum process run more often on a larger table. While there is no exact science to what this percentage should be, lowering it to 10% or less on large tables might be a good starting value.

Now that we know how to trigger a vacuum process manually when necessary, and how to tune individual tables for more frequent autovacuuming, let's talk about what the vacuum process actually does.

A quick word to the wise. The autovacuum process can be disabled in the PostgreSQL configuration. However, DO NOT turn off the autovacuum process on your cluster.

Sometimes users will diagnose server performance issues and see vacuum running frequently and think this is one of the reasons for degraded performance. Even if it is a contributing factor, turning autovacuum off will usually cause more problems than you think it will solve.

Dead Tuples and Table Bloat

The first task for the vacuum process is to deal with dead tuples. When rows are marked for deletion by populating the *xmax* column, they still exist and take physical space on the data pages for the associated table. Once all transactions that contain those rows in their snapshot have ended, these rows serve no viable purpose for querying. That space needs to be cleaned up and be made available for reuse. Otherwise, the table storage footprint grows, more pages of data need to be read to satisfy a query, and database performance suffers at the very least. This is defined as table bloat.

There are two ways to quickly identify the percentage of dead tuples that exist in a table compared to live tuples. Listing 13-3 shows a simple percentage calculation of dead tuples to live tuples.

Listing 13-3. Relative percent of dead tuples to live tuples

```
SELECT n_live_tup live_tupes, n_dead_tup dead_tuples,
       round((n_dead_tup::numeric/n_live_tup)*100,2) percent_dead_tuples
FROM pg_stat_user_tables WHERE relname='rental';
```

live_tuples	dead_tuples	percent_dead_tuples
1 6,367,788	404,311	6.32

Figure 13-7. Output showing the relative percent of dead tuples in a table

Alternatively, Listing 13-4 uses the *pgstattuple* extension to get more detailed information, which includes how much free space is currently available in the table. Note that using pgstattuple requires scanning the entire table, which can cause a significant load, but also provides more accurate information.

Listing 13-4. Detailed tuple information using pgstattuple extension

```
CREATE EXTENSION IF NOT EXISTS pgstattuple;

SELECT * FROM pgstattuple('bluebox.rental');
```

	Row #1
table_len	599,392,256
tuple_count	6,363,746
tuple_len	483,580,480
tuple_percent	80.68
dead_tuple_count	404,311
dead_tuple_len	29,337,736
dead_tuple_percent	6.32
free_space	52,057,616
free_percent	8.69

Figure 13-8. Detailed output from pgstattuple for the rental table

To deal with the table bloat and keep unnecessary growth under control, the vacuum process scans pages of the table and removes all pointers to the dead rows and then frees the space used by that row version. That free space can then be used for new data during an insert operation or for a new row created by an update operation as demonstrated earlier.

Keeping dead tuples at bay is an essential task to keep table data healthy and reduce maintenance overhead. Either monitor dead tuple percentage of large tables on a regular basis or find a monitoring tool that tracks large tables and the growth of dead tuples over time.

Freezing Live Tuples

The second main task that the vacuum process does is to maintain the transaction ID space by "freezing" live tuples so that their XID can be reused in the future without impacting the availability of the data.

As the vacuum process scans a page for dead tuples, it also looks for rows where *xmin* is sufficiently old enough that all current and future transactions should be able to see it, regardless of what the original XID is. This is known as freezing a row, and it allows vacuuming to be run more quickly and reduces some overhead on determining which rows are visible to a transaction.

When the vacuum process runs, it skips over any rows that have been frozen previously. This can save a significant amount of time in the number of rows that vacuum must process, therefore speeding up the overall time to completion.

Furthermore, if the vacuum process determines that all rows on the page are frozen, it will mark the entire page as frozen, reducing the amount of scanning work that the vacuum process must do. It also means that the individual rows don't have to be checked to ensure they are visible to a transaction. If the page is frozen, all rows are visible to all transactions.

There are other nuances and details that govern exactly how and when XIDs are frozen but knowing the main principle of what's happening under the covers is a good first step. For instance, you probably won't ever have to really worry about things like `vacuum_freeze_min_age`.

ANALYZE and autoanalyze

In Chapter 11 we discussed how PostgreSQL uses a cost-based query planner. Based on the statistics about the table and distribution of values in each column, the query planner tries to determine how many rows and how much work will be required to retrieve rows from a table. If those table statistics are outdated, the planner is more likely to choose a bad query plan. Keeping statistics up to date is what the ANALYZE command is for, and the matching autoanalyze process.

Like autovacuum, the autoanalyze process watches for tables that have had enough rows modified (10% by default) to trigger an analyze of the data. This threshold is also based on a percentage of modified rows over the whole table.

Outdated statistics usually present themselves in two ways. Your first hint that column statistics are outdated will likely be a performance regression for some queries. This is easier if you have a tool that tracks the historical performance over time, but it might be very noticeable if your application performance is suddenly impacted.

Once you think there may be some queries that are regressing, you'll likely run an EXPLAIN on a sample query. Your suspicion of outdated statistics will be confirmed if there are nodes where the estimated rows are noticeably higher or lower than the actual count of rows returned from the query. Running a manual ANALYZE on the involved tables can often improve the query plan in the near term (Listing 13-5).

Listing 13-5. Manually analyzing a table

```
-- analyze the rental table because we notice poor row estimates
ANALYZE bluebox.rental;
```

However, it's better for us to tune tables to analyze data more frequently if statistics regularly become outdated. Just like autovacuum, we can set a specific scale factor (percentage) and threshold before autoanalyze kicks in (Listing 13-6).

Listing 13-6. Modifying the analyze scale factor on a specific table

```
-- set the autoanalyze percentage threshold to 5% for this
-- large, update heavy table
ALTER TABLE rental SET (autovacuum_analyze_scale_factor=0.05);
```

Monitor VACUUM and ANALYZE with pg_stat_user_tables

One last word about effectively monitoring and tuning how frequently VACUUM and ANALYZE are being run on your tables. The pg_stat_user_tables view shows the last time these processes were run manually and automatically as shown in Listing 13-7.

Listing 13-7. Verifying the last time analyze and vacuum were run on a table

```
SELECT schemaname, relname, last_vacuum,
 last_autovacuum, last_analyze, last_autoanalyze
FROM pg_stat_user_tables
WHERE relname = 'inventory';
```

schemaname	relname	last_vacuum	last_autovacuum	last_analyze	last_autoanalyze
1 bluebox	inventory		2024-09-05 17:40:08.145 -0400	2024-09-05 17:39:44.014 -0400	

Figure 13-9. Last vacuum and analyze timestamps

You can see that the inventory table in my sample database has been autovacuumed recently, but it hasn't been autoanalyzed yet. However, somebody (Ryan here) manually analyzed the table to update statistics.

The general wisdom in the PostgreSQL community is that autovacuum and autoanalyze should run more frequently than not. You'll often get better performance overall by lowering the thresholds and having these processes run more often.

You know your tables and data best. So, if you see actively updated tables, especially large ones, are not being vacuumed and analyzed every few hours to a few days, modify the thresholds. By delaying this necessary work, you're likely to pay the price somewhere down the line.

Configuration and Maintenance Tasks

Understanding how MVCC works and how to keep your tables in tip top shape with autovacuum and autoanalyze processes are an essential task for any PostgreSQL administrator, even the accidental administrators among us. However, there are a few more configurations and tasks that you need to monitor to keep things running smoothly.

maintenance_work_mem

We discussed this setting in Chapter 5 with other configuration options that are worth your attention. Like `work_mem`, it limits the amount of memory that maintenance tasks can use to complete their assigned work. This includes tasks like building indexes, adding foreign keys, and vacuuming.

When it comes to vacuuming, particularly on tables that often have lots of dead tuples from updates and deletes, having sufficient memory to read in data pages and do the work in larger batches will speed up the work. If the vacuum process doesn't have enough memory to process tables efficiently, there is the potential that the process will continually vacuum the large, active tables and never process others.

There are usually two reasons vacuum has trouble completing its work. The vacuum scale factor is set too high; therefore, a lot of dead tuples need to be processed when vacuum runs. We discussed earlier how to alter a table to specify more appropriate scale factor values.

The other reason is that vacuum doesn't have enough memory to process the number of dead tuples in the table. By default, `maintenance_work_mem` is set to 64MB. In Chapter 5 we discussed raising it significantly to 256MB or even 1GB. Increasing it beyond 1GB will provide more memory for tasks like indexing large tables. However, PostgreSQL 16 and below silently caps vacuum memory usage to 1GB regardless of the setting. PostgreSQL 17 and above remove that silent limit.

As with all memory settings, you must remember that allocating more memory to one process can have an impact on others. If every maintenance worker uses 1GB of memory on a server that only has 8GB or 16GB of total memory, query processing could be severely impacted.

Look to increase this value to keep maintenance tasks like vacuum running smoothly. Keep an eye on overall server health and performance, incrementing changes to this setting more slowly if you have concerns about performance impacts.

Reindexing

Indexes are a key component of a performant database. In some cases, index pages that have become completely empty can be reclaimed for re-use as part of regular operations. However, over time, index storage can become bloated when pages are mostly empty. Reindexing cleans up all the dead space and improves index usage.

There are other rare cases, like with a BRIN index, where the summary value for a range of pages becomes outdated because values in that range of pages have been changed. Although there are mechanisms in place to re-summarize BRIN index entries naturally over time, a reindex will ensure that the index is clean and correct.

Creating an index or reindexing an existing index, takes an exclusive lock by default. However, almost all indexing operations can be done concurrently, which only takes a shared access lock. Concurrent indexing (Listing 13-8) will likely take longer and is completed in multiple phases to avoid heavy locks, but it will not lock the table while it works.

Listing 13-8. Concurrently reindexing a table. Creating an index can be performed concurrently, too.

```
-- rebuild all indexes on a table concurrently
REINDEX TABLE CONCURRENTLY bluebox.rental;

-- rebuild a specific index
REINDEX INDEX CONCURRENTLY rental_rental_period_idx;
```

Fill Factor

Like other database platforms, PostgreSQL supports setting a specific fill factor target for indexes and tables. The default fill factor for indexes is 90%, while the default for tables is 100%. Any time a page of data is created, the process will try to pack the pages with data up to this amount. Having free space on pages for tables and indexes reduces the need for additional pages to be created concurrently.

For indexes, this reduces the need for page splits and the maintenance that comes with it. The recommendation is to pack the pages more densely, say 95%, when the indexed column will not be changed and generally only increases in value (timestamps and counters are examples). This will reduce the overall space needed for the index at the potential cost of cascading page splits, should an index value change on a packed page. Listing 13-9 shows how to set or alter fill factor for an index.

Listing 13-9. Modify the fill factor for an index

```
-- set an index fill factor on creation
-- use a lower value for indexes that will have lots of random
-- entries over time. User a value close to or at 100 for indexed
-- columns that will not change in the future
CREATE INDEX rental_inventory_id_idx ON rental (inventory_id) WITH
(fillfactor = 75);

-- set an index fill factor at a later time
ALTER INDEX rental_inventory_id_idx SET (fillfactor = 95);
REINDEX INDEX rental_inventory_id_idx;
```

Heap-Only Tuples

With table pages, however, having some free space encourages a different optimization known as Heap-Only Tuples (HOT). Because PostgreSQL uses heap storage, new rows can technically be written on any page that has space, or on a newly created page when needed. As rows are written to different pages, even for what would otherwise be sequential data, random page access increases when retrieving data for a query. As we discussed in Chapter 11, this increases the likelihood that PostgreSQL will simply scan the entire table rather than try to fetch a bunch of random pages.

Heap-Only Tuples aim to reduce the proliferation of random pages and heavy index maintenance when rows are updated and there is free space on the same data page. In this case, HOT updates prevent the index from being modified because the pointer is to the page, and a HOT update simply updates the pointer to the new row version on the same page. This keeps index maintenance to a minimum when possible and speeds up row retrieval.

A HOT update can occur when the data being updated is not an indexed column and there is free space on the data page for the new row version. Listing 13-10 shows how to set or alter the fill factor for a table.

Listing 13-10. Modify the table fill factor at creation or alter it later.

```
-- set the fill factor to a specific value at creation time
CREATE TABLE bluebox.inventory (
      inventory_id serial4 NOT NULL,
      film_id int4 NOT NULL,
      store_id int4 NOT NULL,
      last_update timestamptz DEFAULT now() NOT NULL
) WITH (fillfactor=95);

-- Reduce the fill factor to allow more space for new and updated rows
ALTER TABLE bluebox.inventory SET (fillfactor=75);
```

Particularly for tables that you know to be update heavy, it's worth keeping an eye on a few columns in `pg_stat_user_tables` to monitor if HOT updates are occurring (Listing 13-11).

Listing 13-11. Viewing Heap-only Tuple performance on update-heavy tables

```
SELECT schemaname, relname, n_tup_upd, n_tup_hot_upd
FROM pg_stat_user_tables;
```

	schemaname	relname	n_tup_upd	n_tup_hot_upd
1	bluebox	rental	4,489	0
2	bluebox	inventory	4,461	442

Figure 13-10. HOT updates compared to updated rows

When the number of HOT updates (`n_tup_hot_upd`) is growing at a similar rate with the number of updated tuples (`n_tup_upd`), then there is adequate free space for PostgreSQL to keep these modifications within the same data page. If HOT updates are not occurring at a similar rate and you believe that they should be, lowering the fill factor could increase the likelihood of HOT updates taking place.

Listing 13-11 shows two tables from our sample database. If this were a live application and no HOT updates were happening on the rental table as shown, lowering the fill factor to 75% or 80% would be a first step to see if HOT updates would begin to happen.

Conclusion

The vacuum and analyze processes are essential tools to keep a PostgreSQL database running smoothly and queries performant. In most cases you will need to tune specific tables, particularly ones that grow over time and are update or delete heavy. It's a valuable part of maintaining a PostgreSQL database and something that you need to invest time in.

14
Replication and HA

In Chapter 12, we talked about various methods for creating backups of your data and, more importantly, restoring it. We can't say it often enough - your backup strategy is only as good as your ability to restore to the state you need.

However, our organizations, users, and applications require more than just the ability to restore to a point in time if a failure happens. Having the least amount of downtime requires something more than copying data files and replaying the write-ahead log (WAL) to get the database back into a known state. When disaster recovery is needed, this may be your only option, so it's still imperative that you know how to do it as we discussed in Chapter 12.

For high availability, however, we need to have additional replica servers that are kept up to date with the primary and can "take over" at a moment's notice. Granted, "a moment's notice" is subject to a lot of factors. But if the data is being replicated effectively, it should be significantly faster to failover to a replica and continue processing requests.

Cloud Hosted Databases

Before we get into the details of replication and how to enable it in PostgreSQL, it's worth a brief discussion about replication support with most cloud providers.

Depending on the type of replication you require, it can be somewhat challenging to set up, especially if you're managing the server and PostgreSQL cluster yourself. Often, however, the responsibility of managing and maintaining replication is where the real work begins.

Cloud providers know this, and they also recognize that effective high availability implementations are an essential requirement for users. Therefore, they've worked very hard to provide mechanisms for easily setting up replication and managing most of it for you.

If you are new to PostgreSQL, and especially if you are moving an existing project that requires high availability (HA), vendor provided replication tools often reduce the total cost of ownership (TCO) of the database. While most of them don't provide a full "set and forget" implementation, you'll probably get an HA environment setup much faster using their tools. Check with your cloud provider to see what replication options they support with your given PostgreSQL database and where the best documentation is. We introduce some of this information in Chapter 16.

Regardless of whether you're using a cloud provider or not, understanding what types of replication PostgreSQL supports and what's happening under the cover is still important. Let's dive into the details.

Replication

PostgreSQL supports two kinds of replication: physical and logical. Each has different capabilities, and therefore, are typically used for different purposes, or aspects, of a replication and HA strategy.

Physical Replication

Physical replication is accomplished using the WAL in one of two ways: WAL archiving (log-shipping) or streaming. Both rely on transferring the page-level changes recorded in the WAL to a replica server to replay locally.

WAL archiving requires that you have a location to place the files where the replica can access them when needed for recovery. This could be a physically shared disk location, like a shared network drive, or a folder on one of the servers, just as long as the files can be accessed by the replica. 16MB WAL segment files are transferred once they are full and applied by the replication once it arrives.

Streaming replication, on the other hand, streams the data transaction by transaction through a database connection and doesn't require a shared disk location. These two methods can be used in conjunction with each other and there are scenarios when this makes sense. But increasingly, streaming physical replication is the preferred method and what we will focus on in this chapter.

Once set up properly, streaming replication works by replaying the WAL as it is transferred to the replica servers. Because the WAL is cluster-wide, you cannot stream individual databases or database objects. This is used for replication of the entire cluster – all or nothing.

Streaming replication can also be asynchronous or synchronous. When replication is asynchronous, the default, the primary doesn't wait for the replicas to acknowledge that the same transaction was committed before finalizing the commit itself. Assuming the replica received the WAL, there's an understanding that it might be slightly delayed replaying it, and therefore, the replica might appear to be slightly behind the primary.

When streaming replication is synchronous, the primary server typically waits for confirmation from at least one synchronous replica that the transaction was committed. If you have more than one replica, you can specify the ones that must acknowledge the committed transaction, or you can specify that a certain number of replicas must confirm without dictating which ones. This introduces one major concern, and therefore management overhead, with synchronous replication.

If the minimum number of replicas do not acknowledge or are even just slow to acknowledge that the transaction has been committed, then synchronous replication becomes a blocking process. Every transaction on the primary must wait for confirmation, which can quickly put your application in an unusable state because PostgreSQL isn't completing requests. Therefore, if your application requires synchronous replication, we highly recommend that you have at least two replicas and configure PostgreSQL to wait for acknowledgement from a smaller percentage of them, something like 50%-75% of your total replicas. You'll have to consider your tolerance of risk for losing data, or potentially blocking your application if the replicas can't be reached.

Finally, streaming replication cannot be used between different major versions of PostgreSQL. Because this is ultimately a file-level replication, the format of pages can change between major versions, which would make the data incompatible with a newer (or older) version of PostgreSQL. Logical replication can be used to stream changes between different major versions of PostgreSQL, although it has other trade-offs.

Logical Replication

Logical replication, on the other hand, doesn't stream the physical block-level file changes. Instead, it streams the DML table operations that logically recreate the change in the target table. The commands are created by decoding the WAL file on the primary as it is generated and "pushing" forward the appropriate insert, update, or delete commands to the target database. The transfer of these changes is managed through a publication/subscription model where each subscription can have multiple subscribers, and any table can be made available through multiple publications.

There are several specific advantages to using logical replication that simply aren't possible with the "all or nothing" approach of streaming replication. With logical replication you can stream:

- individual table changes

- between different versions of PostgreSQL

- filtered rows of the same table to different subscriptions

- physical replication changes to additional downstream logical subscribers (cascading replicas)

That said, logical replication doesn't replace streaming replication for at least one specific reason; DDL changes. Logical replication is currently data-centric, not schema-centric. It will only stream data modifications, not any of the DDL that you execute on the source tables.

Replication Slots

Replication slots are used to ensure that replication data is kept until the replica (physical), or subscriber (logical) has received the data. Initially added in PostgreSQL 9.4 to solve the issue of WAL logs being recycled if it wasn't streamed after some time, slots are a helpful way to ensure that replication data is not lost. It does come with the downside where the primary server can fill up the disk where WAL is stored if a replica becomes disconnected for a long time, so you must have a monitoring solution in place to track for potential replication issues. This can be done, in part, by watching the `pg_replication_slots` view.

Also, when slots are used for synchronous streaming replication, the primary server will become unresponsive as soon as a replica becomes disconnected that is configured as one of the replicas that must acknowledge the transaction. In this case, you will need to get the replica connected again quickly or reconfigure the replicas that must acknowledge receipt in order to stop the blocking processes. We can't stress this enough, if you are going to use synchronous replication, ensure you have enough replicas, with stable network connections, and only a subset of them must be truly synchronous. The PostgreSQL documentation is a great place to start if you start down the synchronous replication path.

Physical or Logical Replication?

Having multiple replication options provides a lot of flexibility in how high availability can be architected in your PostgreSQL environment. Any replica can be used as a physical primary to another server or even a logical publisher to downstream subscriptions.

If your main requirement is to have a warm, read-only standby replica then streaming replication is all you need. If you need to publish specific tables to additional databases that users can query without impacting the primary cluster, logical replication is your best bet. Or maybe you maintain a database that aggregates multiple datasets for various groups or departments in your company and they need access to it. Rather than allowing them to run ad hoc queries on the primary clustering, likely having to use row level security rules to limit the data they can see, you could use logical replication to stream filtered data to separate read-only databases for each department that they can access instead.

Only you know the high availability and disaster recovery requirements of your organization or application, and there's a good chance you may end up using different replication methods in combination. For the context of this chapter, however, we're going to stick with streaming replication using slots, and two examples of logical replication; filtered and unfiltered.

And finally, it's worth noting that replication doesn't come for free. The more complex your HA environment, the more WAL that will need to be retained for some time, and the more memory and network resources needed to keep downstream replicas in sync. All this comes at a cost which could eventually impact the performance of your application and the experience of end users. Add one method of replication at a time and measure any impact on performance or maintenance effort over time before adding more complexity.

Setting Up Streaming Replication

In Chapter 12, we demonstrated the basics of how to use `pg_basebackup` to get a complete file-level backup of a running PostgreSQL cluster. This is the starting point for enabling streaming replication and must be completed with an instance of PostgreSQL that matches the major version of the primary cluster.

To review at a high level, the basic set up entails creating a role with the replication attribute, configuring a rule in the `pg_hba.conf` file, running `pg_basebackup` from the replica server, and then ensuring that the replication slot is active, and that streaming is running as expected. In general, it's a straightforward process. If you have the correct access and permissions on both PostgreSQL clusters, you can have a replica cluster running without a lot of headaches.

Note: You do need to have direct access to the cluster filesystem to set up streaming replication. Testing these steps on multiple PostgreSQL Docker images through the running shell will not work since they are running the PostgreSQL process as the container entry point. If you try to stop the running process on the replica container to remove the data files (Step 3 below), the container will immediately stop.

For practice, set up virtual machines either locally or in a cloud provider to get some experience using each of these replication methods.

Step 1: Create replication role

Listing 14-1 shows a CREATE ROLE command as demonstrated in Chapter 5, but this time with the REPLICATION role attribute. This will also need to login and have the appropriate authentication mechanism so that the replica can connect easily. In our example, we'll use password (scram-sha-256) authentication. This role is created on the primary cluster.

Listing 14-1. Create a replication role for authentication

```
CREATE ROLE repusr LOGIN REPLICATION PASSWORD 'rep-password';
```

Step 2: Modify the pg_hba.conf file

The host-based authentication file needs to specify a specific rule for the replication user. You can get as specific as you need with the host restrictions, but the database name must be REPLICATION, and the role and authentication method must match the role you just created. Listing 14-2 shows a sample pg_hba.conf rule.

Listing 14-2. A pg_hba.conf entry to allow replication connections

```
# TYPE   DATABASE        USER        ADDRESS          METHOD
host     replication     repusr      192.168.1.2      scram-sha-256
```

You will need to reload the configuration on the primary server for the authentication rule to be recognized (Listing 14-3).

Listing 14-3. Reload the PostgreSQL service for pg_hba.conf changes

```
$ sudo systemctl reload postgresql-16.service
```

Step 3: Prepare the replica cluster

Before we can copy the data to get the starting point for replication, we need to do two things: stop the cluster and empty the data directory.

First, the PostgreSQL cluster needs to be stopped because we need to replace the data files that it initialized when we started it. Usually, the replica cluster is a fresh install, and we can simply replace the data files. If for some reason you are repurposing an existing cluster to be a replica for a primary server, the current data files will be replaced because, remember, you replicate the entire cluster, not individual databases.

With the cluster stopped, the easiest way to prepare for the backup files is to remove everything from the data directory. This doesn't require you to change where PostgreSQL looks for these files when it starts up. Otherwise, if you create a new, empty directory to copy the files into, you'll need to tell PostgreSQL where those files are. Listing 14-4 shows how to clear out the standard data to prepare it for reuse.

Listing 14-4. Remove data files on replica to prepare for pg_basebackup

```
# Reuse the default PostgreSQL data directory. Your path may be slightly
# different depending on your OS, install, and PostgreSQL version
$ rm -rf /var/lib/pgsql/16/data/*
```

Step 4: Create the base backup

From the replica command line, we can start a pg_basebackup with the appropriate flags. Once started, pg_basebackup will automatically put the primary server into backup mode at the beginning out of backup mode at the end. Other database clients will not be affected by the backup taking place.

To begin the backup process, the replica cluster must have TCP/IP access to the primary server. From the command line on the replica cluster, initiate a pg_basebackup. The command shown in Listing 14-5 is slightly different from the basic form shown in Chapter 12. In this case we're using some command flags to set up the replication slot on the primary server for us and to create the appropriate configuration files on the replica to start replaying the received WAL once the backup is complete.

Listing 14-5. Execute pg_basebackup from replica cluster

```
# As the postgres user (or whatever system user owns the process/folders)
$ sudo su - postgres
$ pg_basebackup -h 192.168.1.1 -U repusr -D /var/lib/postgresql/16/data\
    -c fast -R -S 'replica1' -C -P
```

There's a lot there, so let's work it through together. First, we specify the standard connection criteria for the host (-h) and user (-U) that is connecting to the primary. These flags are the same across the tools shipped with PostgreSQL.

Next, we specify the directory (-D) where the data files should be copied to. In our case, this is the standard PostgreSQL data directory on our server that we cleaned out in the earlier step. Remember, this directory must be empty. If it's not, `pg_basebackup` will exit with an error.

The next set of flags are specific to setting up replication and the slot on the primary. If you don't use `pg_basebackup` to help you with this, you'll have to manually add and edit these files after you copy the backup files which takes added effort.

- **-c**: perform a checkpoint on the primary to prepare a starting point for WAL updates and streaming. Using the "fast" option as shown is recommended.

- **-R**: appends connection and slot information to the `postgresql.auto.conf` file and creates the `standby.signal` on the replica server which enables replication to start.

- **-S**: the name of the slot on the primary to connect to for managing streaming replication

- **-C**: create the slot on the primary if it does not exist

- **-P**: show the progress of the base backup as it occurs

Step 5: Start the replica cluster

Once the base backup is done, the replica server needs to be started. Depending on your Linux distribution, this is typically accomplished through the system service with the `systemctl` command as shown in Listing 14-6.

Listing 14-6. Start PostgreSQL on the replica cluster

```
$ sudo systemctl start postgresql-16
```

Once the server is started, we can check the replication statistics views to see the status of replication, first from the primary and then on the replica. Listing 14-7 and Figure 14-1 show the output of `pg_stat_replication` on the primary cluster.

Listing 14-7. Verify that the replica is connected to the primary

```
-- On the primary, check to see if the walreceiver on the replica
-- is connected and receiving data
SELECT * FROM pg_stat_replication;
```

	Row #1
123 pid	24,583
123 usesysid	20,400
ABC usename	repusr
ABC application_name	16/main
⊞ client_addr	172.31.26.132
ABC client_hostname	[NULL]
123 client_port	58,686
⊙ backend_start	2024-09-18 02:43:31.310 -0400
⊞ backend_xmin	[NULL]
ABC state	[NULL]
⊞ sent_lsn	[NULL]
⊞ write_lsn	[NULL]
⊞ flush_lsn	[NULL]
⊞ replay_lsn	[NULL]
⊙ write_lag	[NULL]
⊙ flush_lag	[NULL]
⊙ replay_lag	[NULL]
123 sync_priority	[NULL]
ABC sync_state	[NULL]
⊙ reply_time	[NULL]

Figure 14-1. Output of pg_stat_replication

Listing 14-8 and Figure 14-2 show the output of `pg_stat_replication_slots` on the primary cluster.

Listing 14-8. Verify that the replication slot is active and streaming data

```
select * from pg_replication_slots;
```

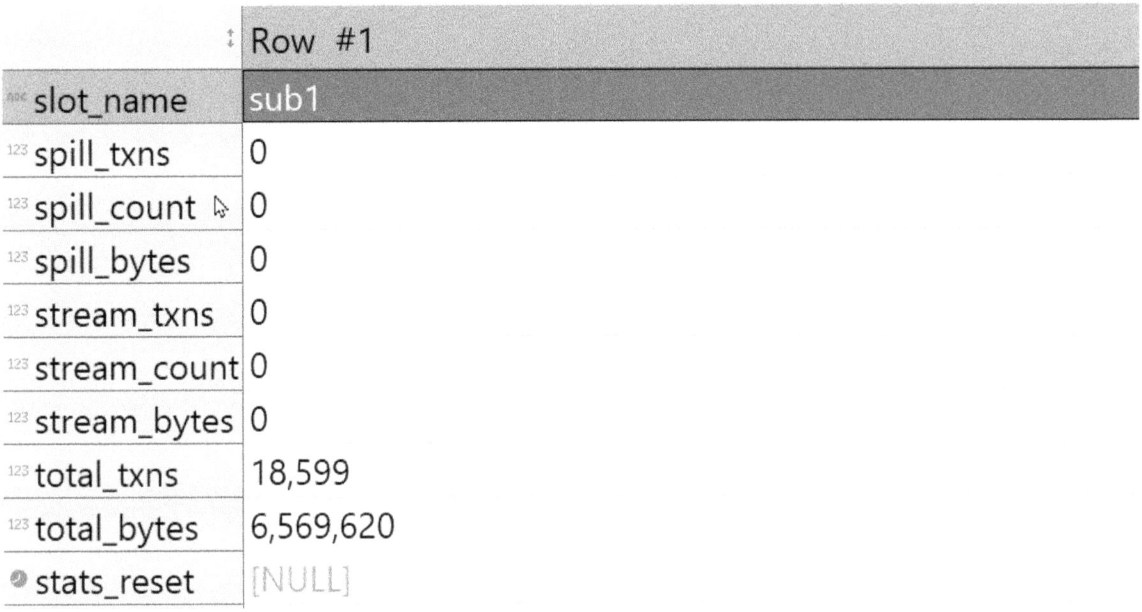

	Row #1
slot_name	sub1
spill_txns	0
spill_count	0
spill_bytes	0
stream_txns	0
stream_count	0
stream_bytes	0
total_txns	18,599
total_bytes	6,569,620
stats_reset	[NULL]

Figure 14-2. Output of pg_stat_replication_slots

Listing 14-9 and Figure 14-3 show the output of `pg_stat_wal_receiver` on the replica.

Listing 14-9. Verify that the replica is connected and receiving WAL

```
select * from pg_stat_wal_receiver;
```

	Row #1
¹²³ pid	27,090
ᴬᴮᶜ status	streaming
⬚ receive_start_lsn	0/30000000
¹²³ receive_start_tli	1
⬚ written_lsn	0/342B8168
⬚ flushed_lsn	0/342B8168
¹²³ received_tli	1
◉ last_msg_send_time	2024-09-19 12:35:50.129 -0400
◉ last_msg_receipt_time	2024-09-19 12:35:50.130 -0400
⬚ latest_end_lsn	0/342B8168
◉ latest_end_time	2024-09-19 12:35:50.129 -0400
ᴬᴮᶜ slot_name	replica1
ᴬᴮᶜ sender_host	172.31.29.76
¹²³ sender_port	5,432
ᴬᴮᶜ conninfo	user=repusr password=******** channel_binding=prefer dbname=replic

Figure 14-3. Output of pg_stat_wal_receiver

From this point forward, the primary server will continue to stream WAL data to the replica. Should the replica become disconnected at any point, the slot that was created will ensure that the primary server keeps WAL data available to stream as soon as the replica reconnects.

With streaming replication in place, the next steps in high availability involve understanding how to failover to the replica. As it stands now, the replica is in read-only mode, so no data modifications can take place. If the primary server becomes inaccessible and you need to promote the replica, it's as simple as executing a command to promoting it. This can be done with either the pg_ctl command line tool (Listing 14-10), or the pg_promote() function on a running replica. Both commands do the same thing, take the replica out of read-only mode and allow data modifications. This will also stop any replication connections to the old primary server.

Listing 14-10. Use the PostgreSQL pg_ctl CLI tool to promote the replica

```
$ pg_ctl promote -D /var/lib/pgsql/16/data
```

Ultimately, however, true HA requires some mechanism to automatically failover to a replica when some failure criteria is met. PostgreSQL does not ship with this kind of functionality built in. Instead, there are several open-source tools available to help you manage the entire high-availability setup, including the steps we just took above to set up the read-only replica to begin with.

The set up and management of these tools and a full-blown HA environment is beyond the scope of this introductory chapter. If you are managing your PostgreSQL clusters on your own, rather than in a cloud hosted database service, then you should check out the available external replication tools and their accompanying documentation. Two of the most popular tools for managing PostgreSQL replication are:

- **Patroni** (https://patroni.readthedocs.io/en/latest/): This is a set of python scripts and associated tools to manage physical replication, and all parts needed for HA.

- **repmgr** (https://www.repmgr.org/): a set of open-source tools provided and maintained by EDB for managing replication.

Setting Up Logical Replication

Logical replication works on a pub/sub model. On the source database, you create a publication with the specific tables that you want to stream DML changes for. This can be specific tables, or you can include all tables. On a target cluster, you then subscribe to the publication and begin receiving data changes. With logical replication, the destination tables must already exist with matching schema, regardless of whether the data is being filtered or not. If you try to subscribe to a publication on another server without the table already existing in the local database, PostgreSQL will return an error.

In each of the examples below, we're going to create two different publications: one that is filtered and one that isn't. We'll subscribe to each of these from different destination databases to demonstrate how the data sent and received is different. As we mentioned earlier in this chapter, there is a lot of flexibility over what data you publish with logical replication. These are simple examples, so modify as necessary.

Step 1: Modify wal_level configuration on source cluster

To start logical replication publications, the cluster needs to be configured to encode the WAL messages with a little more information which allows the messages to be decoded on the target cluster. To do this, you must set the `wal_level` configuration parameter to `logical`. This can only be set at server start, so modify it in the `postgresql.conf` file.

```
#-----------------------------------------------------------------
# WRITE-AHEAD LOG
#-----------------------------------------------------------------

# - Settings -

wal_level = logical                          # minimal, replica, or logical
                                             # (change requires restart)
```

Once the configuration file is changed, restart the PostgreSQL cluster.

```
$ sudo systemctl start postgresql-16
```

Step 2: Create a publication on the source database

Publications are managed per database, so you must make sure you're connected to the correct database to create the publication. Since a publication is for tables, you can specify individual tables, all tables in a schema, or all tables in the database. In Listing 14-11 we create a publication for just one table. At any time, you can alter the publication and add more tables to it.

Listing 14-11. Creating the publication for the rental table

```
CREATE PUBLICATION rental_pub FOR TABLE bluebox.rental;
```

At the same time, for the purposes of demonstration, we also create a filtered publication that will be applied on a different database for the same table, shown in Listing 14-12.

Listing 14-12. Creating the filtered publication for the rental table

```
CREATE PUBLICATION rental_pub_filtered FOR TABLE bluebox.rental
WHERE (store_id > 100);
```

These publications are just the setup of the process. They don't do anything or start storing WAL for the subscription until a slot is created for them. We'll get to that part next.

Note: Logical replication publications and subscriptions are performed by the role that creates them. You need to ensure that the role has the appropriate privileges to select from the table on the publication database and write to the table on the subscription database. Refer to Chapter 5 for a review on granting privileges.

Step 3: Prepare destination databases

For a database subscription to receive and apply data from a source publication, the same objects must exist in both databases. On the target database this can be done by restoring a backup of the source database (with or without data) or by creating individual tables if that suit your needs. If you are limiting the tables of data that are being sent to the target server, you may also have to remove some foreign keys if the related tables do not exist or are not being replicated as well.

For our example, we'll just be streaming data from the rental table, so that's the only table we're going to create in our target database. But again, you could just restore a backup of the database first. Because this is an empty database, we need to create the schema as well as shown in Listing 14-13. We also removed the foreign key constraints.

Listing 14-13. *Creating the destination table on the target database*

```
CREATE SCHEMA bluebox;

CREATE TABLE bluebox.rental (
        rental_id int8 GENERATED BY DEFAULT AS IDENTITY NOT NULL,
        rental_period tstzrange NULL,
        inventory_id int4 NOT NULL,
        customer_id int4 NOT NULL,
        last_update timestamptz DEFAULT now() NOT NULL,
        store_id int4 NULL,
        CONSTRAINT rental_pkey PRIMARY KEY (rental_id)
);
CREATE INDEX idx_rental_rental_date ON bluebox.rental
USING gist (rental_period);

CREATE INDEX rental_customer_id_idx ON bluebox.rental
USING btree (customer_id);

CREATE INDEX rental_inventory_id_idx ON bluebox.rental
USING btree (inventory_id);

CREATE INDEX rental_rental_period_idx ON bluebox.rental
USING gist (rental_period);
```

For the sake of demonstration, we also created a second database called `bluebox_filtered` on the same target server (although it could be on any accessible server) with the same schema and table in Listing 14-13. We'll use this second database to subscribe to a subset of rows from the rental table as shown in the filtered publication in Listing 14-12 from Step 2.

Step 4: Create a subscription on the target

The last step to get the logical replication process started is to create a subscription from another database. This database can be located anywhere as long as the cluster host can access the source database. Also recall that the target database doesn't have to be the same version as the source.

The `CREATE SUBSCRIPTION` command has a number of parameters that can be configured to determine if it should create the slot on the source cluster, what the slot name should be, if it should start streaming immediately or not, and more. The default values for these properties will create everything necessary to start streaming immediately. Listing 14-14 shows how to create a subscription and start streaming data immediately, however, we've specifically set a number of parameters to control how the slot gets created and its name.

Listing 14-14. Create a subscription to the rental_pub publication

```
CREATE SUBSCRIPTION sub_rental
CONNECTION 'host=192.168.1.1 dbname=bluebox application_name=sub1
    user=repusr password=rep-password'
PUBLICATION rental_pub
WITH (enabled=true,create_slot=true, slot_name=rental_pub1);
```

In a second database that will only receive a filtered subset of rows from the second publication (Listing 14-15), we create another subscription. This time, however, we don't add any additional parameters. Since both `enabled` and `create_slot` are true by default, this `CREATE SUBSCRIPTION` does the same thing as above. The only difference is that the slot name for the source publication will default to the subscription name.

Listing 14-15. Create a subscription to the filtered publication

```
CREATE SUBSCRIPTION sub_rental_filtered
CONNECTION 'host=192.168.1.1 dbname=bluebox application_name=sub1
    user=repusr password=replicapw1'
PUBLICATION rental_pub_filtered;
```

In both cases, if the source subscription has the appropriate privilege to the tables, PostgreSQL will begin to stream decoded messages to the target database and apply them.

Step 5: Verify the publication is working

When a subscription is enabled and the source database begins, the first thing each publication will do is stream all the data required to get the target table in sync and ready to receive changes. We can do a quick test by selecting the count of rows that match each publication on the source and then target database. If you recall from Step 3, the table we created on the target was empty because we did not restore it from a backup. However, the subscription will catch things up first and then stream additional changes. Listing 14-16 verifies the row counts on the unfiltered publication and subscription. Listing 14-17 verifies the counts on the filtered version.

Note: When you first start the logical replication process, the target table will not return any rows until the initial data population is complete. On a large table this could take time and may make it appear that the process isn't working.

You can always check pg_stat_activity on the target server a backend_type of "logical replication worker", or one of the views shown in Listing 14-18 & 14-19 to verify that the process is connected and doing work, even before the target table returns rows of data.

Listing 14-16. Verifying row counts on the source and target database

```
-- on the source database
SELECT count(*) FROM bluebox.rental;

count  |
-------+
1024421|

-- on the target database
SELECT count(*) FROM bluebox.rental;

count  |
-------+
1024421|
```

Listing 14-17. Verifying row counts of the filtered publication

```
-- on the source database
SELECT count(*) FROM bluebox.rental WHERE store_id > 100;

count |
------+
594905|

-- on the target database of rental_pub_filtered publication
SELECT count(*) FROM bluebox.rental;

count |
------+
594905|
```

And finally, we can check the progress of the publication and subscription through their respective PostgreSQL stats views on the source and target database. Listing 14-18 and Figure 14-4 show that the slots have been created and have streamed data on the source database. As expected, the filtered slot has transferred fewer transactions and bytes.

Listing 14-18. Logical replication slot statistics

```
bluebox=# select * from pg_stat_replication_slots;
```

	slot_name	spill_txns	spill_count	spill_bytes	stream_txns	stream_count	stream_bytes	total_txns	total_bytes	stats_reset
1	sub1	0	0	0	0	0	0	24,066	8,456,432	[NULL]
2	sub_rental_filtered	0	0	0	0	0	0	16,896	5,924,300	[NULL]

Figure 14-4. *Output of pg_stat_replication_slots*

On the target cluster, we can query the subscription stats metrics shown in Listing 14-19 to see the status of the specific subscription (Figure 14-5).

Listing 14-19. Verify the subscription status on the replica

```
select * from pg_stat_subscription
WHERE subname='sub_rental_filtered';
```

subid	subname	pid	leader_pid	relid	received_lsn	last_msg_send_time	last_msg_receipt_time	latest_end_lsn	latest_end_time
1 1,199,801	sub1	14,989	[NULL]	[NULL]	0/342B8250	2024-09-19 12:51:58.411 -0400	2024-09-19 12:51:58.464 -0400	0/342B8250	2024-09-19 12:51:58.411 -0400
2 1,199,821	sub_rental_filtered	14,988	[NULL]	[NULL]	0/342B8250	2024-09-19 12:51:58.412 -0400	2024-09-19 12:51:58.464 -0400	0/342B8250	2024-09-19 12:51:58.412 -0400

Figure 14-5. Output of pg_stat_subscription

And finally, the ultimate status check is to verify that when data is added or modified in the source database, the changes are reflected on the target. To demonstrate this, we'll add a day's worth of rental data using the generate_rental_history() procedure (Listing 14-20). Then, we'll check the counts on both sides, using the count values from Listing 14-13 and 13-14 as reference.

Listing 14-20. Generate new rental data for the last day using interval math

```
-- Add historical rental data for the last day
call bluebox.generate_rental_history(now()-'1day'::interval,now());
```

After this procedure runs to the end, we can check the total count of rows for both subscriptions and their target databases (Listing 14-21 and 14-22).

Listing 14-21. Verifying row counts after generating new rental data

```
-- on the source database after generating new data
-- the previous row count was 1024421
SELECT count(*) FROM bluebox.rental;

count   |
--------+
1029538|


-- on the target database after generating new data
-- the previous row count was 1024421
SELECT count(*) FROM bluebox.rental;

count   |
--------+
1029538|
```

Listing 14-22. Verifying row counts of the filtered publication with new data

```
-- on the source database after generating new data on the source
-- the previous row count was 594905
SELECT count(*) FROM bluebox.rental WHERE store_id > 100;

count |
------+
597897|

-- on the target database of rental_pub_filtered publication
-- after generating new data on the source
-- the previous row count was 594905
SELECT count(*) FROM bluebox.rental;

count |
------+
597897|
```

Conclusion

PostgreSQL supports both physical and logical replication that can be asynchronous (the default) or synchronous. Each form of replication can also be used in conjunction with the other. A primary physical replication cluster can also publish logical replication data to be consumed by other downstream clusters.

From a replication and HA perspective, cloud hosted database offerings from vendors like AWS or Azure are configured out of the box to support replication and offer failover solutions that require very little work to get started. If you don't have to manage your own clusters specifically, these solutions offer good set ups for HA.

If you are hosting PostgreSQL clusters yourself, either physically or through hosted virtual machines, setting up replication in either form does require direct access to the host server and the ability to change configurations. It is a slightly more involved process to get started, but easy to maintain once you understand the basics.

Logical replication publications and subscriptions will work regardless of where your database is hosted as long as the source database is accessible, and the roles privileges are properly configured on the source. Once configured, however, logical replication offers a lot of flexibility in what table data is published for other database subscriptions to consume. In addition, it is the best choice for doing an upgrade over time to a new major version of PostgreSQL or if you want to stream a specific set of tables downstream.

15
Monitoring PostgreSQL Behaviors

While PostgreSQL is an excellent set of software, things can and do go wrong. Understanding how your system is behaving, what's slow and where you may have problems - as well as the metrics necessary to address those issues - is vital. Even if you use a third-party monitoring solution, or host your databases in the cloud, a full understanding of how to obtain your own metrics will be important for understanding how your databases are behaving. This chapter introduces you to the internal tools available for understanding PostgreSQL operational metrics, covering the following topics:

- A discussion on the importance of metrics

- Collecting server information

- Performance metrics of queries

While there are a number of extensions and third-party tools for monitoring PostgreSQL, we'll stick with the native solutions in this chapter. Even if you use another tool for collecting monitoring metrics, it's important to know how to do this on your own. Further, many of the third-party solutions are using these same mechanisms, so understanding how the native monitoring works helps you more appropriately use the third-party tools.

Knowledge Drives Decisions

The single most important thing you can say about monitoring PostgreSQL, or any system for that matter, is that you need to collect information in order to make informed decisions about that system. While it is entirely possible to ignore metrics and have a well-functioning system, it's very unlikely. You can, of course, ignore any kind of data collection of information about how your system is behaving and use trial and error to make changes for improvements. Eventually, and likely even soon, this approach will lead to serious problems. So, it's best to gather information about the system and how it's behaving before you run into issues.

In general, and there are exceptions to this as we'll discuss, a lot of the mechanisms used to gather information about your PostgreSQL cluster use aggregation. The data is collected in this manner because, generally, it puts less of a load on the system to maintain a relatively small set of data, aggregated, as opposed to a very large, detailed set of data. In short, it's the safer approach. However, that approach comes with a cost. The most important cost here is the ability to compare two values.

It's good to know that, for example, a query runs in about 20 milliseconds on average. However, how fast did it run last week? How fast was it before we added an index? One of the most important keys to using the metrics available is to be able to compare two points. It could be two points in time, this week to last week, or it could be two points after a change, before and after an index is added. Simply having the aggregation, the average, minimum and maximum, isn't always enough for decision making. With this in mind, if you are monitoring your PostgreSQL systems, you need to plan for some form of data storage over some period of time for the information you collect. This will give you the ability to compare two points of data.

The tools built into PostgreSQL for observing the behaviors of the system are extremely lightweight. However, the simple matter is, the Observer Effect, where the observation of an event actually causes changes to that event, absolutely can impact your systems. While you must gather information about the systems in order to better manage them, you have to balance that with negatively impacting the behavior of the system. So while you should use the mechanisms outlined in this chapter, you still have to be dilligent in how you use them in order to ensure that you're not harming your systems.

Collecting Server Information

We have to immediately differentiate between server information that is reflected in how your operating system, container, virtual machine, hardware or cloud platform is behaving, from information about the PostgreSQL cluster running there. This chapter is not going to cover all possible operating systems and environments. Instead, we are going to focus on information about the PostgreSQL cluster. You will want to also take into account how your virtual machine, etc., are behaving as a part of monitoring your systems. However, we won't be delving into all that. There is simply too much to cover here otherwise.

Getting information about your instance and how it's behaving is relatively straightforward. The primary means of observing your server are through the error logs and the Cumulative Statistics System. We'll start by looking at the error logs.

Error Logs

The very first thing you should know about your cluster is if there are errors being reported. While it is possible your packager may have already configured error logging for you, it is useful to walk through how you would set up error logging yourself since, by default, all errors in PostgreSQL go to the stderr stream. To start to log the errors to a file, you have to reconfigure PostgreSQL. It's a simple configuration setting you have to change as shown in Listing 15-1:

Listing 15-1. *Turning on logging*

```
logging_collector = on
```

You should be able to find that setting under the REPORTING AND LOGGING section of the postgresql.conf. It will be set to the default, off. You can uncomment and change it to on, or simply add a new line. Once done and saved, you will have to restart the PostgreSQL service.

When that is complete, you can validate that the logging collector is running by using the SQL code in Listing 15-2:

Listing 15-2. *Validate the logging collector is running*

```
SHOW logging_collector;
```

The output will look something like Figure 15-1:

Figure 15-1. *Output from SHOW logging_collector*

You can control where the log files are kept and their naming standards by making changes to the configuration file. To see the default location, run the code in Listing 15-3:

Listing 15-3. *Finding out where the log files are kept*

```
SHOW log_directory;
```

The path shown will be relative to your data directory for PostgreSQL. The default value looks like Figure 15-2:

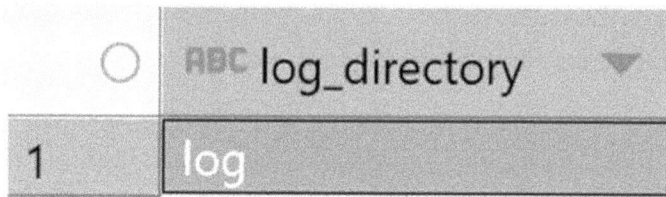

Figure 15-2. *The location of the log files*

You can also see the current log file name, making it easy to track down where the current logs are going as shown in Listing 15-4:

Listing 15-4. *Retreiving the current log file name*

```
SELECT pg_current_logfile();
```

The output here will include the path relative to the data directory again, as well as the current log file. You can see an example in Figure 15-3:

Figure 15-3. *The active log file for a PostgreSQL instance*

By default, the files are named using the date and time when they were created. If we were to navigate to the file location and open it up using an editor, it would look something like Figure 15-4:

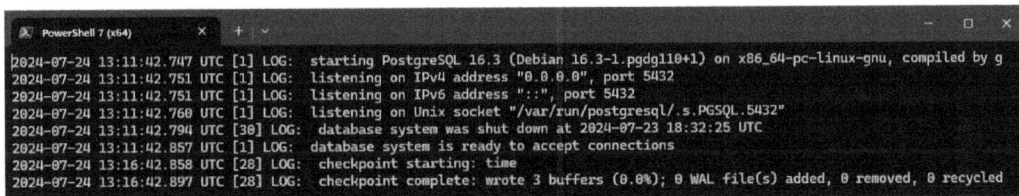

Figure 15-4. *Output from the PostgreSQL log file as the instance starts*

You have a lot of options to control what gets logged and how it is logged. While the default is through stderr, you can add or change the output to:

- `csvlog`: Log output is to a comma separated value file. This is a very common approach to facilitate import to a third-party log analysis tool.

- `jsonlog`: This ouputs the log to JSON format. Once more, this facilitates loading the log into third-party tooling.

- `syslog`: For output to the sylog deamon. It does require making modifications to the deamon to manage the data.

- eventlog: For output to the Windows OS event log. Once again, edits to how the events are captured will be required. This, and syslog, facilitates using third-party logging and alerting software.

As was previously mentioned, the log file names and location are set by default. However, you can directly control them by changing settings in the config file. The logs will automatically rotate based on time or file size, starting a new log file when either threshold is reached. There are a number of additional settings for where your logs are stored defined in the PostgreSQL documentation (https://tinyurl.com/53emnfts).

The information captured by the logs is based on a number of different factors, the first of which are the message levels. The first level, by default, is when a WARNING occurs on the system. A warning comes from potential problems in the code. Heading up in severity you'll see entries in the log when:

- ERROR: Occurs when a command has aborted.

- LOG: Administration information, like the startup & recovery data in Figure 15-4.

- FATAL: Occurs when a session, not just a command, has been aborted.

- PANIC: Occurs when the entire instance, including all database sessions, has been aborted. Appropriately named.

You can change this in the configuration, setting it higher, or lower, to capture less, or more, information.

In addition to errors and warnings, you can also use the log to capture long running statements. This is not enabled by default. However, you can again change the configuration to add this information to your log file output.

Finally, you can configure more directly what is logged in terms of the verbosity and detail that goes into the logs.

It's a very standard practice to bring in extensions and tools such as pgBadger (https://pgbadger.darold.net/) or other third-party options to help deal with logs. You will need to add some mechanism of alerting in order for your logs to be more than just an investigation tool, although they do a great job of that.

Cumulative Statistics System

Built into PostgreSQL is a mechanism for showing internal behaviors known as the Cumulative Statistics System. This consists of, as of PostgreSQL 16, 22 views that represent metrics covering behaviors from indexes, to IO on the system, to behavior of the write ahead log. The information is aggregated and written to disk. It will be available after a controlled restart of the system.

In the event of a system crash, the Cumulative Statistics System is reset. The same thing happens in the event of a failover to a secondary server, a point in time restore, or when the command `pg_stat_reset` is given. The Auto Vacuum process uses information from the Cumulative Statistics, so resetting them should be done cautiously with this knowledge in mind.

Cumulative Statistics are not instantaneous. Processes within PostgreSQL will write out to the system at a set interval, one second by default. Within a transaction, the information retrieved from the Cumulative Statistics will always be the same.

Security directly impacts what is visible. You may only be able to see your own activity in the system, or up to all activity within the system, depending on the role of the login. It's also possible to deny access to this information entirely.

Some of the information is dynamic, meaning it gets updated each time you query it. Other parts are simply accumulated data, based on the activity of your system.

For more details on all this, please see the PostgreSQL documentation (https://tinyurl.com/3bu5n53x).

Retrieving the information is simply a matter of running queries against the system views. One of the most common queries you're likely to run will be against pg_stat_activity. This view shows what is currently happening on the server in question:

Listing 15-5. Querying pg_stat_activity

```
SELECT
       psa.datname,
       psa.usename,
       psa.query,
       psa.xact_start,
       psa.query_start
FROM
       pg_stat_activity AS psa;
```

This will return one row for every server process, whether from a user or the system, active or not. The results of this query are shown in Figure 15-5:

	datname	usename	query	xact_start	query_start
1	[NULL]	[NULL]		[NULL]	[NULL]
2	[NULL]	postgres		[NULL]	[NULL]
3	bluebox	postgres	SET search_path = public,public,"$user"	[NULL]	2024-07-29 08:47:05.276 -0500
4	bluebox	postgres	SELECT c.oid,c.*,d.description,pg_catalog.pg_get_expr(c.relpartbound,	[NULL]	2024-07-29 09:25:04.970 -0500
5	bluebox	postgres	SELECT¶ psa.datname,¶ psa.usename,¶ psa.query,¶ psa.xact_start,¶ psa	2024-07-29 09:36:37.909 -0500	2024-07-29 09:36:37.910 -0500
6	[NULL]	[NULL]		[NULL]	[NULL]
7	[NULL]	[NULL]		[NULL]	[NULL]
8	[NULL]	[NULL]		[NULL]	[NULL]

Figure 15-5. *Current activity on the system*

The columns returned are:

- `datname`: The name of the database where the session is running.
- `usename`: The name of the user logged in and running the process
- `query`: The query being run
- `xact_start`: The start date and time of the transaction
- `query_start`: The start date and time of the query itself, separate from the transaction since a given transaction may have multiple queries

This is just a sample of the information included with `pg_stat_activity`. You can limit the rows returned by adding a `WHERE` clause since these views are just like any other object you query in the database. For our purposes, some very common use cases might be to only include processes where the state is equal to 'active', meaning queries currently running on the system:

Listing 15-6. Limiting the results to only active queries

```
SELECT
        psa.datname,
        psa.usename,
        psa.query,
        psa.xact_start,
        psa.query_start
FROM
        pg_stat_activity AS psa
WHERE psa.state = 'active';
```

pg_stat_activity is an example of a dynamic view that is updated each time you query it.

Another commonly used Cumulative Statistics view is pg_stat_database. This provides information about the database including things such as number of rows accessed, transaction commits and rollbacks and the number of sessions run against the database. For example, to see all the rows that have been read or written to a database, you might run a query like Listing 15-7:

Listing 15-7. Getting the counts of rows, or tuples, from a database

```
SELECT
        psd.tup_returned,
        psd.tup_inserted,
        psd.tup_updated,
        psd.tup_deleted
FROM
        pg_stat_database AS psd
WHERE
        psd.datname = 'bluebox';
```

The results are shown in Figure 15-6:

123 tup_returned	123 tup_inserted	123 tup_updated	123 tup_deleted
17,623,985	3,590,199	244	197

Figure 15-6. All rows read, inserted, updated or deleted for one database

Drilling down inside a database, a very commonly used Cumulative Statistics view is `pg_stat_all_tables`. Here you get information similar to the database including rows that have been read, inserted or deleted, but even more, such as the number of sequential scans or index scans and even the last time Vacuum was run against the table. There are also views that narrow down the selection to either user or system tables; `pg_stat_user_tables` and `pg_stat_sys_tables`.

An example here would be to look for all tables within the public schema that have had sequential scans:

Listing 15-8. *All tables that have a sequential scan*

```
SELECT
        psut.relname,
        psut.seq_scan,
        psut.last_seq_scan
FROM
        pg_stat_user_tables AS psut
WHERE
        psut.schemaname = 'public'
        AND psut.seq_scan > 0
ORDER BY
        psut.last_seq_scan DESC;
```

The relname is the table name. The output looks like Figure 15-7:

	relname	123 seq_scan	last_seq_scan
1	store	4	2024-07-10 09:59:43.336 -0500
2	inventory	4	2024-07-10 09:59:43.336 -0500
3	rental	6	2024-07-10 09:59:43.336 -0500
4	film_crew	4	2024-07-10 09:59:42.992 -0500
5	film_production_company	3	2024-07-10 09:59:42.992 -0500
6	payment	6	2024-07-10 09:59:42.992 -0500
7	zip_code_info	2	2024-07-10 09:59:42.992 -0500
8	customer	4	2024-07-10 09:59:42.992 -0500
9	film_cast	4	2024-07-10 09:59:42.992 -0500
10	production_company	2	2024-07-10 09:59:42.992 -0500
11	film	2	2024-07-10 09:59:41.675 -0500
12	release_type	1	2024-07-10 09:59:19.572 -0500
13	film_genre	1	2024-07-10 09:59:17.498 -0500
14	person	2	2024-07-10 09:59:17.498 -0500
15	spatial_ref_sys	1	2024-07-10 09:59:04.617 -0500

Figure 15-7. Tables that have had a sequential scan

We can drill down even further to look at indexes and index behavior using pg_stat_all_indexes. Here again we have pg_stat_user_indexes and pg_stat_sys_indexes views to break out the data. The information stored includes the number of index scans that have occurred, when the last one was, and the number of rows read. An example query is shown in Listing 15-9:

Listing 15-9. Retrieving index scans from pg_stat_user_indexes

```
SELECT
        psui.schemaname,
        psui.relname,
        psui.indexrelname,
        psui.idx_scan,
        psui.idx_tup_read,
        psui.last_idx_scan
FROM
        pg_stat_user_indexes AS psui
WHERE
        psui.idx_scan > 0
        AND psui.idx_tup_read > 0;
```

Which results in the output shown in Figure 15-8:

	schemaname	relname	indexrelname	idx_scan	idx_tup_read	last_idx_scan
1	public	customer	customer_pkey	4	373,482	2024-07-10 09:59:43.336 -0500
2	public	film_cast	film_cast_pk	2	2	2024-07-10 09:59:42.992 -0500
3	public	film_crew	film_crew_pk	2	2	2024-07-10 09:59:42.992 -0500
4	public	film	film_pkey	12	31,772	2024-07-10 09:59:42.992 -0500
5	public	film_production_company	film_production_company_pk	2	2	2024-07-10 09:59:42.992 -0500
6	public	person	person_pkey	6	511,950	2024-07-10 09:59:42.992 -0500
7	public	production_company	production_company_pkey	2	2	2024-07-10 09:59:42.992 -0500
8	public	store	store_pkey	4	4	2024-07-10 09:59:42.992 -0500
9	public	zip_code_info	zip_code_info_pk	2	38,195	2024-07-10 09:59:43.336 -0500

Figure 15-8. Indexes that have been scanned within the database

We can also focus exclusively on IO through the use of `pg_statio_all_tables`, which also has a user and system view. Now, instead of focusing on tuples, we'll be retrieving the actual blocks that have been affected. This allows for monitoring at a lower level within the system. So, another example would be to see the 8k page blocks that have been read from disk, and those read from memory:

Listing 15-10. *Retrieving the blocks read from heaps*

```
SELECT
        psut.relname,
        psut.heap_blks_read,
        psut.heap_blks_hit
FROM
        pg_statio_user_tables AS psut
WHERE
        psut.schemaname = 'staging';
```

The results are shown in Figure 15-9:

	relname	123 heap_blks_read	123 heap_blks_hit
1	film_cast	4,732	10,166
2	film_credits	1,553	8,855
3	film_crew	4,705	22,148
4	film_detail	558	1,127
5	holiday	5	7
6	release_date	1,248	2,566

Figure 15-9. *Blocks read from disk and from memory*

If you look at the first line, you can see that the film_cast table had 4,732 reads from disk and 10,166 reads from memory.

There are a number of other views available on the Cumulative Statistics. This collection of queries into the views shows examples of how you can gather metrics about the performance and behaviors of your cluster, databases, and the objects within them. There are a number of additional views into the Cumulative Statistics information listed in the documentation, so please use that as a resource. Just remember, since the Cumulative Statistics are an aggregate, you may need to create your own system of collecting them over time in order to have multiple points of comparison.

Query Performance Metrics

Knowing what is happening within your cluster is important. However, one of the primary performance issues you will be addressing regularly is that of the queries running on your system. There are several ways to capture query behavior within PostgreSQL. The first is to capture metrics as you execute a query. The second is to add an extension that let's you proactively capture query metric information. We'll cover both.

Query Metrics at Execution

A very easy way to get performance metrics for a query is to measure them at the time of execution. In order to have a query to consistently measure performance on, we're going to add a simple function to our database as shown in Listing 15-11:

Listing 15-11. The filmcast function retrieves the entire cast for one movie

```
CREATE OR REPLACE
FUNCTION bluebox.filmcast (filmid int)
RETURNS TABLE (filmtitle TEXT,
film_character TEXT,
actor TEXT)
AS $$
  SELECT f.title, fc.film_character, p.name
  FROM bluebox.film AS f
    JOIN bluebox.film_cast AS fc
      ON f.film_id = fc.film_id
    JOIN bluebox.person AS p
      ON fc.person_id = p.person_id
  WHERE f.film_id = filmid
$$
LANGUAGE SQL
```

With this function in place, Listing 15-12 shows how we can use it to retrieve a cast listing for the film "The Fifth Element":

Listing 15-12. Querying the filmcast function

```
SELECT
        *
FROM
        bluebox.filmcast(18);
```

Executing the query within DBeaver, we will see a simple, core metric: the amount of time it took this query to run and retrieve all the rows for the query. You can see this at the bottom of the query results screen as shown in Figure 15-10:

123 row(s) fetched - 0.074s, on 2024-07-30 at 08:02:54

Figure 15-10. The amount of time the query took to run

As a measure, this is adequate for some purposes. However, to get a more detailed view on query performance, we can modify how we query the function. Listing 15-13 adds EXPLAIN ANALYZE to the query:

Listing 15-13. Using EXPLAIN ANALYZE while querying the function

```
EXPLAIN ANALYZE
SELECT
        *
FROM
        bluebox.filmcast(18);
```

The results are shown in Figure 15-11:

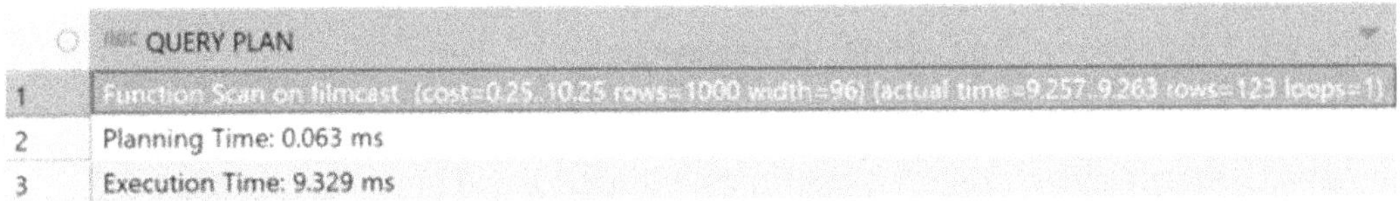

	QUERY PLAN
1	Function Scan on filmcast (cost=0.25..10.25 rows=1000 width=96) (actual time=9.257..9.263 rows=123 loops=1)
2	Planning Time: 0.063 ms
3	Execution Time: 9.329 ms

Figure 15-11. Query timing results and explain plan

A few things to point out in the results. First, you can see both the time it took to compile the explain plan within PostgreSQL and the total execution time, 9.329ms in this example. That helps you understand what is happening within the query. Further, if you look at the explain plan, you'll see that time values are also added to the operators there. This gives you further detail about how a given query is behaving within PostgreSQL.

It's worth noting, using EXPLAIN ANALYZE requires running the query to be analyzed against the system, with all the performance and system load implications that come with that query. Therefore, it's not a good idea to run this without thought, especially against larger queries on bigger systems that may already be under considerable load.

This is a very tactical way to observe query performance and is best used when focused on a query you've already identified as needing work. To better identify which queries you need to work on, you must add a more proactive monitoring approach.

Monitoring Query Metrics

PostgreSQL does not have a means of collecting query metadata by default since this kind of data collection can add overhead to a system. However, it is standard practice to take advantage of an extension, pg_stat_statements, to enable that type of data collection. While using pg_stat_statements is extremely common, it is important to know that it does add some overhead to the system, so enabling it, especially on a system already under stress, should be done carefully. That said, almost every major cloud provider does enable it by default.

The steps to enable pg_stat_statements are as follows. First, you'll need to modify the postgresql.conf file. Listing 15-14 shows the line that must be added:

Listing 15-14. Changes to the postgresql.conf file

```
shared_preload_libaries = 'pg_stat_statements'
```

If you already have values in the shared_preload_libraries setting, you can simply append `pg_stat_statements` using a comma separated list. There are additional properties for `pg_stat_statements` that you can also set within the configuration file. For our purposes here, the defaults will work fine. However, you can change the number of queries captured; the default value is 5,000. You can also change what kind of queries are captured. The default is 'top' which means only queries coming from clients, but you can change it to 'all', which includes queries inside functions, or 'none', which disables data collection.

With that addition to the configuration file, we now need to create the extension, `pg_stat_statements`. The command in Listing 15-15 must be run by a login with appropriate permissions from within the psql utility:

Listing 15-15. *Creating the pg_stat_statements extension*

```
create extension pg_stat_statements;
```

You should see a return of CREATE EXTENSION. However, you can validate that the extension was successfully created by listing out the extensions on your server using Listing 15-16:

Listing 15-16. *Which extensions are on the server*

```
\dx
```

The results will look something like Figure 15-12:

```
                                 List of installed extensions
          Name          | Version |  Schema    |                      Description
------------------------+---------+------------+-----------------------------------------------------------
 fuzzystrmatch          | 1.2     | public     | determine similarities and distance between strings
 pg_stat_statements     | 1.10    | public     | track planning and execution statistics of all SQL statements executed
 plpgsql                | 1.0     | pg_catalog | PL/pgSQL procedural language
 postgis                | 3.4.2   | public     | PostGIS geometry and geography spatial types and functions
 postgis_tiger_geocoder | 3.4.2   | tiger      | PostGIS tiger geocoder and reverse geocoder
 postgis_topology       | 3.4.2   | topology   | PostGIS topology spatial types and functions
(6 rows)
```

Figure 15-12. *A list of installed extensions*

You can see on the second line that pg_stat_statements is now installed with version 1.10.

You will now need to restart the PostgreSQL service in order for the extension to get loaded. We can easily validate if everything is working using Listing 15-17:

Listing 15-17. *Querying pg_stat_statements*

```
SELECT
      *
FROM
      pg_stat_statements AS pss;
```

If you get an error, you may need to check to see which of the preceding steps failed. The first time you run a query, you'll likely see no data at all. The second time you run a query, depending on the load on your system, you may only see the query in Listing 15-17. Otherwise, you should see something similar to Figure 15-13:

#	123 userid	123 dbid	✓ toplevel	123 queryid	ABC query
1	10	39,411	[v]	8,539,980,000,065,055,696	SELECT c.oid, a.attnum, a.attname, c.relname, n.nspname
2	10	39,411	[v]	6,167,162,860,506,190,155	SET application_name = 'DBeaver 24.1.3 - SQLEditor <C
3	10	39,411	[v]	-8,902,887,982,724,596,472	SET application_name = 'DBeaver 24.1.3 - Metadata <bl
4	10	39,411	[v]	1,650,470,535,910,119,993	SELECT * FROM pg_stat_user_functions AS psuf
5	10	39,411	[v]	427,240,950,862,911,343	SELECT * FROM public.filmcast($1)
6	10	39,411	[v]	1,863,558,588,648,808,360	SELECT * FROM pg_stat_statements AS pss
7	10	39,411	[v]	-3,136,912,395,674,931,128	SET application_name = 'PostgreSQL JDBC Driver'
8	10	39,411	[v]	2,323,669,589,107,905,898	SHOW search_path
9	10	39,411	[v]	-4,570,799,927,402,708,811	SET extra_float_digits = 3
10	10	39,411	[v]	5,881,330,753,738,736,544	SET application_name = 'DBeaver 24.1.3 - SQLEditor <C
11	10	39,411	[v]	-1,060,727,637,632,159,469	SELECT current_schema(),session_user
12	10	39,411	[v]	2,741,659,110,022,807,052	SELECT c.oid, a.attnum, a.attname, c.relname, n.nspname
13	10	39,411	[v]	-7,293,484,450,177,423,104	SET application_name = 'DBeaver 24.1.3 - Main <bluebo
14	10	39,411	[v]	853,227,096,929,458,702	SET search_path = public,public,"$user"
15	10	39,411	[v]	2,353,672,630,740,010,998	SET SESSION CHARACTERISTICS AS TRANSACTION ISOL

Figure 15-13. Results from querying pg_stat_statements

The amount of information we get from `pg_stat_statements` is really good. There's a lot to it, but we'll just focus on some basic query metrics here. Also, as you can see above, you'll need to plan to locate your particular query out of the extensive list of queries (up to 5,000 by default, remember, and you can make that number larger). We would recommend tracking down the `queryid` value and then use that for all subsequent queries. Before running this next query, be sure to go back to Listing 15-12 to query the `filmcast` function. Listing 15-18 shows one way to get that value:

Listing 15-18. Finding the queryid for filmcast

```
SELECT
      pss.queryid
FROM
      pg_stat_statements AS pss
WHERE
      pss.query LIKE '%bluebox.filmcast%';
```

In this specific database, the value returned is 427240950862911343. We can then use that to get more interesting information as shown in Listing 15-19:

Listing 15-19. *Retrieving performance metrics for one query*

```
SELECT
      pss.calls,
      pss.total_exec_time,
      pss.min_exec_time,
      pss.max_exec_time,
      pss.mean_exec_time,
      pss.stddev_exec_time
FROM
      pg_stat_statements AS pss
WHERE
      pss.queryid = 427240950862911343;
```

With this query we get:

- `calls`: The actual number of times the query has been run

- `total_exec_time`: across all the calls, what is the total run time

- `min_exec_time`: the fastest time the query ran in

- `max_exec_time`: the slowest time in which the query ran

- `mean_exec_time`: the average, or mean, run time for the query

- `stdev_exec_time`: the standard deviation value for the mean execution of the query

That goes a long way to understanding the behavior of this query. If we were to also capture these values over a period of days, or before and after creating an index, we would have the necessary comparison points to understand our query's behavior in detail.

There is all sorts of additional information in pg_stat_statements, from the rows and blocks read by a query, to blocks written, write time, write ahead log information, and more.

Conclusion

In this chapter we introduced several mechanisms for observing how your servers, databases and queries are behaving within PostgreSQL. All these tools, and more, are useful additions to your tool belt. Just remember that monitoring is best done with multiple data points over time in order to truly understand how systems are behaving. All observation of a system can, to a degree, negatively impact that system. However, without observation (monitoring) of a system, we can't know how that system is behaving. So, we are going to take advantage of these tools that PostgreSQL gives us in order to gain that knowledge of what our systems are doing.

16
PostgreSQL
on the Cloud

Service offerings within the cloud are now a common part of any organization's infrastructure. Whether an organization is 100% in the cloud, or only partially hosting services in the cloud in a hybrid environment mixed with on-premises services, very few do not have at least some services hosted in the cloud. PostgreSQL is no exception. It's extremely common for organizations to have virtual machines (VM) in the cloud and then manage their PostgreSQL environments on these VMs. What's less common but growing is hosting PostgreSQL within the Platform as a Service (PaaS) offerings.

In this chapter we'll explore, in general, why hosting PostgreSQL within one of the PAAS services may be a good fit for some organizations. We'll also discuss the general strengths and weaknesses of hosting PostgreSQL in this fashion.

Then, we'll look at the features and offerings of each of the three largest cloud services organizations: Amazon Web Services (AWS), Microsoft Azure and Google Cloud Platform (GCP). This will be an overview of each of these services.

Since these types of cloud services change extremely rapidly, the broad information within this chapter will be largely applicable for years to come, but many of the details may be subject to change.

Why the Cloud?

The classic definition of the cloud is put simply as "someone else's server." With this definition, why would organizations consider hosting any of their services in the cloud? The shortest possible answers to this question come down to costs and capabilities.

First, the costs. Some organizations have both the money and the need to build their own data centers. They can afford to invest in high availability, disaster recovery, large scale data movement and all the rest of the associated costs that come with running a large scale, or even global enterprise. In fact, they may already have this capacity and are simply maintaining and growing the existing services.

However, many organizations simply don't have the money, or the time, to build out multiple data centers in multiple locations around the world. Further, they simply may not have the need to manage all this on their own. For these organizations, the cloud becomes a cost-effective mechanism for building out a global infrastructure, without actually building out a global infrastructure. By using "someone else's server" to get the job done, these organizations can realize global data management and services for radically reduced costs.

Further, the time it takes to set up a global service within the cloud is orders of magnitude less than it is to do the same thing on your own. A very few commands or clicks of the mouse on many cloud services will have replication set up between multiple locations around the world.

Next, capabilities. There are organizations out there that have extremely capable, and usually larger, IT organizations that have the institutional knowledge and skills to support a large scale and global data infrastructure. They regularly test and develop bigger and better high availability, disaster recovery and other data services because they can.

The vast majority of businesses, small, large and in-between, simply do not have these kinds of IT capabilities within the organization. Developing and growing these capabilities is an expensive and time-consuming process. By taking advantage, once again, of "someone else's server," organizations with a smaller IT team can create global infrastructure for their organization, but much simpler and quicker.

Teams will still need to develop knowledge and understanding of the cloud to maximize the capabilities and benefits for the organization. Further, getting the cloud wrong can be quite costly, and investments in time for training and knowledge development are vital to a successful cloud implementation.

On top of this, some of the cloud service offerings may simply be completely unique. This makes the cloud the one place to go for some types of capability.

While there are other reasons why organizations may choose the cloud, these two are generally the primary motivating factors.

Why Platform as a Service (PaaS)?

If any organization chooses to host data in the cloud, why not simply default to setting up VMs, install PostgreSQL there, and manage it that way? Well, for a lot of organizations, they do just that and it works just fine for them.

As before, when talking about capabilities, we need to consider the internal knowledge and skills of any given organization. Maybe the IT department has development teams who build out applications that generate and consume data through PostgreSQL. However, they don't have the skills to appropriately backup, maintain, protect, and provide high availability for their PostgreSQL databases. Further, they may want some of the functionality within the various PaaS offerings that are unique, such as Query Store on Azure or Query Insights on GCP.

The beauty of choosing a database as a service through PaaS on one of the cloud vendor platforms is that you eliminate the need for a lot of work. You don't have to worry about maintaining an operating system. That's taken care of. In fact, you can't even see the operating system. You also eliminate a lot of standard maintenance tasks. The various cloud vendors all handle backups and provide point-in-time recovery. Many of the cloud vendors offer local and global high availability through their database as a service offerings. You also get the benefits of enhanced security, well beyond the capabilities of many IT teams. You get fundamental monitoring and alerting built into these tools. Finally, you may see unique capabilities offered by the cloud vendor that are not available through VMs, even on the cloud.

These are all reasons to look at PaaS.

There are also a few reasons why a given organization may want to avoid PaaS. The number one reason is that you have a workload that simply doesn't lend itself to being hosted within the database as a service offering. This may be because of bandwidth issues, functions needed within the operating system, or, specific to PostgreSQL, extensions you need to run that are not currently supported by a particular cloud vendor. Also, for many cloud vendors, getting databases into their systems is quite easy. Getting the data back out may be more difficult, as well as costly. Some vendors use proprietary backups that can't be restored to a standard PostgreSQL instance. Because of all this, some organizations do fear having a vendor lock-in, so they avoid using the PaaS offerings.

The cloud, and more specifically, database as a service, is not for everyone. It's best to fully evaluate the costs and capabilities in conjunction with your organization's needs before you make a leap into the cloud.

PaaS Services

All three of the largest cloud services vendors offer support for PostgreSQL within a PaaS offering. Largely, since they are all PostgreSQL or forks of PostgreSQL, there is a sameness to these offerings. After all, it's still (mostly!) PostgreSQL in the internals. The differentiators are in how they manage your PostgreSQL data and in the unique offerings they may have around system management, disaster recovery, high availability, and other functionality.

In the following sections we'll explore the general offerings of each cloud service provider and an overview of some of the unique functionality available. We won't be making a head-to-head comparison and we're definitely not talking price, which is subject to change rather frequently. This is meant as an introduction to each vendor for you to understand which may be a better fit for your needs. Also, it bears repeating, things change rather quickly within the cloud. While the general aspects of each service will age well, some details will be different.

AWS

AWS hosts two versions of PostgreSQL. There is a standard version of PostgreSQL as a part of the AWS Relational Database Service (RDS, https://tinyurl.com/yc6acppj) and a fork of PostgreSQL available through AWS Aurora (https://tinyurl.com/ycx7apue). As with most cloud services, the PostgreSQL offerings require payment. However, as of this writing, there is a free tier of AWS RDS available for testing, learning, and development (https://tinyurl.com/2chk8abu).

AWS RDS

AWS RDS is actually a number of different database offerings that includes PostgreSQL. The core concept is that you will be deploying just a database. That means you won't have to worry about tasks such as configuring and maintaining the server, patching the operating system and PostgreSQL, backups, disk management and provisioning. All of that is managed by AWS RDS.

As of this writing, PostgreSQL versions supported on AWS include: 9.6 through 16. AWS maintains a list of approved extensions. Plus, they are working on a service called Trusted Language Extensions (TLE) framework for PostgreSQL so that you can build and run your own extensions without needing AWS to validate the extension when running through AWS RDS. However, as of this writing, the TLE is just getting started.

Security is fundamental to the way AWS RDS is defined. You have network isolation through the Amazon Virtual Private Cloud. The data is encrypted at rest. You control the keys through the AWS services. Finally, data in transit is also encrypted using Secure Socket Layer. If you choose to expose your PostgreSQL to the internet, there is a built-in firewall that prevents access to any except what you choose to expose.

By default, PostgreSQL running on AWS RDS gets availability protection within a single availability zone. You can add a secondary availability zone for a cost. You can even add additional availability zones and the ability to read from the secondary servers, again for a cost.

Basic monitoring of your PostgreSQL databases is possible within AWS RDS. You get the core metrics of I/O, memory and compute, all through a graphical user interface that you can also query. An example is shown here in Figure 16-1:

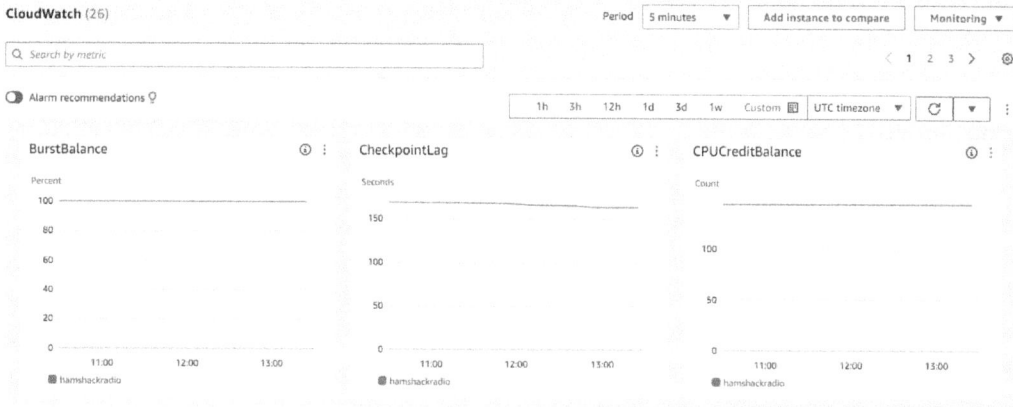

Figure 16-1. *CloudWatch in AWS RDS*

You can read more about PostgreSQL on AWS RDS here: https://tinyurl.com/2jv7wrcx

Listing 16-1. *Creating a PostgreSQL database in AWS RDS*

```
#Creation of an AWS RDS PostgreSQL instance can be done through #the AWS
command line utilities like this:

aws rds create-db-instance `
    --engine postgres `
    --db-instance-identifier newpostgres `
    --allocated-storage 10 `
    --db-instance-class db.t3.large `
    --vpc-security-group-ids sg-007bad1bob21eb88a `
    --db-subnet-group default-vpc-02xxq42area88d03f7 `
    --master-username myusername `
    --manage-master-user-password `
    --backup-retention-period 3
```

Without going into detail, you can see that we pick `postgres` as the `engine`. We then set various traits such as the size of the server through `db-instance-class`. Security is set through several of the values and we close off with setting our backup retention period to 3 days. For more details on the create-db-instance command, go here: https://tinyurl.com/y5w54k94

You can also use the console GUI as outlined here: https://tinyurl.com/2s4j7xet

Once you're connected to a PostgreSQL database within AWS RDS, it's just PostgreSQL. Most of the rest of the material covered in the preceding chapters of the book will apply. You can create database objects, add data and retrieve it, just like from any other PostgreSQL database.

Amazon Aurora

The Amazon Aurora database is not PostgreSQL but a fork of PostgreSQL. Because of this, Aurora is advertised as being PostgreSQL compatible, but not actually PostgreSQL, unlike RDS.

Aurora offers much of the same functionality that is offered by RDS. However, it expands on that capability quite a lot. For example, each Aurora database is automatically across three availability zones, but you only pay for one, enhancing the durability of the database. You also get enhanced performance, especially around I/O. The versions supported are the same as AWS RDS.

Unlike RDS though, Aurora supports a more limited number of extensions. These are specified and controlled by Amazon. You can only choose which extensions to add to your Aurora PostgreSQL database from the supported list and cannot add your own. There are also delegated extensions, an optional addition you can read more about here: https://tinyurl.com/yc435ayr

Security and monitoring, and most of the rest of management of Aurora are the same as with AWS RDS. Also, while Aurora PostgreSQL is a fork of PostgreSQL, working within it while connected is again, almost exactly the same as being within a standard PostgreSQL database.

Azure Database for PostgreSQL

Azure Database for PostgreSQL is a fully hosted database as a service offering within Microsoft's Azure platform. You will not be managing an operating system, disks, or even the PostgreSQL server itself. Instead, you will have a PostgreSQL database within which you'll be able to create tables and maintain data, just like with any other PostgreSQL database.

As of this writing, versions 11 to 16 of PostgreSQL are supported on Azure Database. Patches and upgrades are handled by the Azure system. There is a limited list of extensions available here:

https://tinyurl.com/3uw3dak9

Microsoft has added its own extensions within Azure as well, including the Azure AI extension and others. One of the more exciting extensions is called Query Store. This extension is very similar to a function on SQL Server with the same name. It's a way of capturing query metrics and EXPLAIN plans over time for troubleshooting and query tuning.

Security for Azure Database is extensive. You can set up multi-factor authentication, Kerberos, simple passwords and more. Data at rest and in motion is encrypted. There is a firewall in place if you do choose to expose your database to the internet.

Under the covers, you actually have multiple PostgreSQL databases being maintained to supply you with a high availability solution, built into and a fundamental part of Azure Database. Additional high availability options can be enabled, including zone redundancy, multi-zone backups and more, at a cost. You automatically get a point in time recovery system through automated backups.

Monitoring is available through the Azure portal along with alerting. Figure 16-2 shows an example of one metric being displayed:

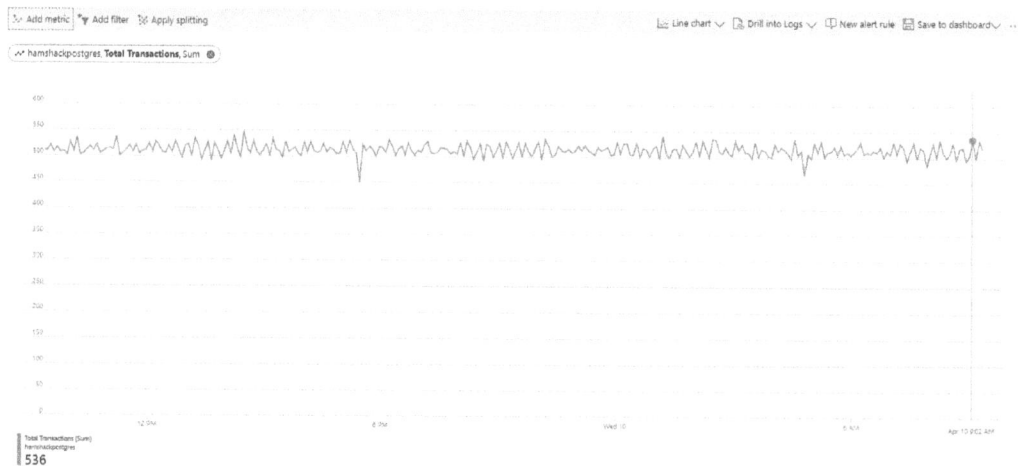

Figure 16-2. Metrics on display in Azure Portal

You can read more about PostgreSQL on Azure here:

https://tinyurl.com/bdd273sa

There is a full set of PowerShell scripts for managing your Azure Database for PostgreSQL. In addition, there is a command line interface for Azure that will also allow you to create databases like this:

Listing 16-2. Creating a PostgreSQL flexible server in Azure

```
az postgres flexible-server create --location eastus \
   --resource-group AzureDevOps --name mypostgresqldb \
   --admin-user myusername --admin-password mypassword
```

We define `postgres` immediately in the command line and then only have to define the location, name of database, and some security settings. More details on how to use `flexible server create` are available here:

https://tinyurl.com/mutwcjrf

It's also possible to create your Azure Database for PostgreSQL through the GUI portal. Details on that are available here:

https://tinyurl.com/yryurpeb

Once connected to a PostgreSQL database on Azure, it's largely the same as being connected to any other PostgreSQL database. The whole idea of platform as a service requires that type of behavior. A free tier for development and testing of PostgreSQL is available:

https://tinyurl.com/bddyksv8

Google Cloud Platform

Google Cloud Platform (GCP) has two versions of PostgreSQL, a standard PaaS offering through GCP Cloud SQL for PostgreSQL and an expanded fork of PostgreSQL called AlloyDB for PostgreSQL. As with the other services, for the most part, once you're inside one of these PostgreSQL databases, it operates in most of the same ways as a PostgreSQL instance would be running within your own servers.

Cloud SQL for PostgreSQL

Cloud SQL for PostgreSQL is a fully hosted version of PostgreSQL that offers managed instances of PostgreSQL. Point in time recovery is offered through a backup system maintained with GCP. Data in motion and at rest is encrypted within the GCP system.

At the time of this writing, versions 9.6 through 16 of PostgreSQL are supported on GCP. You can, for a cost, set up replication between multiple zones with automated failover. A limited list of PostgreSQL extensions that are supported can be found here: https://tinyurl.com/bdesw2sp

There is monitoring built into the Google Cloud Platform. It covers the basics of CPU, memory and the rest.

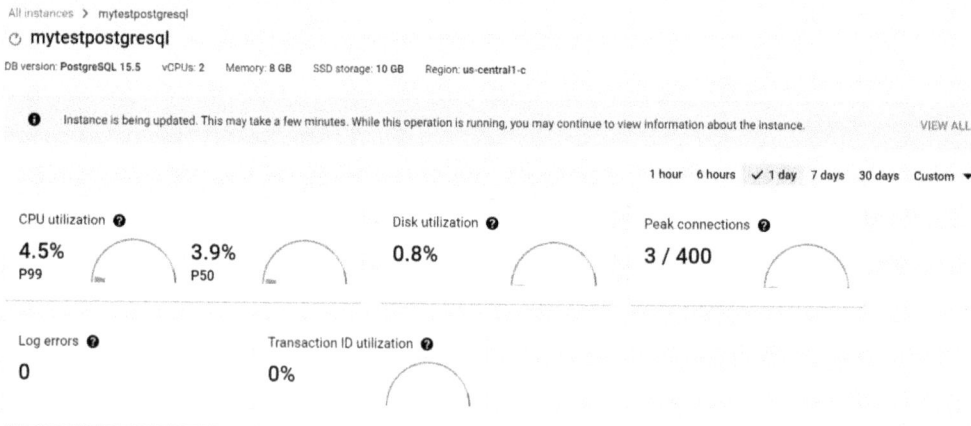

Figure 16-3. Monitoring PostgreSQL on GCP

There is also a query monitoring solution that can capture query metrics. In addition, you can add explain plans by enabling a cloud flag on GCP.

You can read more about Cloud SQL for PostgreSQL here: https://tinyurl.com/52kekavd

You can control and create databases through the gcloud command line, or a console on GCP. Creating an instance of Cloud SQL is accomplished similar to Listing 16-3:

Listing 16-3. Creating a Cloud SQL for PostgreSQL server

```
gcloud sql instances create mytestpostgresqldb \
--database-version=POSTGRES_16 \
--region=us-central1-c \
--zone=zonal \
--tier=db-perf-optimized-N-4
```

The minimums for creating a Cloud SQL database are a bit different. We name the database as PostgreSQL by picking the specific version of the database using `database-version`. Then it's just setting the location information. For more on using the gcloud command line go here: https://tinyurl.com/mrxs69yp. As of this writing, there is no free tier available for Cloud SQL on Google Cloud Platform.

AlloyDB for PostgreSQL

In addition to the Cloud SQL databases, a fork of PostgreSQL is available through the AlloyDB. This is listed as PostgreSQL compatible, meaning that while it is a fork of PostgreSQL, there may be distinct differences in behavior. AlloyDB is different than Cloud SQL in that it is customizable for vCPU, memory and storage. Additionally, depending on the tier chosen, up to 99.99% up-time and up to 35 days point in time recovery. Further, through AlloyDB Omni, you can install and run this database locally as well as host it on the Google Cloud Platform.

AlloyDB is, as of the time of writing, compatible with versions 14 or 15 of PostgreSQL (as well as a preview of 16). You can read more about AlloyDB here: https://tinyurl.com/5yxcfyym

AlloyDB is actually a cluster of virtual machines with shared storage. This allows you to have one machine acting as the principal for data collection, but other VMs can be used as readable secondaries, offloading some of the work. This also adds redundancy and resiliency to your PostgreSQL instance.

Operations within the AlloyDB are mostly the same as within any other PostgreSQL instance. Monitoring is a little different since you're monitoring both an instance of PostgreSQL, but also a cluster of virtual machines. Figure 16-4 shows this in practice:

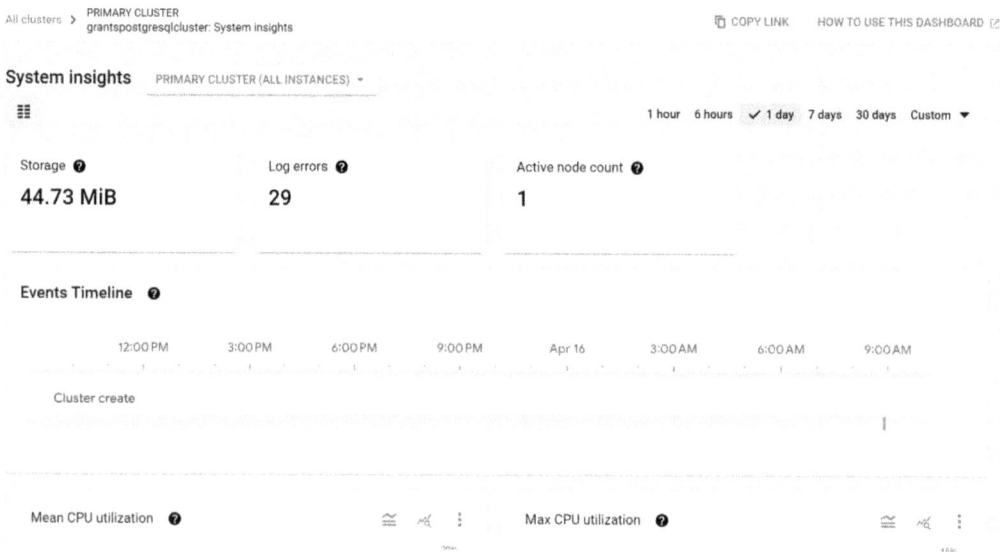

Figure 16-4. *AlloyDB cluster being monitored*

Conclusion

PostgreSQL is fully supported through Platform as a Service offerings by all the major cloud vendors. In addition, there are numerous smaller vendors offering Postgres based DBaaS solutions with their own trade-offs, many of which can run inside the major cloud vendors. As outlined in this chapter, these PaaS offerings provide a lot of management and support for organizations that may not otherwise have the internal skills to appropriately support PostgreSQL. However, choosing to go to the cloud is not free, either in terms of money, time, or knowledge, you will have to spend all three to successfully implement PostgreSQL on any of the cloud vendor's platforms.

17

Where To Go For More Learning

At the beginning of this book, we mentioned how PostgreSQL is a mature project with decades of development under its belt, and as would be expected, the software, community, and ecosystem around PostgreSQL are quite large; far too large for any one resource to cover in its entirety. The purpose of this book is to act as a starting point for learning PostgreSQL. To master PostgreSQL, more information will be needed. This chapter guides you on some of the best resources out there for learning PostgreSQL, and, how best to take advantage of those resources. In this chapter we'll cover:

- PostgreSQL documentation

- Books that help you learn PostgreSQL

- Events that include PostgreSQL

- Online PostgreSQL resources

As with the rest of the book, the information in this chapter is an introduction to what's out there, not a complete listing of all available resources. The most important aspect of using the resources listed here is to ensure that they are either the up-to-date version or the correct version for your PostgreSQL servers.

PostgreSQL Documentation

We reference the PostgreSQL documentation multiple times throughout the book. The reason we do is because that is your primary resource for official information about PostgreSQL. We always start most of our learning with the PostgreSQL documentation. Not only is it a useful resource, but, like PostgreSQL, the documentation is open source, so you can even contribute to making it better.

While the PostgreSQL documentation is your starting point, there are a few things that you have to keep an eye on. If we start with the root location for the documentation (no tinyurl for this one example), https://www.postgresql.org/docs, you'll see the following (as of this writing):

Documentation 📄

    View the manual

Manuals 💻

You can view the manual for an older version or download a PDF of a manual from the below table.

Online Version	PDF Version
17 beta	A4 PDF (14.5 MB) • US PDF (14.4 MB)
16 / Current	A4 PDF (14.3 MB) • US PDF (14.1 MB)
15	A4 PDF (13.7 MB) • US PDF (13.5 MB)
14	A4 PDF (13.4 MB) • US PDF (13.3 MB)
13	A4 PDF (13.0 MB) • US PDF (12.9 MB)
12	A4 PDF (12.7 MB) • US PDF (12.6 MB)
Development snapshot	PDF version not available

Looking for documentation for an older, unsupported, version? Check the archive of older manuals.

Translated Manuals

- Chinese
- French
- Japanese
- Russian

Figure 17-1. PostgreSQL documentation landing page

Two important points to note. First, you have various versions of PostgreSQL mentioned. The most important one, as of this writing, is the one for "16 / Current". The PostgreSQL documentation is designed so that "Current" always refers to the latest stable major version of Postgres. You will also note that version 17, which was in beta testing when this image was taken, is also available for use. When version 17 is officially released, the "Current" link will point to that version instead, and in this case, version 12 will be removed as it will go end-of-life. Another point is that there are translations of the manual to various languages linked in the right sidebar, helping make this documentation more accessible.

However, the one key to using the PostgreSQL documentation successfully is to keep an eye on the version. While most search engines will automatically point you to the "Current" documents, this isn't 100% the case and sometimes you will be pointed to an older version of the docs. Similarly, frequently when people link to the documentation from their own blogs and websites, you'll find that they've linked to older versions of the documentation. Figure 17-2 shows the current version of the Indexes page (located here: https://tinyurl.com/3eztm6kk):

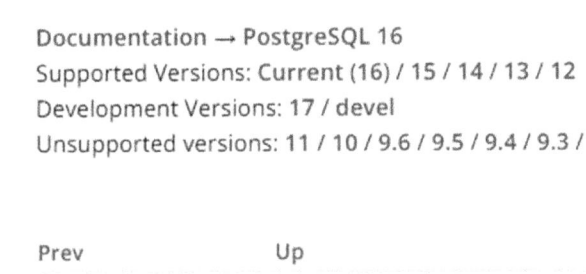

Documentation → PostgreSQL 16
Supported Versions: Current (16) / 15 / 14 / 13 / 12
Development Versions: 17 / devel
Unsupported versions: 11 / 10 / 9.6 / 9.5 / 9.4 / 9.3 /

Prev   Up

Chapter 11. Indexes

Table of Contents

11.1. Introduction
11.2. Index Types
      11.2.1. B-Tree

Figure 17-2. The "Current" documentation on indexes

While Figure 17-3 shows version 13 of the same landing page:

Documentation → PostgreSQL 13
Supported Versions: Current (16) / 15 / 14 / 13 / 12
Development Versions: 17 / devel
Unsupported versions: 11 / 10 / 9.6 / 9.5 / 9.4 / 9.3 / 9

Prev   Up

Chapter 11. Indexes

Table of Contents

11.1. Introduction
11.2. Index Types
11.3. Multicolumn Indexes

Figure 17-3. Version 13 of the documentation on indexes

While these look almost the same, they're not. The key is to note which version of the documentation you're on. If you look at the top of both Figures 16-2 and 16-3, you'll note that it says what version of the documentation you're currently looking at:

Documentation → PostgreSQL 13

Figure 17-4. The label that tells you the version of the documentation

You can also see this if you look at the two URLs:

https://www.postgresql.org/docs/13/indexes.html
https://www.postgresql.org/docs/current/indexes.html

Notice that version 13 is in the URL, as is "current".

The reason this is important is because you need to ensure that you're looking at the appropriate documentation. Something that works in the latest version of PostgreSQL may not work in version 13. Conversely, things that worked in 13 might not work in the latest version. If you're seeking to learn, you need to ensure that the version you're reading up on applies to the version you're using. Otherwise, you'll have a sometimes-painful process.

While the documentation is extremely good, it's not always laid out in a way that is conducive to how people learn. There also aren't pathways of learning through the documentation. This is why, despite how powerful the documentation is overall, there is a need for other resources to help you in your learning.

Books on PostgreSQL

There are many books on PostgreSQL, including the one you're reading. While no doubt all of them are worthy of your attention, we're going to call out just a few that might stand out from the crowd.

NOTE: None of the links provided here are affiliate links.

The Art of PostgreSQL

The Art of PostgreSQL (https://tinyurl.com/t5veh94e), by Dimitri Fontaine, is one of the most recommended books on PostgreSQL. The book itself focuses primarily on building applications with PostgreSQL , so it's clearly a must read for developers. However, well written SQL is just as important for working in analysis, report writing, or when supporting PostgreSQL, making this an informative read for just about anyone working within PostgreSQL.

Dimitri Fontaine has extensive experience working in development in general and specifically open-source development. He is a major contributor to PostgreSQL itself, so comes from a place of real knowledge and understanding.

Database Administration: The Complete Guide to DBA Practices and Procedures

Database Administration: The complete Guide to DBA Practices and Procedures (https://tinyurl.com/a8h3vxuu) was written by Craig S. Mullins. This isn't a book on PostgreSQL. Instead, it's a book on the job of the Database Administrator. However, since so many people are doing DBA work, probably without worrying about the title, or have stumbled into the job as "accidental" DBAs (you'll also hear "incidental" or "reluctant" DBAs), knowledge of what's necessary to get the job done makes a big difference in learning PostgreSQL.

Craig Mullins has over 40 years of experience within IT. This is the second edition of the book and is much more modern than the first. Mr. Mullins also wrote several other books on databases and development.

PostgreSQL Query Optimization: The Ultimate Guide to Building Efficient Queries

PostgreSQL Query Optimization: The Ultimate Guide to Building Efficient Queries (https://tinyurl.com/3t952jet), by Henrietta Dombrovskay, Boris Novikov and Anna Bailliekova. The second edition of the book improves on the original, expanding the information available and updating it based on new functionality. You'll get most of what you need to help improve the performance of your PostgreSQL instances.

Henrietta Dombrovskaya has over 40 year's experience within IT and fourteen working with PostgreSQL in particular. Boris Novikov is a database expert and university professor teaching at both undergraduate and post-graduate levels. Anna Bailliekova is a data engineer with more than twelve years of experience in IT.

PostgreSQL Events

Nothing quite beats in-person learning. From the ability to ask specific questions, to the hallway conversations between and around sessions, live, in-person learning has many advantages. There are a number of in-person events and resources that you should know about so that you can take advantage of them as a part of your continued learning within PostgreSQL.

User Groups and Meetups

One of the best in-person resources will always be local user groups, meetups and the like. Not only can you learn from the other attendees, but these are also your peers going through many of the same tribulations you are. You can network with them to make contacts that may help you in your career in other ways as well. Local groups act as a support network and a learning resource.

One of the best places to go for local PostgreSQL resources is right back to postgrsql.org. There is a listing of local user groups under the community page (https://tinyurl.com/3xcaee9n). These are broken down by country and city, so you can track down the one that's right for where you live, or even where you're visiting.

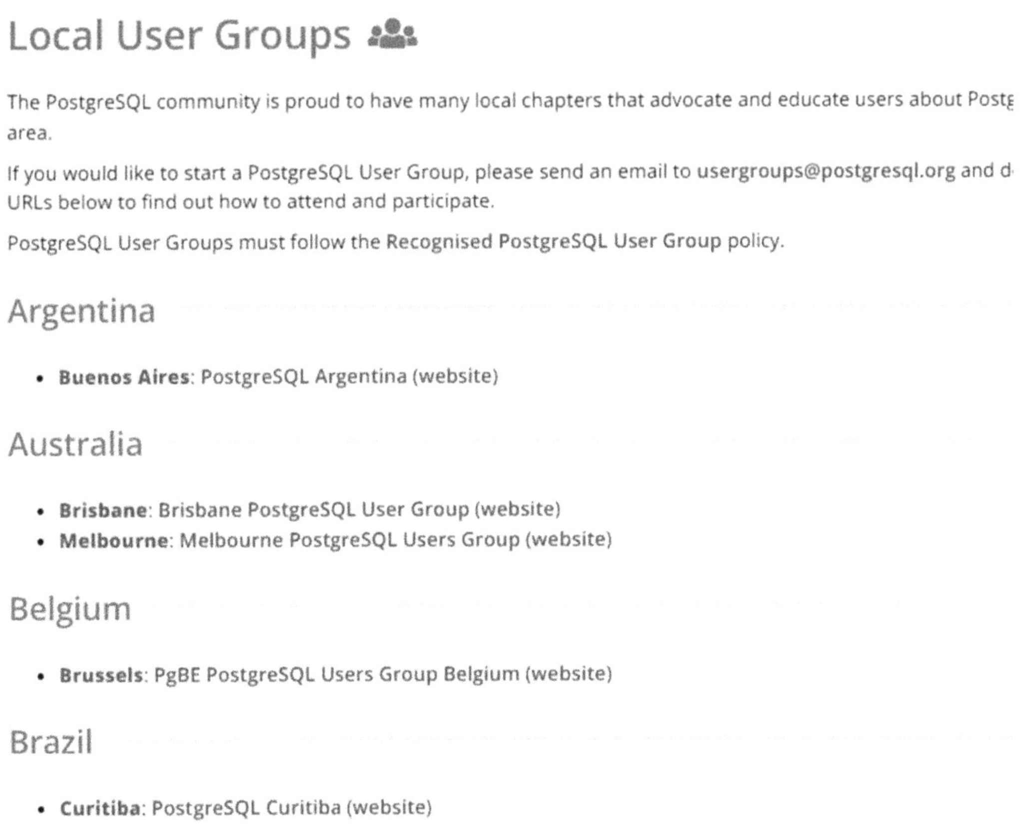

Local User Groups 👥

The PostgreSQL community is proud to have many local chapters that advocate and educate users about Postg area.

If you would like to start a PostgreSQL User Group, please send an email to usergroups@postgresql.org and d URLs below to find out how to attend and participate.

PostgreSQL User Groups must follow the Recognised PostgreSQL User Group policy.

Argentina

- **Buenos Aires**: PostgreSQL Argentina (website)

Australia

- **Brisbane**: Brisbane PostgreSQL User Group (website)
- **Melbourne**: Melbourne PostgreSQL Users Group (website)

Belgium

- **Brussels**: PgBE PostgreSQL Users Group Belgium (website)

Brazil

- **Curitiba**: PostgreSQL Curitiba (website)

Figure 17-5. Local User Groups on the PostgreSQL.org page

Another source for local resources to help you learn PostgreSQL is to look to MeetUp (https://www.meetup.com/). There may be some overlap between what's listed in MeetUp for your area and the Local User Groups listed above. However, a lot of different groups may be teaching PostgreSQL locally. Just as an example, a group in Washington DC called "Data Wranglers DC" meets on various database topics, including PostgreSQL. Another example is the "Berlin Accounting Tech" Meetup that will be hosting an event called "Building an Accounting Ledger with Postgres and Python." In addition to simply searching through MeetUp, there is a designated PostgreSQL page (https://www.meetup.com/pro/postgresql/).

Local Events

A local event is organized much less frequently than a user group. These may be annual or semi-annual and are meant to be a little more regional in scope. There are many different ones organized along different lines. Here are three examples:

PGDay

The PGDay events are organized under the umbrella of the PostgreSQL Community Conference rules (https://tinyurl.com/bfxkmw9n). There are a number of them in different locations around the world. These are typically a one-day event, focused exclusively on PostgreSQL, and often run by one of the User Groups listed on the communities page of PostgreSQL.org.

While these are local and regional events, they draw speakers from around the world. You'll be seeing the kinds of presentations that you'll see at the larger, international events. Upcoming PGDay events will be listed on the Events page of the Community section of PostgreSQL.org (https://tinyurl.com/mtsp2bfx).

DataSaturdays

DataSaturdays are a more generic type of regional event. Instead of a focus exclusively on PostgreSQL, these may include all sorts of other data platforms and other data-focused content. However, they regularly have PostgreSQL content, and some of it from the same speakers that you would see at much larger, international events. These events are organized locally and run under the rules outlined at the DataSaturdays website (https://datasaturdays.com/). Also, they're not just on Saturday so pay attention to the details and date of the event when you are planning to attend.

SQLSaturday

SQLSaturday started life as a Microsoft Data Platform only event. However, over the years, these one-day, local events, held all over the world, and just like DataSaturdays, held on every day of the week, have grown and expanded to the point where, the SQL in the name does include PostgreSQL sessions. While you won't see as much PostgreSQL content at these events, it is there and growing. SQLSaturday events are organized and run locally under the rules outlined at the SQLSaturday website (https://sqlsaturday.com/).

International Events

Generally, the larger events are almost always multi-day, paid affairs. They are often organized by larger groups of people that are probably not even local to where the event is taking place. These are likely to include one or more days of full-day content, often referred to as pre-cons, meaning pre-conference events. They will then have one or more days with multiple tracks, hosting a very large variety of content. Frequently this is where you'll see, and meet in person, some of the more well-known speakers. These events often draw attendees and speakers from around the world.

PGConf.EU

From a PostgreSQL perspective, PGConf.EU is the conference to attend. PGConf is organized and run by the governing body of PostgreSQL. It is considered not merely a premier event in general, but the showcase for PostgreSQL.

The .EU events are held in various locations around Europe. The 2023 event was in Malta. The 2024 event was in Athens, Greece. Upcoming events will be held in other locations.

In terms of in-person events, this is, without a doubt, the single best resource for PostgreSQL users (we'll talk more about developer resources at the Hackers Conference below). That's best in terms of the number and quality of sessions, as well as the people presenting them. That's not to say others are not good, especially when you consider they draw from a lot of the same speakers. However, PGConf.EU is very well established within the PostgreSQL community and draws from a larger speaker pool.

PGConf.NYC

Run by the US PostgreSQL organization, PGConf.NYC is another event that draws on both an international attendance and an international pool of speakers. While not as large as PGConf.EU, it's still one of the larger PostgreSQL specific in-person events you could attend.

PGConf.Dev

The PGConf.Dev, formerly PGCon, conference is specifically focused on those individuals who are contributing to PostgreSQL development. As such, it doesn't offer as many general knowledge sessions as many of the other conferences on this list. Instead, it is focused on how to contribute to the PostgreSQL project itself. If you are interested in moving into this aspect of PostgreSQL, or want to get deeper into the PostgreSQL internals, this is probably the single most important conference. The event used to be held exclusively in Ottawa, Canada, but moved to Vancouver in 2024, and will be held in Montreal in 2025.

Postgres Conference

Postgres Conference is a privately run non-profit event focused on training and networking around Postgres technology. The event itself has sessions lead by acknowledged industry experts. It very much focuses on collaboration between the industry and the end-users. In addition to the in-person events, they regularly host online webinars as well.

PASS Data Community Summit

Only within the last two years has the PASS Data Community Summit embraced PostgreSQL as a fundamental aspect of the event. However, this large, in-person event, usually held in Seattle, WA, is quickly becoming an established destination for PostgreSQL learning. There have been dedicated tracks and pre-cons available on PostgreSQL, with sessions by many of the same people you would see at PGConf.EU or Postgres Conference.

Developer Conferences

Everything mentioned so far has either been conferences dedicated to PostgreSQL, or conferences dedicated to databases and data management. However, there is a lot of PostgreSQL learning available at a whole host of large scale, international events such as:

- FOSDEM

- THAT Conference

- ScalePyCon

Online Resources

To say that there are a lot of resources online for PostgreSQL is probably the understatement of the century, and the century is young. The trick then becomes finding those resources that are generally respected and are worth your time pursuing.

Aggregations

One of the best places to go to get access to online PostgreSQL material has to be Planet Postgres, which is a part of the PostgreSQL.org (https://planet.postgresql.org/). It mostly consists of blogging, but you'll also see webinars and podcasts go by as well. It's voluntary whether people publish through Planet Postgres, but it's still a great resource.

Another place to go for a broad set of contributions is the PostgreSQL Slack (https://postgresteam.slack.com). There are several channels, but of special interest to someone just starting is the Beginners channel. You will find several different channels focused on various kinds of knowledge. There's also a channel on Events if you're looking for something along those lines.

Simple-Talk is an online magazine run by Redgate Software. It pays authors and goes through a rather rigorous editing process, making it a lot more than a blog. You can find a lot of content focused on PostgreSQL there (https://tinyurl.com/bdu22u3j).

Cooper Press publishes a PostgreSQL email newsletter weekly. This acts as an aggregator of blogs and other online content. You can sign up at their web site (https://tinyurl.com/59dv39zw).

Another place that can be a handy place to get a lot of information quickly is X, formerly Twitter. Specifically, going to the #pghelp hash tag, you'll see excellent questions and answers from a very active community. You can either ask questions and learn that way, or, read through people's questions and answers to learn.

One more source for questions and answers, as well as a broad source of information, would be Stack Exchange, but more specifically, the DBA part of Stack Exchange (https://dba.stackexchange.com/). Here again, you can ask questions, answer questions, or simply search to read about topics that you're attempting to learn.

Podcasts

If you enjoy learning by listening, then podcasts are the way to go.

One of the best podcasts out there is Talking Postgres with Claire Giordano(https://talkingpostgres.com/). She and her guests talk about just about everything there is to know about PostgreSQL. She has a very extensive backlog of episodes, so there's a lot to learn.

Another good podcast to learn PostgreSQL from is postgres.fm by Nikolay Samokhvalov and Michael Christofides (https://postgres.fm/). They cover a very wide set of topics, but they all revolve around PostgreSQL. Postgres.fm also has a very extensive backlog of episodes providing more learning.

One more podcast is Scaling PostgreSQL, hosted by Creson Jamison (https://www.scalingpostgres.com/). This weekly show is a little more focused in its topic, as clearly stated in the name. If you're looking to make your PostgreSQL bigger and faster, then this is your podcast.

Blogs

Trying to name individual blogs that are useful will be a difficult undertaking. Instead, we'll focus on a few blog aggregators. The first, we've already mentioned, is Planet Postgres. That would be the main place to start.

PGSQL Phriday is a monthly, themed, blog aggregator run by Ryan Booz but hosted by different people every month (https://www.pgsqlphriday.com/). A person is assigned a given month, and they get to think up a topic, question, or challenge, that a whole host of bloggers then go and create content for. It's been running for 17 months now, so there's a lot of content to pick from.

A slightly different blog aggregator is the PostgreSQL Person of the Week, published by Andreas Scherbaum (https://postgresql.life/). It's not exactly an aggregation of blog posts. Instead, it's a collection of interviews with various people who are involved with the PostgreSQL community. Many of them, however, do maintain blogs, so it's a way to get to know someone to decide if their blog is worth your time.

Webinars

While there are lots of YouTube channels publishing PostgreSQL content, here we'll focus just a few of the regular webinars associated with PostgreSQL, treating video similar to how we treated blogs.

It's a little unfair to call it just an online seminar, because Posette (formerly CitusCon) is much more of an event (https://tinyurl.com/2z2x9nd2). It covers a very wide range of PostgreSQL content. The most recent one hosted 42 sessions by experienced speakers. You can also watch content from earlier events, representing a large collection of content related to PostgreSQL.

Mentioned earlier, Postgres Conference runs a webinar series annually. The link is the same as the one published earlier. The content comes from a variety of people and covers many topics.

Ryan Booz has been running a regular online seminar series entitled PostgreSQL 101 (https://tinyurl.com/y5bd7ttn) hosted by Redgate Software. Clearly, if you're just getting started with PostgreSQL, this series is targeted at you.

One last online resource is the "Postgres for All" meetup, which functions just like any of the in-person MeetUp events, but instead is online. They provide an interactive platform for those learning and working in PostgreSQL (https://tinyurl.com/4b3xybyd).

Conclusion

The goal of this book is to give you the information you need to get started with PostgreSQL. However, we know that this topic, PostgreSQL, includes a lot of information. We're assuming you're going to need more than just our introduction. That's why we included so many other places to learn in this chapter. Whether you want to just go to your local meetup, travel to a large international conference, or learn online at home, we've covered a lot of that material.

Hopefully, you'll find this book helpful. Best of luck on your journey to learn PostgreSQL.

Index

A

Active Directory, 85
Aggregate, 201
AI, 142
AlloyDB, 305, 307, 308
ALTER, 89, 101, 102, 104
ALTER DATABASE, 113, 114, 115, 116, 118, 119, 122
ALTER EXTENSION, 130
ALTER FUNCTION, 181
ALTER ROLE, 89
ALTER TABLE, 122
ANALYZE, 193, 194, 195, 196, 197, 208, 210, 216, 247, 248
anonymous code block, 29
ANSI SQL, 18, 19, 27, 28
Append, 201
APT, 34
array, 14, 23
asynchronous, 257, 275
Aurora, 300, 303
Auto Vacuum, 283
auto_explain, 214, 215, 216, 217, 218
autoanalyze, 247, 248, 249
autovacuum, 243, 244, 245, 248, 249
available extensions, 126
AWS Aurora, 17
Azure Data Studio, 45, 65, 66, 67, 68, 69, 70, 71
Azure Database for PostgreSQL, 303, 305
azure_ai, 144

B

backup, 255, 260, 262, 263, 269, 272, 299, 302, 306

BEGIN, 167, 168, 169, 170, 171, 172, 173, 175, 176, 177, 178, 179, 180, 182, 183, 185, 186, 187, 188
BIGSERIAL, 148, 149
block, 166, 167, 168, 169, 170, 172
blocking process, 257
blocks, 166, 168, 169, 182, 189
BRIN, 153, 157, 250
B-Tree, 153, 154, 155, 156, 206, 207, 208
BUFFERS, 193, 195, 196, 197
BYPASSRLS, 89

C

cache hit ratio, 75, 76
case, 24, 25
CASE, 171, 173, 174
Cloud SQL for PostgreSQL, 305, 306, 307
cluster, 18, 19, 83, 84, 87, 88, 89, 90, 91, 104, 146, 255, 257, 259, 260, 261, 262, 263, 267, 268, 270, 273, 275, 278, 279, 289, 290
commit, 257
Commitfest, 6, 7
composite index, 210
CONCURRENTLY, 153
CONNECT, 92, 94, 95, 98
CONNECTION LIMIT, 89
consistency, 238
container, 43, 44
contrib modules, 124
contributors, 2, 5, 6, 7, 9, 10
COPY, 20
cost estimate, 159
COSTS, 193
covering indexes, 213
CREATE, 88, 90, 92, 93, 94, 95, 98, 100, 102, 103, 104, 127, 146, 148, 149, 150, 151, 152, 154, 155, 156, 157, 171, 180, 182, 183, 185, 187

CREATE DATABASE, 109, 112, 113, 118, 119, 120, 121, 146, 228, 229
CREATE EXTENSION, 125, 129, 135, 293
CREATE GROUP, 88
CREATE OR REPLACE, 182, 183, 185, 187
CREATE PUBLICATION, 268, 269
CREATE ROLE, 88, 90, 103, 112
CREATE SUBSCRIPTION, 270, 271
CREATE TABLESPACE, 120
CREATE USER, 88
createdb, 113
CREATEDB, 89, 90
CREATEROLE, 89, 90
Cumulative Statistics System, 279, 283
currval, 153
Cursors, 186, 188

D

datatype, 148, 153, 154, 155, 156, 162, 163
DAY, 26
DBeaver, 45, 59, 60, 61, 62, 63, 64, 65, 72, 170, 171, 291
dead tuple, 240, 244, 246
dead tuples, 238, 243, 244, 245, 246, 247, 250
Debian, 34
debug, 170
DECLARE, 159, 167, 168, 169, 172, 173, 175, 176, 178, 179, 182, 185, 186, 188
deduplicated, 206, 207
DEFAULT PRIVILEGES, 101, 102, 104
DELETE, 165, 171
detail, 165, 169, 170
dirtied, 196
disaster recovery, 255, 259, 298, 300
DO, 29
Docker, 43, 260
domain, 163
DROP DATABASE, 116, 117, 228
DROP EXTENSION, 130
dump, 221, 222, 223, 224, 225, 226, 227, 228, 229, 230, 231

E

effective_cache_size, 81
ELSE, 173, 174, 176, 178
END, 167, 168, 170, 171, 172, 173, 175, 176, 177, 178, 179, 180, 182, 183, 185, 187
errcode, 170, 171
ERROR, 282
error handling, 165, 166, 171
error logs, 279
escape characters, 167, 168
exception, 169, 170, 171
exclusive lock, 244, 251
EXIT, 175, 176, 177, 178
EXPLAIN, 17, 77, 82, 191, 192, 193, 194, 195, 196, 197, 199, 203, 208, 210, 216, 217, 304
EXPLAIN ANALYZE, 77, 291, 292
extension, 11, 14, 15, 16
Extension Registries, 131
extension versions, 127
extensions, 10, 124, 300, 301, 303, 304, 306
    drop, 130
    install, 128, 135
    update, 129, 135
Extensions, 14, 123

F

failover, 255, 266, 267, 275
FATAL, 282
FDW, 161
file_fdw, 217
fill factor, 251, 252, 253
flexible-server create, 305
FOR, 175, 176, 177, 178, 186, 188
FOR LOOP, 175, 176, 177
Foreign Data Wrappers, 161
FORMAT, 193
function, 169, 173, 175, 179, 180, 181, 182, 183, 186, 187
functional index, 208, 209
functions, 149, 151, 153, 158, 159, 162, 163

G

GENERIC_PLAN, 193
GIN, 153, 156, 157
GiST, 153, 155, 156, 157, 161
GRANT, 93, 94, 95, 96, 100, 101, 103, 104, 105
Group, 201
GROUP BY, 201

H

HASH, 151, 154, 155
Hash Join, 200, 201
Heap-Only Tuples, 252
high availability, 255, 256, 259, 266, 298, 299, 300, 304
hint, 170
hit, 195, 196, 197, 198, 204, 205, 211, 212, 213
hooks, 125
HOT, 252, 253
hypopg, 142

I

IDENTITY, 149, 150, 152
identity column, 148
IF, 165, 166, 171, 172, 173, 175, 176, 178, 189
index, 153, 154, 155, 156, 157, 161
Index Scan, 197, 198, 199, 209, 211, 212
info, 169, 187, 188
INHERIT, 88
INOUT, 160, 183, 184, 185
INTERVAL, 27
isolation level, 237, 238

J

JIT, 82, 89

K

Kerberos, 85, 304

L

LATERAL, 27, 28
LIMIT, 22, 23, 25, 26, 28
Linux, 31, 33, 34, 36, 38, 43, 45, 46, 52, 54, 59, 60, 66, 90, 91
LIST, 151
log, 170
LOG, 282
log_fdw, 217
logical, 256, 258, 259, 267, 268, 270, 273, 275
Logical Replication, 258, 259, 267
LOGIN, 87, 88, 90, 94
log-shipping, 256
LOOP, 174, 175, 176, 177, 178, 179, 187

M

materialized, 161
Merge Join, 200
MONTH, 26, 27
Multi-version Concurrency Control, 237
Multi-Version Concurrency Control, 78
MVCC, 78, 79, 237, 238, 239, 243, 249

N

n_tup_hot_upd, 253
n_tup_upd, 253
Nested Loop, 197, 198, 200, 201
nextval, 153
node, 192, 194, 195, 196, 198, 199, 200, 201, 202
nodes, 76, 77, 195, 196, 197, 198, 199, 200, 201, 216, 217
NOLOGIN, 87, 88, 91, 93, 94, 103
notice, 165, 169, 185

O

OPEN, 186, 187
ORDER BY, 201, 210
OUT, 160
OVERRIDING SYSTEM VALUE, 150

P

PAAS, 297, 299, 300, 305
page, 108, 256, 288
pages, 195, 196, 198, 199, 206, 207, 208, 209, 210, 213
PANIC, 282
parameters, 151, 152, 158, 159, 160, 169, 181, 182, 183, 184, 185
partial indexes, 209, 210
partitioning, 151
PASSWORD, 88, 89, 90
Patroni, 267
pg_available_extension_versions, 127, 135
pg_available_extensions, 126, 135
pg_basebackup, 225, 226, 227, 228, 231, 233, 234, 235, 260, 262, 263
pg_cron, 16, 138
pg_ctl, 266, 267
pg_current_logfile, 281
pg_dump, 222, 225, 228
pg_dumpall, 225
pg_hba.conf, 83, 84, 85, 86, 260, 261
pg_hint_plan, 16, 137
pg_partman, 140
pg_promote, 266
pg_restore, 223, 225, 229, 230, 231
pg_settings, 110, 114
pg_sleep, 179
pg_stat_activity, 283, 284, 285
pg_stat_all_indexes, 287
pg_stat_all_tables, 286
pg_stat_database, 285
pg_stat_statements, 128, 136, 214, 292, 293, 294, 295
pg_stat_sys_indexes, 287
pg_stat_user_indexes, 287, 288
pg_stat_user_tables, 245, 248, 249, 253
pg_statio_all_tables, 288
pg_statio_user_tables, 76
pg_switch_wal, 233
pg_trgm, 141
pgAdmin, 36, 37, 42, 45, 51, 52, 53, 54, 55, 56, 57, 58, 59, 61
PGAdmin, 17

pgai, 143
pgBadger, 282
pgBouncer, 78
pgPool-II, 78
pgrx, 124
pgstattuple, 246
pgvector, 143
PGXN, 131
pgxnclient, 131
physical, 256, 257, 258, 259, 267, 275
Physical Replication, 256
pl/pgsql, 124
PL/pgSQL, 165, 166, 167, 172, 174, 179, 188, 189
Platform as a Service, 297, 299, 308
point-in-time recovery, 299
port, 39, 40, 44, 48
postgis, 137
PostGIS, 133
postgres, 86, 90, 99
postgres.ai, 133
postgres_fdw, 139
postgresql.auto.conf, 263
postgresql.conf, 75, 232, 233, 234, 279, 292
primary, 255, 257, 258, 259, 260, 261, 262, 263, 264, 266, 275
procedural language, 165, 166, 171
procedure, 169, 179, 180, 183, 184, 185
procedures, 158, 159, 160
psql, 35, 44, 45, 46, 47, 48, 49, 50, 51, 72, 229
PUBLIC, 96, 97, 98, 147
PUBLIC role, 147
publication, 258, 267, 268, 269, 270, 271, 273, 275

Q

QUERY, 180, 182, 187
query execution, 125
Query hints, 137
Query Insights, 299
query plan, 191, 192, 193, 195, 198, 199, 201, 202, 215, 216, 217, 218
query planning, 125
query processor, 202

Query Store, 299, 304
query tuning, 191, 199, 214

R

raise, 169, 170, 171, 172
RAISE NOTICE, 173, 175, 177, 178, 179, 185,
   187
RANGE, 151, 152
RDS, 300, 301, 302, 303
read, 196
READ, 171
read-only standby, 259
Recovery Point Objectives, 220
Recovery Time Objectives, 220
reindexing, 251
replica, 255, 256, 257, 258, 259, 260, 261, 262,
   263, 264, 266, 267, 268
replication, 255, 256, 257, 258, 259, 260, 261,
   262, 263, 264, 265, 266, 267, 268, 269, 270,
   273, 275, 298, 306
REPLICATION, 89, 261
Replication slots, 258
repmgr, 267
restore, 255, 269, 272
RETURN, 177, 180, 182, 187
REVOKE, 93, 96, 98
role, 18, 19, 84, 85, 87, 88, 89, 90, 91, 92, 93, 94,
   95, 96, 97, 98, 99, 100, 101, 102, 103, 104,
   105, 112, 113, 115
row version, 238, 239, 240, 241, 246, 252
row versioning, 238
RPO, 220, 221, 228, 235
RTO, 220, 221, 235

S

scale factor, 244, 248, 250
schema, 13, 19, 21
Seq Scan, 192, 194, 195, 197
sequence, 148, 149, 152, 153
sequential scan, 199, 200, 206, 208
Sequential Scan, 199
sequential scans, 80, 206, 209

SERIAL, 148, 152
SET, 78, 89, 103, 104
SETTINGS, 193
setval, 153
shared buffers, 74, 81
shared_buffers, 75, 76, 77, 81
SHOW, 232, 280
snapshot, 238, 241, 245
Sort, 201
statistics, 247, 248, 249
stored procedures, 158
streaming, 256, 257, 258, 259, 260, 263, 266,
   269, 271
subscription, 258, 269, 270, 271, 273
Subtransactions, 160
SUMMARY, 193
Supabase, 133
superuser, 146, 160
SUPERUSER, 88, 90
synchronous, 257, 259, 275

T

table bloat, 245, 246
tablespace, 110, 112, 120, 121, 122
Tablespace, 120, 121
TABLESPACE, 151
template, 146, 147
template0, 108, 120, 146, 147
template1, 108, 112, 117, 118, 119, 146, 147
TEMPORARY, 92, 94, 98
TEXT, 21, 29
THEN, 165, 166, 171, 172, 173, 175, 176, 178,
   189
Timescale, 133
TIMESTAMP, 21, 23
TIMING, 193
TOAST, 20
transaction, 237, 238, 239, 240, 241, 242, 243,
   247, 257
trigger, 162
triggers, 162
trust, 85, 86
Trusted Language Extensions, 301
tuple, 19

Types, 162

U

Ubuntu, 33, 34, 35, 48, 52, 53, 59
UNION ALL, 201
UPDATE, 165, 171, 176
USAGE, 92, 95, 98, 103, 105
using, 170

V

Vacuum, 286
VACUUM, 79, 243, 244, 248
VACUUM FULL, 243, 244
vacuum process, 238, 239, 243, 244, 245, 246, 247, 250
variable, 168, 169, 172
variables, 159, 165, 166, 168, 169, 182, 189
Vector, 142
VERBOSE, 193, 196
view, 160, 161

W

WAL, 193, 220, 221, 225, 226, 227, 231, 232, 233, 234, 235, 255, 256, 257, 258, 260, 262, 263, 266, 268, 269

WAL archiving, 256
WAL segment files, 256
wal_level, 268
warning, 169, 172, 173
WHILE LOOP, 178, 179
Window Aggregate, 201
Windows, 31, 33, 36, 38, 40, 41, 42, 44, 45, 46, 52, 53, 54, 59, 60, 66
WITH FORCE, 117
WITH TIME ZONE, 21, 23
work_mem, 76, 77, 78, 79, 202, 204, 205, 249, 250
Write Ahead Log, 219, 220, 221, 225
write-ahead log, 255
written, 196

X

XID, 239, 240, 241, 242, 243, 247
xmax, 239, 240, 241, 245
xmin, 239, 240, 247

Y

YEAR, 26, 27

www.ingramcontent.com/pod-product-compliance
Ingram Content Group UK Ltd.
Pitfield, Milton Keynes, MK11 3LW, UK
UKHW051901280125
454351UK00009B/249

9 781036 902377